WHERE
RIVERS
MEET

Muriel Marshall

NUMBER FOURTEEN:

The Elma Dill Russell Spencer Series
in the West and Southwest

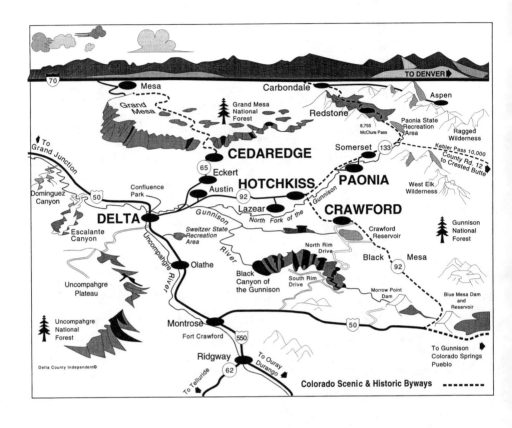

Colorado Scenic & Historic Byways - - - - - - -

WHERE RIVERS MEET

Lore from the Colorado Frontier

BY

Muriel Marshall

TEXAS A&M UNIVERSITY PRESS

College Station, Texas

The paper used in this book meets the minimum requirements
of the American National Standard for Permanence
of Paper for Printed Library Materials, Z39.48-1984.
Binding materials have been chosen for durability.

Library of Congress Cataloging-in-Publication Data

Marshall, Muriel.
    Where rivers meet : Lore from the Colorado frontier / by Muriel Marshall. —
1st ed.
        p.   cm. — (Essays on the American West / sponsored by the
Elma Dill Russell Spencer series ; no. 14)
    ISBN 0-89096-686-9 (alk. paper). — ISBN 0-89096-687-7 (pbk. :
alk. paper)
        1. Gunnison River Region (Colo.)—History.   2. Uncompahgre River
Region (Colo.)—History.   3. Colorado—History, Local.   I. Title.
II. Series.
F782.G9M27   1996
978.8´41—dc20   95-40368
                                                                CIP

To Eric, Andy, & Alan Niemand

ALSO BY MURIEL MARSHALL

Uncompahgre (Caxton)
Red Hole in Time (Texas A&M University Press)

FICTION
Lovely Rebel (Rinehart)

CONTENTS

ILLUSTRATIONS

ACKNOWLEDGMENTS

My warmest gratitude goes to members of the Delta History Book Committee who, on their own, conceived this project marking a century and a decade since the first homesteader drove stake at the area at the confluence of the Uncompahgre and the Gunnison Valleys. Special thanks to Linda Loftis, who heads the committee; Robert Jay and Gordon Hodgin who recruited the support of townspeople and organizations; Ben Walker who reproduced scores of photographs from Delta County Historical Society files; and the creative work of committee members Deborah Doherty, Millard Fairlamb, Alfred and Mary Gallegos, Donald Malone, David Mangum, Margaret Stewart, and Sobeda Torrez.

I join the committee in thanking the people who gave of their means as well as their memories. Many are direct descendants of early settlers, as can be seen by the historic names they honor.

Pat Musser, honoring the Aebi family; Katharine Amsbary Hedgcock, honoring Judge Albert E. Amsbary; Jo Gore, honoring Elias and Ellen Beach; Jo Gore, honoring Floyd and Dora Beach; Catherine Brown, honoring A. Allen Brown; Bob Bruton, honoring Olin Bruton; Margaret Stewart, honoring King L. Banks; Mildred Heddles, honoring John Calhoun; Rosamond Edmunds, honoring Phillip "Bud" Edmunds; Evelyn Farmer, honoring Joseph Raymond Farmer; Jo Gore, honoring Wayne Gore; Genevieve Hammond, honoring Henry "Hank" Hammond; Kenny Henwood, honoring the Harrington family; Jack and Bernice Musser, honoring Morgan Hendrickson; Loretta Hinton, honoring Floyd A. Hinton; Shirley Hodgin, honoring Gordon Hodgin; Carrie Johns tenBensel, honoring Wilbur Johns; Beth Johnson, honoring Mr. and Mrs. W. Ruel Johnson; Greg Kaup, honoring Meredith "Babe" Kaup; Jim Kendrick, honoring Donald Kendrick; Jack Lowe, honoring Ben and Ruby Lowe; Cleo and Bill Merritt, honoring Judge Guy Merritt; Ray Meyer, honoring Arthur R. Meyer; Inez Mowbray, honoring James Mowbray; Jack and Bernice Musser, honoring the Musser family; Lois Pritchard, honoring Letitia Crabill Hillman Obert; Renata Osborn, honoring Thomas W. Osborn, Jr.; Virginia Harding, honoring William H. Overbay; the Castle-Parker family, honoring Charles Edwin Parker; the Castle-Parker family, honoring Edith Castle Parker; Les Renfrow, honoring Clyde

Renfrow; Jackie Renfrow, honoring Melvern Renfrow; Gordon O'Brien, honoring the Oscar Roatcap family; Gordon Hodgin, honoring Julius F. Schmidt; L. J. Springer, honoring Melvin Springer, Sr.; Esther J. Stephens, honoring R. W. Stephens; Rod Stewart, honoring Judge Clyde Stewart; Alberta Swaim, honoring Orville Swaim; Dorcas D. Ween, honoring the Stockham family; Helen Sukle, honoring John Sukle; Charles Swanson, honoring Oscar B. Swanson; Ray Veatch, honoring Homer Veatch; Robert Warner, honoring W. W. Warner; Helen Wigram, honoring Edward L. "Ted" Wigram; Dorothy Honnen, honoring Capt. James J. Winton; Linda Loftis, Mark Loftis, Shane Loftis, and Maxine Wheatcroft, honoring the twentieth-century pioneers; Mary E. Baker.

WHERE
RIVERS
MEET

1

While Wagons Wait

They gathered at the last stop before the Indian reservation. Tents everywhere. Flocks of covered wagons, like white geese, all pointed one way—west. Axles greased, tongues hanging. Ready. Waiting.

Unlike the wagons of the gold and silver boomers who hit Gunnison City in the summer of 1880, these were not loaded with miners' picks and shovels. These 1881ers were headed for free land, to stake out farms, raise cattle, start businesses, and build towns down there on the Western Slope of the Rockies, just as soon as the Utes were escorted out.

At least three of those waiting knew where one of the new towns would be: a hundred miles to the northwest on brushy land where two rivers came together, the Uncompahgre and the Gunnison. These men were a Kansan called Gov. George A. Crawford, who would incorporate the town; W. O. Stephens, who would provide the land, though he didn't own it yet; and Sylvester Huffington, who guessed a mile wrong about exactly where the town would be located. Governor Crawford even had a name for the town—Uncompahgre. Of course, all this depended on getting there first.

What was holding things up? The 1880 treaty opening a third of the state of Colorado to settlement had passed Congress in June, over a year ago. By September of last year, the Utes had ratified it, as three-fourths of their males put an X beside squiggles said to be their names, agreeing to move to the new reservation over in Utah. In December, the president of the United States had declared the reservation open to settlement. Right now, a thousand troops were stationed at Fort Crawford down there in the middle of the Uncompahgre Valley, waiting to ease the Indians out and the settlers in—and in the meantime keeping them apart.

Fort Crawford had reason to be cautious about allowing settlers onto the reservation before the Utes were taken out. Not only because the Indians, enraged at being driven from their ancestral home, might cause trouble, but also because some recklessly overeager white man might trigger it. Not long ago, on the very road most of the settlers would travel to reach the Uncompahgre Valley, a band of Utes had ambushed and overpowered officers who were bringing a wagon-freighter to trial in Gunnison City. The freighter had shot the son of Ute Chief Shavano in an incident that very well could have started an Indian war. The band of Utes, scornful of white justice, meted out their own punishment with a rifle and threw the freighter's body over a cliff.

As the story of that ambush made the rounds among the restless settlers, it became not a single bullet that had killed the freighter but prolonged torture that grew more ghastly with each telling. Some of the men who had considered riding backcountry trails to "sooner" on the best land decided to wait for the official word.

Huffington and Stephens had their wagons and tents in which to wait out the delay. Stephens may have still had his house. He had come from Missouri to live in Gunnison City, but one winter at nine thousand feet had been enough cold for him. Huffington had come from Kentucky the summer before with his wife, four children, two teams, and two wagons, with the family milk cow tied behind.

"Grandpa was way, way early," Nelson Huffington recalled. "The Ute treaty hadn't even got through Congress yet, so while he waited, he hired on with the railroad construction. The tracks still had a long way to go before reaching Gunnison."

As for Governor Crawford, he had come by train as far as rails had been laid. A former Kansas governor, he had become a professional creator of towns. Working just ahead of the expanding railroads, he had founded several towns in Kansas and now was waiting to get his plats on some of western Colorado. If the governor was staying at a hotel, he was scarcely more comfortable than the tent people. The only hotel in Gunnison City at that time was a huge shed with rows of cots. The shed was lit by a bank of candles at one end that the guests routinely extinguished at midnight by shooting them out with their pistols.

Destined to play prominent roles in the settlement at the confluence of the Uncompahgre and the Gunnison rivers were two business and professional men who had no intention of going there. For them, things were fine right there in mine-booming Gunnison City. But druggist Trew Blachly, for whom nothing ever went right, was destined to die a dramatic death at the confluence; and lawyer A. R. King, for whom it seems that nothing could go wrong, was to serve so outstandingly at the confluence that he would be appointed Judge of the Colorado State Court of Appeals.

Upon finishing law school, A. R. King of Kewanee, Illinois, courted Annie Caldwell, a neighbor farmgirl, and then came west alone, determined not to drag her into pioneer life until he had established a practice large enough to support a nice home for her. That took three years.

By contrast, Trew Blachly married a cosmopolitan girl, Dellie Bradley, a senior at Oberlin College and daughter of a physician-missionary in Bangkok, where she had been born. Well-staffed with servants, the Bradleys' fine teakwood house stood in a landscaped compound across the river from the Siamese royal palace. Her mother taught the many children of the King of Siam's wives (preceding the famous teacher, Anna Leonowens, whose tenure is depicted in *The King and I*). Dellie and her brothers and sisters played with the royal children.

Trew married Dellie a few weeks after they met and brought her to Monument, Colorado, the first of eight towns where the couple perched temporarily as he followed the advancing railroad, setting up his combination grocery and drugstore in the front half of whatever was available to live in—tent, barn, cabin. At Gunnison City, Trew built a six-room brick house, using money Dellie's mother lent to ease her life and perhaps to help her achieve her dream of owning a piano. Then and thereafter, Trew operated by mortgaging everything, including the piano Dellie later bought for herself by giving piano lessons.

The drug business was good. As wagons arrived daily from all over the nation, the crowded camp was plagued with treatable afflictions: heat-fainting, flies, bedbugs, mosquitoes. The diarrhea called summer complaint created a run on castor oil and extract of opium. With extra cash as a borrowing base, Trew Blachly speculated in mining and land.

Earlier that year, without waiting for the official word and apparently unnoticed, one wagonless family—two men, a young woman, and two very tiny children— had passed through town and right on into the reservation.

Three weeks after the United States, on Dec. 6, 1880, ratified the Ute treaty— months before the Utes could be coerced into doing so—the George W. States family was having a Christmas gathering back in Michigan. They shared exciting letters from kinsman Herb Castle, who had gone west and was a burro-packer to the San Juan mines.

"He described this land of wondrous beauty, the opportunities presented in the opening up of this vast Western Slope empire: 'millions of acres where land-hungry people by diligence and hard work could build homes.' It was an exhila-

rating prospect." So his grandson, Dr. G. W. States, reminisced in a series of
articles in the *Delta County Independent.*

All the family members decided to dispose of their property and move
as trail-makers to the land of the Utes. Herbert Castle and Grandfather
States were the Caleb and Joshua of their respective tribes.

In February 1881 Grandfather States, his daughter Eliza (Mrs. Herbert
Castle) and her two children, Eva and Ira, age 4 and 2, left Michigan for
the end of the Rio Grande Railroad construction.

Here they were met by Herbert Castle with saddle mules and pack
burros to transport them and all their earthly possessions to the
Uncompahgre Valley. Wanting to be among the very first to the valley,
they lost no time and proceeded at once through the snows of winter.

Herbert Castle had been mule-skinning in the San Juan Mountains long enough
to know where not to go in the dead of winter. Instead of taking his family out
around Otto Mears Road, which swooped up over The Blue, treacherous in winter,
he followed the new railroad grade right down through the bore of Black Canyon.

Construction crews with surveyors in the lead were along the route
preparing the way for the coming of the iron horse. Some crews were
working (far ahead of the track) in dark narrow Black Canyon. In many
places the giant walls had to be blasted away to make a place wide enough
for this narrow track. This was quite a while before a train ever entered
the canyon.

At one place where the river was slow and the ice thick they camped
for the night with the flowing river gurgling beneath them. It was the
only level place they could find to bivouac for the night. On the ice they
piled rocks, built a fire, and fried their fish and venison. It was a devious
and perilous trail to follow in winter, especially with two small children.

Most of the time the children rode in quilt-lined soap boxes rigged on
each side of the burro, but in particularly dangerous places the mother
carried the youngest child in her arms. They all went down the canyon,
windswept, and sometimes biting cold, without a child having even the
sniffles. The air was dry and as free from germs as the North Pole.

Eliza was carrying little Ira when

they rounded a point of rock and came suddenly upon a construction
crew of Irishmen at work. The sight of the pack train, a woman on a mule

with a babe in her arms, took the crew by such a surprise they dropped their tools, took off their caps and threw them in the air, while one Irishman shouted, "Behold the Virgin Mary and the Child Jesus!"

After many days in the Canyon, other days on the trail leading out, the battle with the snows on Squaw Hill Pass, they looked out at last over the broad valley, their promised land.

But they couldn't enter. It was only March, five months before the Utes would finally leave. So they set up camp along the Uncompahgre River, under the protection of Fort Crawford.

Some land-hungry pioneers had come even earlier than the States and Castle party. As John Obergfell told it, he and Henry Hammond came hunting gold in the San Juans in the late 1870s, soon after that portion of Ute lands was ceded. They noticed how fat the Indian ponies were that came from a certain valley, the Uncompahgre. Both men were into blooded horses, so they trailed that valley to see what kind of feed had put on so much winter fat. They found it just downstream from where two rivers came together. Mentally staking out 160 acres each to be filed on as soon as the Utes were out and filing was legal, they returned to Salida.

Obergfell figured out a way to be close enough to watch over his selected piece of land and keep anybody from jumping his unstaked claim. He joined the cavalry stationed at nearby Fort Crawford. He couldn't resist going down now and then to look at the property, drag up some logs, and get started on a cabin, however. The cavalry caught him at it and locked him in the guardhouse, and that is where he was when all the wagons started for the promised land. He was released at the same time the Utes went out and arrived at his "homestead" just hours too late. J. C. Cole already had staked it out. Obergfell had to move over one set of stakes.

Impatient at the long delay, "sooners," singly and in groups, slipped into the reservation on horseback to stake out claims ahead of the rush.

One group of six included town-locators Sylvester Huffington, W. O. Stephens, and Henry Hammond. Governor Crawford would follow when the Utes were out and everything was neat and legal. Upon reaching the Uncompahgre, the party was held up by the soldiers at Fort Crawford, but not for long. Continuing on downstream for about thirty miles, they came to "the spot," the confluence of the Uncompahgre and the Gunnison.

W. O. Stephens staked out a quarter of a section of bottomland that took in most of the wedge between the two rivers. To Sylvester Huffington, the bottom-land on the other side of the river looked better. It was not as marshy, and there was more of it for a town to expand into. Henry Hammond chose land well south of the place, where mesas on both sides pinched together overlooking the confluence. The land was higher out there, and the area in the valley was just about limitless. Hank Hammond always had big ideas. Among the tools they had packed in were simple surveying instruments. Huffington had had experience as a surveyor, so all their corners were square. These corners were unrelated to corners anywhere else on earth, however; the men had beaten not only the other boomers, but also the land survey. Hayden's survey had been too vast to deal with the nitty-gritty of section corners, and Gunnison's survey had concerned railroad lines only.

Others of the party—George Moody, Abe Butler, McGranahan—staked land nearby, and all began chopping down cottonwoods and building cabins on their claims.

You had to have something that looked like a house; stakes and tents did not protect squatters' rights. And with no official survey and no land office to register a claim, squatters' rights were all they had. The cabins were small, with dirt floors and dirt roofs. The latter were made by bending saplings over a ridge log from wall to wall, covering the saplings with a layer of anything soft and handy that would hold dust—sagebrush, leafy branches, cattail reeds—and then shoveling a thick layer of dirt on top to shed rain. Doors and windows were holes.

Fort Crawford soldiers caught two of the group in the act of soonering. George Moody, his cabin only half finished, was ordered off the reservation, and Henry Hammond was arrested. Perhaps his cabin was more noticeable than the others, or perhaps he himself was too conspicuous (Hank was noted for being noticeable). In any case, he was invited to spend the duration of the wait in the fort's guardhouse.

Slipping back to Gunnison City in mid-August, the sooners found tensions higher than ever. The railroad track had reached town and was aimed like a battering ram at the rock cliffs west of town, at the stubborn Utes, and at the sluggish U.S. government. Summer was edging toward fall. If the wagons didn't start soon, they stood a good chance of getting caught on a high pass in a blizzard.

Must there be another fight? With Chief Ouray dead almost a year now, was there any chief powerful enough to force the Utes to go peaceably? To make things even shakier, the United States itself was virtually without a chief. President Garfield, shot by a fanatic in July, was too ill to act, and there was no rule about who should take over when a president was still alive but not functioning.

The reports of those who had seen the land were reassuring. At wagon tail-gates, around evening campfires, in saloons, or hunkered down in the straw of

George Moody and the cabin he "soonered" at the confluence in 1881. Utes were long gone by the time he'd added that screen door, but gun is still handy. Courtesy of Delta County Historical Society.

livery stables, the sooners described what they had seen: two great long valleys floored with wide benches of flat farmland, gently walled all around with mountains two miles high. There was a door at the north end, where the two merged rivers had carved an exit, creating an easy, all-season way in and out. The Salt Lake Trail, it was called, though it was really a wagon road. At the other end lay Santa Fe, New Mexico. Canyon trails led in all directions, but, except for that doorway down at the confluence, everything was uphill: up over Grand Mesa, up over Marshall Pass, up over Cochetopa Pass, up over Red Mountain Pass, up over Dallas Divide, up over the Uncompahgre Plateau, up over McClure, up over Kebler. Named or as yet unnamed, all trails merge here, just as the rivers do. To come into the valley by any of these passes is a little like climbing a ladder to enter the house by an attic window.

Putting a town down at that confluence was a natural thing to do. You could see that place had been a favorite gathering point for Indians since time out of mind. Stripped cottonwood saplings marked where they'd bark-fed their ponies in winter, and that big tree standing alone on trampled earth obviously had been the focal point of tribal council meetings.

The place lay right on the highway, you might say, between the ancient Spanish civilizations to the southeast and the burgeoning ones in Utah, California, and Oregon. The railroad survey line passed alongside the confluence and then, a few miles downstream, entered a canyon so deep and narrow that no competing townsite could be located for fifty miles.

The place had everything needed for agriculture and industry—water for farm and millwheel, land, grass, encircling mountains protecting against foul weather, fish, wild fowl, big game, timber, clay for bricks, coal, building stone. Yet not too much, noted these men, many of whom were escaping eastern industrial cities. Not so much and not so boundless as to engender a sprawling ugliness, such as all too often characterizes important crossroads.

Waiting, they counted the possibilities like coins. Twelve million empty acres, a third of the state of Colorado; 175,000 acres of farmable land in that one valley alone. No need to feel bad about pushing the Utes out, they weren't using it— three thousand Indians in twelve million acres? Why, that was four thousand acres for each brave, squaw, and papoose! And only eighty of them had ever tried to farm an inch of it, according to Chief Ouray himself.

Virgin opportunity. Wide open country. Virtually untouched by man.

Well, not quite.

2

The "Old Ones" Left Sign

Thousands of years before the six "town-locators" set stake in the virgin soil of the river delta, this place had been peopled. Not by Cliff Dwellers, not by Basket-Makers, Utes, or Navajos. Nobody knows who these inhabitants were.

They left groups of stone circles at widely spaced sites on the slopes of the Uncompahgre Plateau and the lower benches of Grand Mesa. Some of these clusters of stone circles are not far from town—one lies out by Roubideau and one on the side of Grand Mesa, near what would be Pipeline Road when there was a pipeline. If these sites were noticed at all, they were dismissed as stones placed to hold down Ute tipi edges in windy weather. Some very strong winds must have been postulated, for the rocks were piled three and four courses deep to form low, mortarless masonry walls.

In the early 1940s, Betty and Howard Huscher of the Colorado Museum of Natural History came through doing research for their book, *The Hogan Builders of Colorado*. (They used the word *hogan* to mean "home," as it translates from the Navajo, and not merely the earth-covered structures the Navajos were living in at that time.)

The low circular wall provided a base for the hogan roof of poles and brush, and could have served inside as a bench or shelf. Unprotected by cliff overhang, any wood that might have yielded tree-ring dating had weathered to dust long before; but shards of blackish pottery are said to date from very ancient times and seem to link these people with others in Alaska and Siberia, substantiating the theory that the folks called "Native Americans," like the rest of us, came from someplace else—in this case, from Asia via the iced-over Bering Strait.

The Huschers wrote: "This region [the confluence region] may prove to be one of the most important because of the high percentage of off-type potsherds which turn up there . . . One site just north of Delta consisted of several circular houses (probably at least five) of piled basalt 'niggerhead' boulders on the very top of a conical hill of Mancos shale and a higher hill nearby with three additional circles."

You won't see those Pipeline Road circles now. The story got around that the piled rocks marked Indian graves. People dug into them with shovels, hoping to unearth beadwork, pottery, weapons, and turquoise that had been buried with the dead to ease their journey to the Happy Hunting Grounds. Nothing was discovered. Later someone tackled the site with a bulldozer; by this time, there was a Pipeline Road with a bulldozer as part of the scene. Again nothing was found. Some fool even tried to aid excavation by using dynamite.

Predating everything discovered so far in the area are two Folsom points found near Black Canyon in the summer of 1939. They are estimated to date back twenty or thirty thousand years.

Utes, coming into this area later, regarded these relics of an earlier race as spiritual evidence of the power of the "Old Ones," and, far from disturbing the site, avoided going near.

As for later cultures, a group of Colorado University students under Dr. William Buckles spent the summer of 1963 excavating ancient Ute campsites in the area. They concentrated on the lower Roubideau Canyon at Christmas Rock Shelter, so named because R. P. Maupin and W. E. Goddard carved their names and the date on the cliff there on Christmas Day of 1888. By studying campsite strata— one year's camp ashes built on sediment covering last year's—and by overlapping similar evidence gathered from older "digs," they corroborated former archeological findings indicating that the Utes were here some thirteen hundred years ago. Having only stone tools and weapons, the tribe lived but little better than their ancestors had as Paiutes in the deserts to the west. Archeologists at other sites, using ever more exact tools, have traced this culture back ten thousand years.

According to an illustrated brochure put out in the early days by H. H. Tammen of Denver, the mummified body of "an Indian Maiden" had been found near Delta on February 25, 1884, by a party of miners working twenty feet underground. The illustrated brochure advertised Tammen and Company's Curio Shop, "dealers in Minerals and Indian Relics."

Perhaps coincidentally, in May of 1884, the *Delta Chief* reported that an Indian mummy, belonging to R. E. Eggleston and reportedly stolen by the Taylor Museum, had been retrieved and was to be exhibited in New Orleans. Whether this was the same mummy is not known. In his many newspaper articles, Eggleston referred to the sandstone and marble mines in the canyon below town. These mines may have begun as natural caves, a favorite place for Indian burials. If this was the same mummy, Eggleston later may have sold it to Tammen.

The Utes were a "hunting and gathering" people. In the spring they separated into family groups, each following its accustomed circuit into the mountains to hunt game, roots, seeds, and, as they ripened, berries. The Utes hunted deer for meat to eat and to dry for winter; they tanned hides to make buckskin clothing and leather totebags; and they wove blankets of strips of rabbit fur. They were not potters, but they were so skilled at basketry that their woven utensils were watertight and served as kettles, the contents being heated by dropping hot rocks into the vessels.

Without agriculture to increase the land's yield, with no tools but sticks and stones, with no domestic animal except the dog (employed as both a pack animal and an emergency food supply), scrounging off the land required a lot of territory per capita just to stay alive.

Nature relentlessly controlled population. Always on the brink of starvation, these people could be decimated by a dry year or a hard winter. No one grew old. When you were unable to walk to the location of seasonal food, you died. Nutrition was so poor that few bones older than forty years are found among remains of the Ute-Paiute cultures.

Childhood hardly existed. For the safety of the people, lest a howling child alert the enemy, a newborn was taught never to cry aloud by having nose and mouth pinched shut at every wail. Even for a babe so vociferous he showed signs of intending to become a chief, this lifetime lesson took less than half an hour. An infant was bound immobile in a papoose basket, carried (along with a gathering basket) on mother's back or propped against a tree by the cooking fire. As for the girl-child, as soon as she could walk, she was burdened with as much as she could carry and still keep up with the clan.

If she could not keep up, or if the clan had to run for its life, she had to be left behind. An extra baby put such strain on the family clan that a practical religious ruling made twins taboo; the surplus child was deemed to be possessed of an evil spirit and laid beside the trail to die or to be rescued by his own kind, as the Spirit willed.

The existence of this twin taboo was confirmed by people living in the town that once had been part of the Ute reservation.

For all their deprivations, the Ute-Paiutes were not lacking in enterprise. With only patience and bow and arrow for weapons, they were ingenious at hunting, as several local hunting blinds attest. Willis Aldridge described one on the slope of

When the ancient Ute Council Tree loses a branch, Indian medicine men come from the Reservation, hold blessing rites and make ceremonial drums of the wood. Recent photo courtesy of the Delta County Historical Society.

Grand Mesa. Above a spring on a deer trail, they had laid a low sandstone wall to crouch behind, topping it with round black lava rocks like heads looking over. Deer frequenting the spring would get so used to seeing the black rocks that they wouldn't notice when one had grown black hair. Trailing autumn to the lower valleys, Ute families gathered at the confluence of the Uncompahgre and the

Gunnison Rivers to set up winter camp in the shelter of cottonwoods. They fashioned small dwellings of poles and brush, sealed with shredded juniper bark. Most families had not seen each other since early spring, so it was here along the river bank that Ute social life took place—athletic contests, games of chance, and dances such as the Bear Dance, giving the young folk a chance to meet and fall in love with someone not a blood relative.

The *suuvupu tawaavi,* a certain cottonwood at the confluence of the rivers, the tree that whites later would call the Ute Council Tree, was the focus of the encampment. In its shadow, they worked out problems between bands, conducted rituals to placate the lurking *uruci,* and prayed to the *sinawavi* for an easy winter and plenty of *toonapi* berries next fall.

Mountain-based Utes had a better grip on staying alive than Digger tribes to the west, whose homes were holes in the ground; but even here in the shelter of bluffs and trees, lasting out a winter was touch-and-go. Snow-driving winds pierced the walls of the brush wickiups despite the cedar bark stuffing. Snow buried firewood. In a long winter, the gathered food ran out, rabbits became scarce, ice made trap-fishing difficult, frozen ground locked food-roots away. The winter moon that spans our February and March was called Moon of Chewing Rawhide because, by that time, the people often were reduced to boiling and eating the leather that they wore.

Winters were endurance ordeals, time when life processes shut down, a kind of grim hibernation like that of the bear but without the blessing of unconsciousness. That the bear awoke each spring, resurrected from this symbolic death, was occasion for enormous hope and joy. The spring Bear Dance, celebrating the bears' survival, was and is the chief ritual of the Ute.

Down in New Mexico, in about 1630, the Utes made their first contacts with the Spanish—and with the horse. It was like thunder after lightning. They took to horses instantly, becoming superb riders, trainers, breeders. It was as if they'd been created split-legged just so they could straddle a horse. To get horses they would trade anything they owned—tanned buckskin, clothing, baskets. They captured Paiute Indians and sold them as slaves. They sold their own sons to get horses—though this was not so terrible as it sounds. From the Spanish *padres* and *hacendados,* the boys learned (or got a chance to learn, if they were so inclined) techniques of herding sheep, raising cattle, farming, mining, milling, and thinking in another language. Then, about the time they achieved a full set of adult male muscles, they could slip home, much more valuable to the tribe because of their enforced sojourns. Trading your son for a horse was a little like sending your son to Harvard, except that you got paid for it instead of the other way around. Several of these ex-slaves became tribal leaders. Chief Ouray was one. His parents had sold him or farmed him out (historians differ) to the Spanish at Taos when he was a child.

Slave trading—usually of half-starved Paiutes or Goshutes—became such big business that the main route was named for it: the Old Slave Trail, or the Old Spanish Trail. An alternative stretch of that trail between Salt Lake and Santa Fe ran down along the Uncompahgre, crossing the Gunnison near the confluence.

The horse transformed the Utes. In less than fifty years, they changed from leaderless, wandering families to chief-led bands of hunter-warriors of such reputation that the Spanish at Abiquiu found it advisable to make a treaty with them as early as 1675. Sweeping onto the plains, in enemy Comanche-Arapaho territory, they could slaughter enough buffalo in half a moon to keep them in jerky, pemmican, grease, and tipi leather for a whole year; and then race back, losing the pursuing enemy in intricate mountain trails they alone knew.

Life beside the converging rivers changed greatly. Thanks to the pack-power of the horse, the Utes now could have mobile homes—big, strong tipis made of buffalo hide that withstood any kind of weather and were equipped with appliances (pole-controlled flaps) to vent smoke out the smoke-hole, no matter where the weather was coming from. Food was plentiful and more varied, as swift raids on Rio Grande farming communities provided corn, wheat, honey, dried fruit, and vegetables.

Under the protection of braves ready to ride at a moment's notice in case of attack by enemy or slave-trader, camp life became very relaxed. In this safe place, children were free to be noisy, running and yelling at games such as *kanapi sikunikat,* shooting arrows at willow hoops sent rolling down the river bank, and engaging in wrestling matches, shinny, foot races, horse races.

Horse racing was so prevalent that every get-together—Bear Dances, medicine sings, weddings—culminated in races. Gambling, a favorite Indian pastime, was even more fascinating after the Indian got the horse. It was much more exciting to bet on whose horse would win a race than on whether *wisa-nipi* would come up heads or tails. Racetracks became a part of any location where Utes were accustomed to set up camp. At least two Ute race tracks still can be made out from a helicopter circling the confluence of the Uncompahgre and the Gunnison. One is on a low bench of the Uncompahgre Plateau and another in the 'dobes north of town. They are made of earth so hoof-beaten that, more than a century later, it still shows the scar, unable to grow quite enough shadscale, grass, and sage to match the land around it.

If there had been a flag flying over the delta of the Uncompahgre during the 1600s, it would have been the Spanish *bandera*. At this time Spain claimed, without challenge, the entire western half of what is now the United States. True, some Russians had settled along the Pacific in the Northwest, and there was that colony of British subjects along the Atlantic seaboard, but both those colonies seemed more interested in pegging down what they had—establishing homes, farms, and trade—than in the glories of exploration and conquest.

Then, toward the end of the century, the French showed signs of trying to muscle in. After floating all the way down the Mississippi, LaSalle claimed its entire drainage for France, and soon French traders were threading the western branches of that river and poking their canoes into the Rocky Mountains.

Upon seeing how well the French were getting along with the Plains Indians, the Spanish became alarmed. They themselves were still trying to recover from the revolt when the Pueblos had kicked them (temporarily) out of New Mexico. So they sent an army of a hundred men down the South Platte to drive the French out. Six Spaniards survived the French-Indian battle. After that the Spanish gave up on the eastern slope of the Rockies and turned their attention westward.

In 1765, Governor Cachupin of New Mexico sent Don Juan Rivera and his party to take a look at what Spain owned up north. Rivera came exactly as far as the confluence of the Uncompahgre and the Gunnison, then turned around and went back home. Nobody knows why. History is more mystery than anything.

He came by way of Pagosa Springs, went west to the Dolores River, swung north as far as Paradox Valley, crossed the Uncompahgre Plateau, and headed down the Uncompahgre River. At the confluence with the Gunnison, he carved a cross, his name, and the date on a cottonwood tree and then packed up and returned to Santa Fe.

His report must have been favorable, because, during the next decade, Spanish explorers seeking gold and silver followed his trail. Signs of their quest remain—map names such as La Plata ("Silver"), tumbled earth where they placered, lost tools—but only three (who sneaked in, unofficial and unsanctioned) left their names to history. In 1775, Pedro Mora, Gregorio Sandoval, and Andres Muñiz came as far as the confluence, "where at the mouth of the Uncompahgre they examined the young cottonwood on which Rivera had carved a cross." Then they went home.

Things were looking up for the Spanish. At the end of the French and Indian War, France ceded everything west of the Mississippi to Spain, and the British colonies along the Atlantic were too busy gearing up for what they would call the Revolutionary War to covet anything west of the Ohio.

But by this time, those Russian settlements in the Northwest were creeping southward, threatening the Spanish hold on the West. To forestall them, the Spanish created a chain of California missions. To keep in touch with them, the Spaniards needed some method safer than going straight west from Santa Fe through hostile Apache lands, where just about everybody except another Apache was routinely slaughtered.

Two Spanish priests, Fathers Domínguez and Escalante, were outfitted and dispatched to find a safe route to California by swinging north and then west. They hoped to travel through the lands of friendly Indian tribes all the way. Being Franciscans, they wore long robes of coarse gray cloth gathered at the waist with a rope and topped by a pointed hood to shield their shaven heads from the sun. They had taken vows to own no possessions, to walk barefoot, and never to ride a horse unless long distances required it. This was going to be a very long distance indeed, and Father Domínguez rode most of the way, but Father Escalante, according to his diary, had no trouble keeping his vow because he had a painful case of piles and riding nearly killed him.

With eight companions, the priests left Santa Fe in July 1776, just a few days after a group of British subjects on the Atlantic coast had signed a Declaration of Independence telling their sovereign where to get off.

The priests, their cattle (for fresh meat on the road), and herders followed the route taken by Rivera, but evidently they didn't leave the Dolores River soon enough. They became entangled in thorny riverbottom brush between canyon walls and had to slash and struggle their way out. Their difficulties gave the river its name—*dolores* means "pains." Missing the Indian trail over the Uncompahgre Plateau, they climbed an incline so steep and stony that it made the horses' feet bleed.

At the top they met a Ute, the first they'd seen on the trip. This is not incredible—in midsummer, Indians would have been gathering foodstuffs as high in the mountains as they could get, and the priests, seeking to map an easy route, had avoided mountain heights by threading low passes.

Hiring the Ute as a guide, they were led down to the Uncompahgre River and out across the 'dobes (now Peach Valley) to the river we call the Gunnison. Father Escalante christened the latter El Río de San Javier, though noting that Utes already had named it Tomichi. At the cove where Austin someday would be located, the Fathers paused to preach to friendly (and apparently cheering) Utes gathered along the rim above and then proceeded up the North Fork, over Grand Mesa, and west to Utah Lake. There—feeling winter coming on—they scrapped the trip and circled southeastward back to Santa Fe.

Escalante never reached California, and he missed the Uncompahgre-Gunnison confluence by a mile or so.

3

Four Nations Owned the Confluence

To keep those pushy French trappers out of Spanish beaver streams, New Mexico had a law stating that only Spanish citizens could trap in Spanish territory, which included most of the Rocky Mountains. Antoine Robidoux, a member of the French-Canadian Robidoux family that was operating a large fur and trapper-supply business out of St. Louis, got around the law by going down to Santa Fe and getting himself naturalized. Better than that, he married a Mexican girl and became president of the town council. The trappers he set to work in the mountains back of Taos and Santa Fe soon decimated the beaver population, so Robidoux began scouting for new territory.

He found it on the western side of the Rockies and built a trading post–fort in the very center of that vast area, choosing a spot near where a stream the Indians called Uncompahgre emptied into another river that trappers then were calling Blue River. The Ute name for this second, larger river was Tomichi, a name still carried by the river's source above Gunnison.

We do not know exactly where Robidoux's trading post was, but there is a fair chance that someday someone will come upon an artifact—perhaps a hand-molded bullet, a couple of bright blue glass trade beads—that will tell history buffs where to start looking.

We can surmise that the post was not small. As a supply base for crews of trappers working streams in an area several hundred miles in all directions, it had a large storage building, described as a log structure with dirt floor and roof. The building must have been big enough to store total replacement supplies for trappers—from guns and saddles to sugar, shirts, and the cinnamon and other spices that, mixed with the beaver's own castoreum, made trap bait. Since it would have been dangerous to operate a trading post in Indian territory without trading with Indians, there would have been extra storage space for Indian trade items (all of the above except beaver-bait spices, plus cotton and wool yard goods, beads, and abalone and other colorful seashells). The trading room would have been large, for it had to serve as a social center for both Utes and trappers, who often would see each other nowhere but here. Other structures would store baled hides and the machine that baled them, and house guards and workers, trappers stopping over, and wranglers moving trade-in horses. Hooves being the only means of power and transportation, there would have been many horses and mules coming and going, requiring picket corrals and expanses of pasture.

The first consideration in selecting a site would have been safety. Though the Utes were a friendly people, they were showing signs of resenting the increasing encroachment by Spanish from the south, French from the north, English from the east. And by now the Utes were as powerful as they would ever be. There was always the chance that a band, primed by grievance or whiskey, might attack. So we can assume that Robidoux's trading post was well stockaded and situated in open country, not overlooked by nearby bluffs where an enemy, bow or gun in hand, could look down into it and pick off post personnel headed for cellar or latrine.

Taking all this into consideration, William M. Bailey, in his book, *Fort Uncompahgre* (1990), deduces that the trading post probably stood on the south bank of the Gunnison River two or three miles below its confluence with the Uncompahgre and just upstream from a wide shallow ford. Situated near this ford, the trading post would have been right on the "highway"—that is, on the intermountain fork of the Old Spanish Trail between Santa Fe and the Great Salt Lake. From the evidence, Bailey envisions a spread of many structures enclosed in a protective stockade, with additional cabins of Mexican workers up Roubideau Creek, where indeed log foundations of an old building were found by J. D. Dillard in 1894.

Now you have some idea where to look for those beads and bullets.

The flags flying over Fort Uncompahgre and over Robidoux's Uinta Mountain post were Mexican flags. Shortly before Robidoux established his fort in 1825, Mexico won its independence from Spain. A first-hand description of these two posts comes to us from a not unbiased guest, preacher Joseph Williams. On the return leg of a two-year round trip to Oregon, he visited both places, staying longer than he liked: "This delay was very disagreeable to me on account of the wickedness of the people, and the debauchery of the men among the Indian women. . . . Mr. Roubideau [*sic*] had collected several of the Indian squaws and young Indians to take to new Mexico [as slaves]. . . . the Spanish would buy them for wives."

Enforced wifehood could have been an improvement in lifestyle for them, as Williams goes on to say: "I heard the mountain men tell of the miserable state of Indian root diggers. Numbers of them would be found dead from pure starvation . . . [they] gather crickets and ants and dry them in the sun, and pound them into dust, and make bread of it to eat." Williams pronounced the trappers at the fort "fat, dirty, idle and greasy."

The first wheel tracks over the Rockies—and down to Fort Uncompahgre— were made by Robidoux, who was hauling freight in the two-wheel mule carts so prevalent among the Mexicans in Santa Fe. Williams verifies that, as early as 1842, Robidoux was using full-sized wagons, noting that, five days out from Fort Uncompahgre, Robidoux picked up a wagon which "he had left there a year before. He hitched his oxen to it and took it along."

As a business venture, Fort Uncompahgre failed. It was created just a little too late to catch the crest of the beaver felt hat craze. For two or three decades, there was a worldwide mania for felt hats made with beaver fur. They were in such demand with both civilians and the military that one hundred thousand pelts a year poured from these mountains into markets at home and overseas. The hats came in many shapes, but the usual style was the one you see on Christmas card carolers—tall, gray, with brim curved elegantly.

Suddenly, just as capriciously, the fad was silk top hats. The beaver market crashed. And it was a good thing, too; the beavers had almost been wiped out. Faced with crushing debt, Robidoux trading post shifted its focus to Indian barter. Antoine's debt for Taos Lightning alone was so great that in October, 1840, the distiller was trying to collect through the U.S. government.

The Utes were now hostile, at war with Mexico—as were most nearby tribes after the uprising in which the Pueblos succeeded in killing Charles Bent in the governor's office at Santa Fe. They attacked and burned Robidoux's trading post in the Uinta Mountains and attacked Fort Uncompahgre. Just what happened to the structure at the junction of the rivers is unknown. Some historians say it was burned, while others contend that it wasn't, noting that later explorers wrote of seeing the ruins of the fort and did not mention fire. Structures as extensive as the ones described above do not weather away to nothing in just thirty-six years—the time between Robidoux's abandoning the fort and the arrival of the first Anglo settlers. It is possible that a flood ripped through, changing the river channel, and that those beads and bullets you're looking for are at the bottom of the Gunnison.

If there had been a flag flying over the wedge of land between the Uncompahgre and Gunnison rivers on February 2, 1848, it would have been pulled down and the Stars and Stripes run up. When the treaty of that date ended our war with Mexico, the confluence of the rivers, along with the rest of the continent west of there, became U.S. territory.

Almost the first thing the government did after acquiring all that land was to start building a railroad across it. At the outset, a military survey crew passed through the confluence area headed for the West Coast.

But one of the West's most picturesque figures beat the survey crew by one year. In spring, 1852, Uncle Dick Wootton, famous trapper, hunter, gold prospector, and general entrepreneur, left tracks along the Uncompahgre where Delta is now. Nearly ten thousand tracks, in fact; but he came near leaving his bones there, too.

Learning that fat sheep were selling in California for ten times what they would bring in Taos, New Mexico, Wootton extended his credit as far as possible, bought nine thousand sheep, and collected a crew to help him herd them halfway across the continent. The crew consisted of twenty-two armed men, eight goats, and a dog—in addition to a *remuda* of saddle horses and enough pack mules to carry six months' worth of supplies for the party. Traveling slowly at grazing speed—so the sheep would arrive on the coast even fatter than when they left home—they had little trouble except for swimming the spring-flooded streams. Until they reached the Uncompahgre, that is. There a band of about a hundred Utes under Chief Uncotash demanded toll for passing through their lands. While the haggling was going on, Uncle Dick noticed that the Indians had divided into small squads, each squad standing beside one of his men. He realized that the Utes were only pretending to bargain and meant to kill his crew and steal sheep, horses, and mules. Outnumbered and as good as dead anyway, he jumped off his horse to take on the chief. Uncotash had the same idea, and they hit the ground together. In a wrestling match, Uncle Dick proved more powerful and quicker. Beneath Uncle Dick's lifted knife, Chief Uncotash called his men off and began toll negotiations.

> Crossing the Grand River [the Colorado, which was in flood that year, as all the rivers were] a little later was a dangerous business and it took me nearly two days to accomplish it . . . I had eight trained goats and a shepherd dog, which was worth more to me than four times the number of men would have been. The goats led the flock, and the dog brought up the stragglers. Two of the goats were picked out every day to act as leaders and they could be guided as easily as a well-trained yoke of oxen. When we had a stream to cross the two goats were driven into the water

just as you would drive a team of horses and they took the sheep across safely.

Uncle Dick Wootton's fame was such that, when Brigham Young learned he was in Salt Lake City, he invited him home to dinner. This put Uncle Dick in a bind because of what the rivers had done to his clothes.

> I hesitated a little about accepting because I didn't know how many of the Mrs. Youngs I might be presented to and I wasn't looking as handsome as I always liked to when going into the company of ladies.
>
> I had on a buckskin suit when I left home, and was still wearing that same suit. It had changed wonderfully in appearance, however, and it wasn't for the better, either. Swimming a dozen or more Rocky Mountain streams had spoiled the fit . . . and had been particularly disastrous to my trousers. Every time they got wet the legs stretched out a few inches, and every time this happened I had cut them off at the bottom. When I entered the Salt Lake Valley and got into a hot, dry climate I learned that I had made a mistake in cutting off those trousers. They commenced to shrink, and when I got into Salt Lake I should have been in just the fashion if knee breeches had been the style.

Just before the Civil War riveted national attention on North and South, there was a push to connect East and West by railroad. Engineers surveyed four possible routes. In 1853, one of those survey parties, commissioned by Secretary of State Thomas Jefferson and headed by Capt. John W. Gunnison, came into the confluence area over Cochetopa Pass and down the river that later was named for the captain. The entourage consisted of sixteen freight wagons, six mules to the wagon; an ambulance; and a lighter rig carrying the survey instruments. Ahead of the survey party was Captain Morris of Fort Leavenworth, with a detachment of thirty men, bridging streams, clearing a trail, and keeping Indians at a safe distance. The party frequently was accosted by howling Ute bands, who realistically perceived the railroad survey as an invasion of their lands.

Gunnison and his party detoured around Black Canyon (though the railroad itself did not) and reached the confluence of the Uncompahgre and the Gunnison rivers on September 15. They passed the Robidoux trading post, finding it in ruins; crossed the Gunnison at the ancient ford; and continued on their way into Utah and death. A band of Paiute Indians attacked them, killing Captain Gunnison and all but four of his party.

Four years later, in 1857–58, a U.S. Army wagon train, consisting of fifty or so wagons with three hundred men, led by Col. William Loring, struggled through the confluence area in the dead of winter on a desperate mission. They had been sent to Fort Union, New Mexico, to fetch supplies for Colonel Johnston's starving dragoons and infantry near Fort Bridger, after their supply train had been burned during the Utah War. If Fort Uncompahgre was visible when those wagons slogged through, no mention is made of it in the available Army records. But even that early, they were following visible tracks cut by iron wagon wheels long before the reservation was opened. When the first settlers spoke of the road from the confluence across the "Stinking Desert" to the Colorado River, they called it the Old Salt Lake Wagon Trail.

Nor was Fort Uncompahgre noted by Ferdinand Hayden, reluctant physician turned avid geologist, who headed the U.S. Geological Survey of the Territories when it came through the area about 1879. A man who hated indoor work and loved the wilds, Hayden fired up the nation to find out what was on, under, and above the lands it had acquired. He thoroughly recorded not only the lay of the land, but also its geology, botany, and ethnography. By 1879, when he reached the Uncompahgre, he had seen it all, so his comment, while overlooking the Uncompahgre Valley, is especially poignant: he would make his final home on this spot, if only the cursed deskwork back east would allow him to.

The discovery of gold on Cherry Creek in 1858, the influx of gold seekers—and accompanying profiteers—along the east, south, and north slopes of the Colorado Rockies put the Utes in a treaty squeeze. As early as 1675, though they had had the horse for less than fifty years, the Utes were already powerful enough that the Spanish thought it prudent to make friends of them by treaty. This arrangement worked well for the Utes. As Spain's hold on the country weakened, theirs grew. They reached their pinnacle of power in the following century, defeating tribal enemies and hunting and trading when and where they chose over a vast territory inside and outside what eventually became the state of Colorado.

Then, in 1849, the Utes, who had no calendar but seasons and moons, began descending a ladder of dates into oblivion. That was just after the United States won the Mexican War, acquiring all land to the Pacific. Indian Agent Calhoun succeeded in getting the Utes to sign a treaty recognizing the sovereignty of the United States. By that fatal signing, though they were not removed from any lands, they conceded nationality. Ouray was only a teenager at the time of the signing. Had he been chief, the fate of the Utes might have been different.

In 1863, additional treaty-like negotiations for the first time put the Utes inside named boundaries, depriving them of more than half of the immense country they had ranged since acquiring the horse. In 1868, they lost the vast agricultural and ranching potential of the San Luis Valley by treaty, as Spanish land-grant holders asserted their rights under the agreement that ended the Mexican War.

In 1873, the Utes were treated out of most of the San Juan country, because the U.S. government could not restrain the rush of prospector-miners seeking the gold and silver it contained. The Utes' holdings were reduced to merely the Western Slope of Colorado.

In 1880 . . .

Ouray was chief of the Utes when the most notorious person who ever camped at the confluence came through—Alferd Packer, the cannibal.

Packer was on a chain-gang, working Salt Lake City streets, when he was pointed out as a man who knew how to get to those fabulous gold veins in the San Juans recently ceded by the Utes. Twenty men made up the party that paid Packer's fine, freeing him to lead the expedition. Their first mistake was starting too late in the year. They had three hundred miles to go, just to reach the foot of the mountains they must cross to get to Saguache; and their average speed was ten miles a day. Time and supplies were lost when their raft buckled crossing Green River. It was well into November when they forded the Gunnison at the confluence and continued up the Uncompahgre to Chief Ouray's winter camp.

After Ouray was assured that they had not come to settle on the reservation but merely were passing through on their way to the San Juans, he warned them of snow-buried trails, ice-rimmed canyons, and blizzard-swept passes in the two hundred or so miles still between them and their goal. He offered them the hospitality of his camp until spring. Half of them took him up on the offer. The other half, splitting into two parties, went on, struggling through deeper and deeper snow, up steeper and steeper slopes, in country devoid of game because the game had better sense than to be there. The party not led by Packer dragged into the Indian Agency near the top of the pass emaciated and nearly starved to death. Packer arrived later, fat and vigorous, having survived on the bodies of his five companions after killing and robbing them.

In 1876, Colorado Territory—Utes and all—became a state, and counties were created right out across the Indian reservation. Gunnison City became the county seat for close to a third of the Western Slope, including the Uncompahgre and Gunnison valleys. The Utes ignored this high-handed usurpation; after all, the counties were just lines on paper. Probably nothing would have been done about their attitude, for a while at least, but a few Utes precipitated the removal of them all. Nathan Meeker, founder of the failing commune at Greeley, Colorado, got himself appointed Indian Agent to the White River Utes. He set out to change his charges in one year from hunter-warriors, proud and free atop spirited horses, to plowmen plodding a furrow behind equine rear ends. He made the fatal mistake of ordering the tribe to plow up the grassy valley where its ponies wintered—including the race track.

In the resulting uprising, Meeker and several agency people were killed, Meeker's wife and daughter were abducted, and troops sent to subdue the Utes were adroitly ambushed.

When White River Ute runners reached Ouray at his hunting camp on the Gunnison, he at first considered suicide, either by his own hand or by joining the futile revolt. He was sick. Sick physically: he was suffering from a kidney ailment that would soon be fatal. And sick spiritually: he had spent his life trying to save his people—stalling, maneuvering, yielding a little here and a little there, having seen that, when Indians tried to fight back, they were wiped out.

In 1880 . . . The response to the Meeker Massacre was a foregone conclusion, as Ouray had anticipated. Within weeks, treaty terms were proposed in Washington that eventually expelled all but Southern Utes from Colorado and placed them within the confines of a Utah desert reservation. Chief Ouray tried one final stall, stipulating that before the treaty could be enforced, the signatures (witnessed marks) of three-fourths of the male Utes must be obtained. At the time of Ouray's death, few Utes had signed. Paying out of his own money two silver dollars per *X*, Otto Mears finished the job. He knew that, given the vengeful fury of the times, the Utes would be annihilated if they didn't agree to go.

They delayed as long as they could, finding excuses—stray horses to round up, final ceremonies at sacred places in the hills. One Ute, Colorow, staged a futile war against cannon and cavalry, perhaps hoping that he would be killed and his bones remain behind.

The long march began, with Indians trailing down the Uncompahgre Valley, crossing the Gunnison at the ford below the confluence, rounding the smoke-colored Horn, and setting out across the desert. Fort cavalrymen rode behind the Indians, not so much to drive them out as to keep the wagons back. The first settlers came in on the dust of the departing Utes.

One man was breasting that tide. He was a young fellow, William McGinley, who had come onto the reservation too early, suffered the usual "sooner" run-in with the guards at Fort Crawford, and been released on September 3. He rode down to the Uncompahgre confluence, where he spent a jolly evening: "We arrived and camped a little north of where the town of Delta now stands. There were one or two companies of soldiers down toward Roubideau crossing. . . . they induced me to get into a poker or penny-ante game, which I did. We were getting along fine when all at once the bugle sounded, with instructions to break camp and march" to Fort Apache, where General Carr had been jumped by Arizona Indians.

So it wasn't a full military complement that escorted the Utes out of Colorado. In the confusion, McGinley and his party slipped away and rode down to the Grand River. Returning, they dodged the files of departing Utes riding dejectedly toward them on the wagon road. When they arrived back at the confluence, a group of settlers, defending their new land, took McGinley and his party for Utes who had decided not to leave and greeted them with guns.

4

Utes Dammed Out, Settlers Flood In

On September 14, 1881, the U.S. Army gave official permission for settlers to enter the reservation, but few wagons had waited for that. With the first rumor that the Utes were on the move, wagoneers had cracked accelerator whips over their horsepower and took off, their yearning stretching way ahead of the horses.

Most went by way of Otto Mears' Lake Fork Toll Road, over Son-of-a-Bitch Hill (later sanitized to "The Blue"), over Cerro Summit, and past Whiskey Cutoff. By this route wagonloads of liquor had reached Ouray miners without infringing reservation regulations barring it. But some settlers chose to angle northwest over Black Mesa to the North Fork of the Gunnison. W. O. Stephens was one of a party that made this choice, as his daughter Nellie remembered eighty years later:

> We loaded our possessions in a covered wagon, with mother's feather-
> bed and quilts on top, and set out over Black Mesa headed for the
> Uncompahgre by way of the North Fork of the Gunnison. There was no
> road over the Mesa, they cleared a path through trees. To get the wagons
> down off the Mesa, trees were felled and tied to the wheels. Even so it
> was necessary to station a man at each wheel as the vehicles were lowered
> over the edge.

One campfire meal especially impressed this child of seven: "Once we were guests of some cowboys who had killed a beef and cooked it in a wash boiler."

Sylvester Huffington started late. There was no hurry; his land was staked and his cabin roofed, and every extra day he worked with the Denver and Rio Grande Railroad (D&RG) made him $1.50 richer, plus another dollar if he worked his own team on the earth scraper.

At dawn on September 20, Huffington's two wagons were loaded, his wife and four children were aboard, and he was bending to hook tug to singletree when a boy came running from the telegraph shack. "The President died! President Garfield died last night!" Since Mrs. Huffington was a distant cousin of Garfield, the death had special meaning for them.

Perhaps the wounded president's incapacity and death had delayed action; at any rate, though the Utes had been removed by early September and the army officially welcomed settlers in mid-September, it was June of the next year before the federal government got around to proclaiming Ute lands open for settlement. By then, thousands of homesteads had been staked in the Uncompahgre, Gunnison, and Grand River valleys.

Smallest of the Huffingtons was four-year-old Oscar, whose most vivid memory of that trip was lying on the bedding in the back of the wagon holding the rope that linked the wagon to the spotted milk cow trailing along behind.

The trip from Gunnison to the confluence of rivers took four days—remarkably good time, considering that even with today's bulldozer-straightened highways, the distance is more than a hundred miles.

"We would have made the trip a day sooner but one morning all of our horses had disappeared. My father was afraid the Indians had stolen them. He and the young man he'd hired to drive the other wagon hunted all day for the missing horses. They found them, but we couldn't get anywhere that day."

The first settlers to arrive at the spread of land between the two rivers found it already occupied—by a tent store (one with wooden walls and a canvas roof) bearing the sign "McGranahans & Butler Emporium." Soonering the sooners, the McGranahans are said to have been operating somewhere on the reservation since 1879. Apparently, though cabin-builders were ordered out, they were allowed to remain because their stake-out was considered a trading post and not land preemption.

Just as they'd planned, the McGranahans' store formed a nucleus around which the wagons gathered as they came threading down the Uncompahgre Valley. Tents were put up randomly; there could be no streets until a town was laid out. One of the wagons, labeled "Vanderventer Vehicle Store," offered to take merchandise wherever settlers staked claims. And they were staking homesteads in all directions. Riding through the yellowing cottonwoods, they found and "located" all

McGranahan and Butler's store replaced their Ute trading-post tent in the sagebrush just months after the reservation opened in 1881. Courtesy of Delta County Historical Society.

the farmland along the nearby river banks in a matter of weeks. Sylvester Huffington, who had guessed wrong about where the town would be, hurriedly pulled up stakes and put them down again on the other side of the Gunnison. He also had to hurry the building of a second cabin to beat the stork; the town's first white baby, Della Huffington, was born on March 20, 1882. Having the only milk cow in town, he set his oldest child to delivering warm milk by the bucket.

When town-creator Gov. George A. Crawford arrived, he worked fast. He organized a town company. Selecting squatter W. O. Stephens' claim for the "Main" section, he and the company laid out the town, though it would not be platted officially for many months. Finally, he gave the new town its name, "Uncompahgre," then dashed off to do the same things again at the confluence of the Gunnison and Grand rivers, before somebody beat him to it.

The usual way to launch a town was to pick a likely spot along a railroad survey, buy somebody's claim, plat it out in lots, and sell the lots as settlers poured in. Nellie Stephens wrote, "When Father took up his ranch he agreed to sell it to Gov. Crawford if they succeeded in making a town. Not every town that was planned and plotted really turned out to be a town."

To help railroads extend lines into new areas, the government gave them free land along the route—not merely right-of-way, but with some lines a twenty-acre depot tract every ten miles in addition. Any or none of those depot spots might become a town. By whim, for profit, or because of difficult terrain, the road might change its original survey and bypass a burgeoning townsite altogether. The Denver and Rio Grande Railroad at times made a point of slightly bypassing towns established on its projected route, preferring to reap profits by creating its own settlements as it went.

In such cases, the railroad owned stock in the town company, and its officials customarily were memorialized by having something named for them. Besides deeding half the town company's stock to the railroad, the town named three of its streets for D&RG officials: Palmer, the president; Dodge, the general manager; and Hastings, the assistant general manager. Meeker Street commemorated the massacre that had triggered the evacuation of the Utes, opening the land to settlement and making the town possible.

Eaton Avenue was named for Gov. Benjamin A. Eaton, who already had had an entire town on the other side of the Continental Divide named for him. The governor dented history so lightly that he scarcely makes the index in history books; a century's worth of people using the street named for him have supposed that the name is a corruption of *eatin'*, because, as the main route of access to the railroad station, it was lined with restaurants. Special and imposing as it is, Eaton Avenue apparently was created by accident. When the town was laid out in neat rectangles, the D&RG depot was a couple of boxcars on a siding. Somebody someplace else—on the other side of the Rockies, probably—decided on the depot's location, and the company put it where that individual had pointed his finger. It had nothing to do with the layout of the town. Eaton was carved through the intervening streets at an angle, so as to connect town and depot, and it was made wide to accommodate dray and buggy traffic to the hotels, stores, and eating houses that always clustered around depots. A few of these early structures survive—most notably, the ornate Eldina Hotel. As laid out, the new town included five hundred acres which the town company bought from three squatters—W. O. Stephens, Sylvester Huffington, and a man named Andrews. Each was paid ten town lots. For about eight months, town lots were free. A settler could pick any lot he wanted except for certain lots assigned to churches, library and reading room, and three public squares reserved for courthouse, schools, and park.

In December, 1881, Governor Crawford came up and finished the job of legally incorporating what he called the Uncompahgre Townsite. Three of the town company's directors were D&RG officials: David C. Dodge, William A. Bell, and R. F. Weitbreck. The latter was replaced by D&RG's man, William Hastings, who visited the town and liked it so much that he built a house on Garnet Mesa.

Other members of the town corporation were Crawford himself, its president; Harvey Bailey; M. C. Vanderventer; and Charles L. Anderson.

When the town was nine months old, it started charging for those lots, $100 to $150 each, depending on location. In June the platting was completed. Henry Hammond cleared the townsite of sage and greasewood, receiving $800 and four corner lots for his work. One of those lots is on the northeast corner of Main and Second, where eventually he built a big turreted brick house that still stands. The McGranahan brothers roofed their business so quickly that some history probers doubt that the brothers actually began by selling cornmeal and button shoes from a tent.

That December visit was about the last the town saw of Gov. George Addison Crawford. While he was upcountry hiring Samuel Wade to survey and plat his two towns, a claim jumper staked off some of his Grand Junction townsite. The resulting lawsuits kept Crawford occupied in the few years remaining before he died.

In spring of 1884, the newspaper published a letter from Crawford tensely urging the town company to prove up on the land the town was sitting on. The editor, perhaps unaware that the man was dying, commented: "Gov. Crawford keeps promising us a big hotel and flouring mill, nothing comes of it." He did, however, in his last official act, deed a lot to the town on which to build a fire-hose house. When Crawford died that year, 1891, he left the "expressed will that his memory be perpetuated in a library building in the city of his founding." Though no library was established, he does not lack a memorial. Crawford Avenue was named for him, and his body rests in a tomb on Waterworks Hill, overlooking that other confluence, the Gunnison and Colorado rivers.

With surveyor Samuel Wade's town plat to go by, the footpaths and wagon ruts winding between tents straightened into streets. The foundation logs of new cabins were lined up with the boundaries of town lots. There were twenty-five hundred lots. In March, 1883, the *Delta Chief* was advertising business lots at seventy-five to three hundred dollars and residential ones at twenty-five to one hundred dollars.

Nina Aldridge Peterson described those first cabins. They were small, some only eight by ten feet, with dirt floor and dirt roof. A blanket was hung up for a door, cloth sacking tacked across the unglazed window. Some wives covered the dirt floor with the wagon canvas laid over a pad of cattail reed, while others stretched that canvas above cookstove and table to keep earthen-roof dust from sifting down onto the food. After men had time to hunt, bear and deer hides served as rugs. Real windows and doors came with the railroad track and the town's first hardware store.

Louisa Koppe described the furniture in a similar 1882 cabin: sprucewood chairs with seats woven of willow, cupboards and bureaus made of drygoods boxes with calico curtains, a rough board table, and beds made of cottonwood boards with straw ticks, "but we had feather ticks that mother brought from Georgia." Since lifting logs to wall height was next to impossible for one man alone, "cabin raisings" were joint efforts made into social events. Women and children gathered for a shared noon meal. To make life easier for newcomers, the people of the town erected a floored tent—later replaced by a house—that provided free shelter for a newly arrived family during the week or so it would take to raise a cabin of their own.

Nor did tents disappear from the townscape.

A plague of tuberculosis was sweeping the eastern states. Called consumption because it reduced the body literally to skin and bones, the disease was fatal and had no cure. All a doctor could do was prescribe light-weight air that could be handled more easily by sick lungs. Dry, high-altitude air is light, so patients were advised to go to the mountainous West and live in a tent or in a sanatorium, typically consisting of several stories of screened porches. "Merry Lungers" the consumptives were called—or called themselves—because the victims usually were young, in their twenties, and because the disease often produced a strange, nervous exhilaration in the dying patient. The house-tents had wooden floors, three-foot wooden walls, and wood-framed doors that often were beautifully paneled. A canvas stretched over the tent kept it cool under summer sun. Many of these young people died—among them, the town's founder, Governor Crawford—but a surprising number recovered. The word got around. Mile-high Delta, situated in the cloud-parting rain-shadow of the Uncompahgre Plateau, had about the driest, lightest air anywhere around. The Servite order of Chicago built a large brick monastery on Garnet Mesa especially for its tubercular young men who were studying for the priesthood. Wealthy families furnished their sick with everything to make a tent luxurious—carved oak chiffoniers, central draft lamps, patented rocking chairs. But many desperate families had spent everything just to send their children here, leaving them nothing to live on. More consumptives came than the tiny community could handle. Patients crowded the newly constructed county poorhouse south of town and died there pitifully. One of many single-paragraph obituaries noted: "Nick Strang, 21, young German, died of tuberculosis at the county home. No relatives or friends." The situation eased after a minister toured Colorado churches, explaining the situation and pointing out other salubrious locations.

Main Street was changing rapidly. Hank Hammond opened his livery stable, enlarged it to include a saddlery, and on the side ran a race track on his homestead. J. J. Barker set up a blacksmith shop prepared to "fix anything from a needle to a threshing machine" and then added so much stuff that the place became a virtual hardware store. R. M. McMurray began building a drugstore. Harvey Bailey was fixing to open a bank. Vanderventer went into the hotel business, establishing the Uncompahgre House, bearing the town's name, then sold it to Dr. J. H. Yarger, who had big renovation plans but died one month later of peritonitis after accidentally stabbing himself with a dissecting knife.

Lumber to build "real" houses was beginning to come down from sawmills located on the Uncompahgre Plateau.

Coal for forging, heating, and lime burning was first dug where exposed by river erosion west of the town. Of poor quality, this coal was never used after Joe Rollins, prospecting on the slopes of Grand Mesa, discovered an outcrop of the vast sheet of coal riding on the striking sandstone formation named for him.

Every male, including business and professional men, staked out land. Even if you never had mined or farmed a lick in your life, you couldn't pass up an investment that got you 160 acres for merely $1.25 an acre and living on it a few months of the year. If you never turned a hand toward the required improvements—fencing, buildings, and plowing—you could sell your relinquishment for higher and higher prices, as valley land was locked up by corner stakes. Homesteader-attorney A. E. Amsbary followed the homestead law scrupulously, establishing his family in a cabin on his California Mesa claim and walking to the office each morning. Considering the poundage he carried, he probably needed the exercise.

Sometime that first spring, between his canvas and roofed business enterprises, M. C. Vanderventer prowled the plateau and came upon a mystery he described as

> a chunk of bullion weighing nearly 12 pounds which looked as if it had been melted and run into a frying pan. One edge had a hole as if when cast a cobble stone had been placed in it before cooling, and then knocked out. When found it had a short rope through it for packing. Sent to Gunnison, an assay showed its worth at $400 a ton. From different pieces of similar metal around the old camps of the Utes it is believed the Indians smelted the mineral from the ore and used it in making bullets.

Others discovered veins of copper in Unaweep Canyon and deposits of sulfur along the North Fork. Nearer home, semiprecious jewels, chiefly garnets, were turned up in the first years of plowing the mesa east of the new town, giving Garnet Mesa its name. Harvey Bailey had some of these gemstones—opal and chalcedony—cut for pin and ring sets in Denver; by the time he founded the Delta County Bank, he stood behind his window on opening day resplendent in local jewels. Where the opals came from, no one knows, but the garnets probably washed down from the rim of Black Canyon. You may still find garnets in the mica schists at Morrow Point, some nested in the twinned staurolite "fairy crosses" that produced them.

The new settlement between the rivers had geography problems. The nearest post office was at Fort Crawford, the old Cantonment Military Post thirty miles upstream, and the county seat was Gunnison City, more than a hundred miles away.

In applying for a post office, the town company rejected Crawford's "Uncompahgre" as being too unwieldy a town name to spell or speak. Following postal regulations, the company submitted five names, from which postal officials would select the first not already existing in the state. Delta topped the list— suggested because the wedge of land between the rivers was shaped like the letter *D*, or *delta* in the Greek alphabet. The choice reflected the unusually high percentage of college graduates among those who pioneered in the confluence area.

If they didn't know how inconvenient it was to be a hundred miles from the county seat, they learned after their first election, when a man on horseback made the trip carrying their forty-four votes in the requisite locked ballot box. They'd had a little trouble finding a box with a lock, but W. O. Stephens' wife had donated her keepsake box.

In September 1882, the railhead arrived, workers having blasted and graded and laid a hundred miles of track through mountainous terrain in eleven months, using nothing but dynamite and horsepower. The construction crew came through so fast that it barely took time to sidetrack two boxcars to serve as the Delta depot. The reason for the breakneck construction speed was that D&RG President Palmer was racing to connect Denver and Salt Lake City by rail before some other railroad beat him to it. General Manager Dodge rampaged up and down the route, fuming about slipshod construction that would result, he forecast, in rails bending under the weight placed on them and every damned bridge having to be replaced inside two years.

The next year, the state legislature finally got around to dividing big, ungainly Gunnison County into four counties, three of which had to find names for themselves. George Moody, reminiscing in the *Laborer* in 1907, described the process: "We wanted to name our county 'Dodge,' Grand Junction wanted to name theirs 'Palmer,' both after D&RG officials. But when Montrose wanted to name theirs 'Mears' after Otto Mears (owner of that *other* railroad), that busted the whole scheme, and the names we now have were finally agreed upon." Delta was designated county seat because only Delta, of five embryo towns in the newly mapped county, was on the railroad line.

In October of that year, the survey came through. Squatters (which was everybody) learned the boundaries of what they were squatting on, and the town found out where it is on the face of the planet—the southeast quarter of Section 13 and northeast quarter of Section 34, Township 15 S, Range 96 W; and the southwest quarter of Section 16 and northwest quarter of Section 19, Township 15 S, Range 95 W.

Eighteen months after the first covered wagons pulled into the brushy wedge between two rivers, a full-fledged town had sprung up. There were three general mercantile stores, two livery stables (one of which—Hank Hammond's, of course—was operating a biweekly stage line up the North Fork), a bank, two drugstores, a newspaper, three saloons (complete with billiard tables), a boot and shoemaker, a barber shop with a tin bathtub in the back room, three churches in the process of organizing, two schools, a county courthouse (a log cabin on the alley at Fourth and Main so bug-infested that citizens feared for county records), a hotel, a bakery, a watch-repair jeweler who was also into real estate, a laundry, a meat market, a combined bookstore–post office (where you could buy cigars and shoot dice until the owner put up a sign forbidding the latter), two blacksmith shops, a saddlery–harness shop, a jail of sorts, three lawyers, three doctors, a county judge, a milliner-dressmaker, and a health spa (a windowed structure built over the sulfur spring below the juncture of First Street and Crawford Avenue, complete with benches where you could sit and sip medicinally smelly water).

The courthouse was a "stockade" log cabin. That is, the citizens didn't take time to miter-cut and lay up logs, but simply dug a trench and stood the logs on end. The first criminal case sounds like something out of today's newspapers—child abuse. An upriver man had fathered his own grandson. He was convicted, but the new makeshift jail was so porous that he escaped that night.

In March, 1883, publisher Robert Blair complained in his newspaper: "Delta needs a good lawyer or two. Court will soon open, but as yet there is no one to practice before it." By August, the town had three lawyers, and a few months later there were five.

One of the first attorneys was A. R. King, who gave up his practice in Gunnison and moved to Delta on the recommendation of lawyer friend Albert Amsbary. In August, King, a native of Kewanee, Illinois, and a graduate of Union College in Chicago, advertised his services in the paper. In November he was named county judge, and in January he had helped to organize a building and loan company. He built a four-room house on Main Street—at the time, the only painted house in town. Then he went back east, married his waiting sweetheart (who had been his student in school), and moved her west in the relative luxury of a passenger train.

Keeping a window eye out for horse thieves? Delta County's first jail lurked beside a stable. Photograph 1974 by Muriel Marshall.

After the initial excitement of her arrival, he remembered that he had promised to get her a piano, so he bought her one of the only two in town. It was in a saloon.

Annie Caldwell King, a Midwestern farm girl, never had been in a saloon before. She took it all in: barstools, spittoons, bar with scuffed foot-rail, back-bar shelves holding kegs and bottles, bartender counting cash that he pawed from his apron pockets, pictures of ladies wearing not a stitch. She went over to the Chickering Grand and began playing the only thing she knew by heart: hymns.

Judge King became a leader in legal affairs in the town, in the county, and eventually in the state. He was named to the newly created State Court of Appeals in 1911. His wife was also promoted, according to the etiquette of the time being known from then on as "Mrs. Judge King."

Mrs. Judge King—who had had to read a book to learn how to serve her first "company" dinner—gradually assumed social leadership in the town. After King built Annie a fine house on Garnet Mesa, she regularly held "afternoons at home." These formal events were attended by ladies in ballooning leg-o'-mutton sleeves with enormous hats atop their expanded, backcombed hairdos. Alighting from chauffeured carriages, they dropped their calling cards on a tray before entering the parlor.

"Garnethurst," Annie named the new house, and she had that address-name printed on her own calling card.

Though not the largest house ever built between the two rivers, Garnethurst has become the most notable, for two reasons. First, its several owners—even those who owned the building when it served as the town's first hospital, after the King family moved to Denver—have realized its historic value and preserved it with as few changes as possible. Second, the Kings' daughter, Ula King Fairfield, wrote and published a book, *Pioneer Lawyer,* about Garnethurst and its founding family. Though the book long has been out of print, a copy of it "goes with the house" when it passes from owner to owner.

Garnethurst, with its lacy wood gables, carved newel posts, and fancy banisters, is a classic. Present owner Maxine Wheatcroft and her daughter Linda Loftis are working to keep it that way, by listing the property in the change-deterring official rosters of state and national historic buildings.

Another of Garnethurst's claims to fame is that it was regularly cleaned and polished by the mother of the future world champion prizefighter, Jack Dempsey. Celia Smoot Dempsey was brought to the Rockies from West Virginia in a covered wagon by her hard-drinking, fiddle-playing, wanderlusting husband Hyrum. Tiny and full of energy and devotion, Celia was the one the family (it eventually numbered thirteen children) depended on to keep food on the table in the intervals when Hyrum had tired of one job—ranching, mining, roadwork, whatever—and hadn't found another that he liked.

Settling first at Manassa, the Dempseys came to Delta when Jack was nine. They lived in a little house just north of the present post office. Hyrum worked in the brickyard, Celia "did cleaning," and the children did chores for people.

When Jack was ten years old, attending fourth grade in Central School, he had a before-school job, earning ten cents a morning for sweeping the sidewalk in front of J. D. VanVolkenburgh's store just across the alley. The boy's build and speed came to John Maxwell's attention. Maxwell, railway agent for the D&RG, was much interested in boxing, and he promoted "smokers" on the Western Slope. Seeing Jack dashing down the alley to his job every morning, Maxwell remarked that the kid was certainly well built for only ten.

It is possible that Maxwell launched Dempsey on his career. The family moved back to Manassa, but Maxwell kept him in mind, and when Jack was sixteen or so, Maxwell brought him back for several boxing events in Delta and the surrounding vicinity. Maxwell saw him as "a rough and tumble kid" but one with promise. The teenage "kid" wasn't idly waiting for fame. He got a job at the Delta brickyard.

Jack Dempsey had a warmth and a strength of character that kept him "The Champ" in people's hearts long after succeeding world champions had come and gone, their names forgotten. But it was probably Annie King's character, the impression she made on him as a boy, that led him to stay in touch with the Kings.

"I had not supposed Jack Dempsey would remember our family," Ula wrote, "as he lived so short a time in Delta, but a few years ago, he telephoned my mother from the Denver airport. He said he wanted to hear her voice; that his mother had spoken so many times of her." Far away in New York City, Jack Dempsey knew when Annie King died. His own mother died at about the same time, and he had just come through a divorce that almost cost him custody of his children. He was deeply involved in trying to serve in World War II, despite his age. With all this, still he knew when Annie King died and wrote her bereaved ones of his sorrow.

Growing up the only girl in a family of boys, Ula King's memories of childhood in early Delta tend to cite her brothers' exploits: "Fred let me hold the gunnysack to catch the prairie dogs he drowned out of their holes. . . . He also collected birds' eggs, raised rabbits, and dug caves." Fred was a good hunter, an outstanding trap-shooter, and enough of a gunsmith to load his own cartridges. "He seemed very expert as he rammed in the powder, wads and shot, and neatly capped the shells."

In those days, most boys had been given guns by the age of ten, as a kind of initiation into manhood. The presentation was accompanied by serious training in the use of and responsibility for the weapon—to such effect that, though the newspapers reported numerous misplaced bullets fired by adult males in or out of their right minds, no children seem to have made that kind of news. Well, there was that eleven-year-old standing on a railroad embankment who bet his two pals he could put a .22 bullet through the windows of a moving passenger coach without hitting anybody. He couldn't.

The confluence was heaven—and a frontier university—for boys. There, under the guise of adventure and play, they practiced at manhood by prowling willow banks and cattail swamps in search of food for the family table. They hunted cottontail rabbits, quail, and ducks. They fished and seined for trout and whitefish, bringing home proud catches. They hunted frogs at night, with lanterns in the early days and flashlights later. In the latter case, as Paul Edwards remembers, they had to cook the catch themselves, because mothers were squeamish about frying food that kept kicking in the pan.

Fred King grew up to become "one of the most famous trapshooters in the nation," as well as a practicing lawyer and a Texas oil man. In turn, his son Rufus, at age fourteen, competing against grown men, won the Grand American Handicap at Vandalia, Ohio, when he broke twenty-four out of a possible twenty-five targets in the shoot-off before a gallery of eight thousand people.

The railroad was the most important thing in town, and Eaton Avenue's angle emphasized the fact. All other streets squared with each other, but Eaton Avenue took off on a wide, tree-lined, forty-five-degree slant that ended smack against the brand new brick depot like a mall leading to a castle. Actually, the avenue was like a park, just made for promenading. Strolling down Eaton Avenue in the late afternoon to see the train come in was part of the town's social life—the hubbub of people arriving and leaving, the somnolent chuffing of the little narrow-gauge engine taking on water, the bustling conductor and brakies, the baggage handlers with their high-wheeled carts, the postal agent in the mail-car door catching tossed bags of mail that he would sort into wall boxes in his moving post office as soon as the train got started again. The Delta House hack met every train. People said whenever the Delta House team heard the train whistle, the horses would head for the depot, swing around, and back the rig up to the loading dock, precise to the inch, whether anybody had hold of the reins or not. Sometimes the driver would show off to prove it, reins tied to the whip socket, arms folded while the team performed.

Ula and her friend Katharine Amsbary Hedgcock vividly described traveling by narrow-gauge. Even after the tracks were broad-gauged in valleys on either side of the Continental Divide, the railroad between them, up over the highest pass in America, was still narrow-gauge. This meant that all passengers and freight had to be unloaded and reloaded twice—at Montrose and again at Salida. "The ride through Black Canyon was a thriller," Katharine wrote. "In later years, an observation car without a top was provided for those who wished to crane their necks to see the tops of the forbidding canyon walls—just a flatcar with bolted chairs. Smoke and cinders drifted back on the passengers, but the views were worth it. Two engines were put on at Sargents to pull the train over Marshall Pass."

At the bottom of its slot, the Gunnison River bounced from wall to wall, forcing the railroad track to cross innumerable bridges. Ula, who made the trip at a very early age, remembered those black walls vividly: "miles of deep and narrow gorges, shadowed by towering cliffs . . . Straight into the sky pointed an unusual rock formation called Curicanti Needle. At the risk of getting cinders in our eyes, we leaned out of the windows in order to see its very top."

But what most enthralled tiny Ula was the ladies' washroom, and the sight of railroad ties flashing by at the bottom of the china toilet hole. "It was fascinating, mesmerizing! Mother sympathized with my reluctance to leave, but she made it plain that there was nothing between my plump little limbs and the track below, and that if I should buckle up and fall through, I would never be seen again."

The *Delta Chief's* biggest story of its first year concerned the Denver and Rio Grande Railroad. The D&RG's General Manager Dodge had been right; when crews working both ways connected rails at Green River, linking the oceans, crews went back and began replacing most of the quick-built bridges. They didn't finish the replacement at Delta soon enough.

In the dark of night, its passengers all asleep, an eastbound train started across that quick-built bridge at the mouth of Roubideau Canyon. It was late May, flood season. The engineer, feeling the bridge give way under him, had just enough time to jerk whistle and brakes before the engine and mail car tumbled into the rampaging Gunnison River. By braking and not jumping, he saved his passengers' lives—the rest of the train hung teetering on the canyon brink—but lost his own life.

Six months later, when that little narrow-gauge engine, Number 107, had been salvaged from twelve feet of water, overhauled in the D&RG's Denver shops and put back on the line, it killed another engineer. On its second run, it hit a boulder on the track west of Delta near Escalante Canyon. No engineer would touch the throttle of Number 107 after that.

5

The Awesome Power of Water

When Herbert Castle had snugly ensconced his little "Madonna of the Mule" in a cabin on the north side of the Gunnison River, he went back to driving pack trains for the mines to get some ready cash. Eliza Castle and her father, George States, planted the "first garden" in North Delta. Carrying water in buckets from the river, they produced enough potatoes, corn, beans, and squash to feed the family through the following winter.

To go to town, they crossed a bridge that, though it couldn't have been more than a few months old, already was known as the Old Cottonwood Bridge, or, as one letter to the editor dubbed it, the "Poor Excuse" for a bridge. In February of what would be the worst flood season Deltans would ever know, the county (at Hart's urging) bought that bridge (and the responsibility for improving it) for eight hundred dollars. About nine weeks later it was gone, and a character called Ark Hall was seen in a slough, gunnysack seine in hand, saying he was "trying to catch Hart's bridge." That was the last time anybody cracked a joke about the Flood of 1884.

It had been a winter of heavy snow, but the people of Delta didn't know how unusually heavy, having only two previous winters to judge by. They wrote home about spectacular red sunsets but didn't attribute them or the massive snowfall to the eruption of the weather-altering Krakatoa volcano on the other side of the world. They heard tales of people killed in avalanches, of mine towns completely buried, of roofs crushed in Durango, and of cross-country snowshoe travelers resting on telephone pole crossbars; but maybe this was the norm. On all sides of town, the mountains became blank white walls, their granite and basalt bones buried and invisible. Every flake of snow on this side of four mountain ranges had to pass the confluence on its way to the sea. There were no dams to hold the snowmelt back or slow it down.

When Herbert Castle and his brother Newton, returning from the mines, crossed the Poor Excuse to get home, it was still standing. The brothers set about building a toll bridge upriver at the mouth of Forked Tongue Creek to give Surface Creekers heading for town the option of bypassing the gumbo clay 'dobes. When the county commissioners noted the Castles' expertise, they hired them to beef up the Poor Excuse. By then, the Forked Tongue Creek bridge was nearly finished, so the Castle brothers cut and rafted three thousand feet of bridge-logs down to the Delta site. Spring came on quick and hot. Waters rising suddenly swept the logs in the general direction of the Gulf of Mexico. (The Castle boys were nothing if not good businessmen; the county paid them $571 for those lost logs.)

From May 14 to July 2, the newspaper chronicled disaster. First the Poor Excuse went, cutting off North Delta; then the Hotchkiss bridge went, the new Tongue Creek bridge went, and the abutments of two bridges in progress—at Paonia and on the Uncompahgre—were swept away. The replacement D&RG bridge, "rebuilt last spring with stone piers to last forever," was washed out. Delta became "the western terminus of railroad travel, as passenger trains lay over and returned east each morning." Then track and bridges in Black Canyon failed. Every town in the Uncompahgre and Gunnison valleys was cut off from every other and from the world. Supplies began to run low, a flour famine loomed, and the newspaper, running short on paper, came out "on the half-shell"—two pages instead of four.

River islands snagged piles of driftwood that deflected raging waters, which in turn cut away farm after farm.

Impromptu ferries up and down the rivers were ripped from their moorings, and wagons trying to ford the North Fork and Uncompahgre were swept away. A woman in one of those swamped wagons made it to shore in rushing water, despite corsets and numerous petticoats. Ten workmen desperately trying to save the railroad bridge swam for their lives as their scow capsized.

Yet there is no record of a single drowning. The Castles were given some of the credit for this. They rigged a toll ferry to put people safely across the turbulent river to North Delta. The *Delta Chief* noted, "The Castle boys handle transfer over the river well. They are at home on treacherous water. The Ferry Skiff starts at the big gate on Johnsons' ranch on the north side of the river and lands at Sulfur Spring at the foot of Main Street. A distance of something over a mile."

According to Ute memory, an even bigger flood had occurred twenty-two years earlier, when flowing water covered the valley, bluff to bluff—more than two miles wide. The first settlers recalled evidence of this flood: "a mountain of driftwood piled against the end of Garnet Mesa. High-country pines. They'd come a long, long way." There is no record of any subsequent flood approaching this magnitude, but before Blue Mesa and other dams restrained the rivers, they were prone to gouge out new farmland. They regularly picked on certain places, one being the Scottie's Cabins motel, which routinely flooded "bed-level" when the rivers went on their spring rampages.

Giving up on rebridging, at least for the foreseeable future, the county commissioners ordered two cable-boat ferries, each twelve by thirty feet. One was to run between Delta and North Delta, and the other at the mouth of Black Canyon, where mail, stagecoach, freight wagon, and buggy traffic had to cross the Gunnison to go up the North Fork. They gave the Castles ten days to build the boats; however, their man, John Chapman, didn't quite make the deadline. Five weeks later the paper announced: "Ferry cable swung into position, running next week."

Mrs. Newt Castle described that ferry traffic: "There were many travelers across the Gunnison in 1884 going to Oregon and other places farther west. The wagons they took apart, loaded the running gear on the boat and towed the wagon box as if it was another boat. The horses they led by a halter rope, and a man sat in the back seat and held the rope. It took several trips across to convey some of these parties."

Because there were many streams and no bridges, westward trekking wagonbeds usually were built as watertight as boats, to keep contents dry while crossing.

Ferries, fords, and low-water log bridges ruled cross-river traffic at the confluence until 1911, when the Campbell Switch Bridge was built down near the supposed site of old Fort Uncompahgre. On the main road (the old Salt Lake–Santa Fe Wagon Trail), its approach hugged the south side of the river almost to the canyon drop-off, ignoring North Delta altogether. If you lived in North Delta and needed a fly swatter or a pound of axle grease or if you wanted to see *Uncle Tom's Cabin* at the AnnaDora Opera House—and the river was too high to ford or the ferry cost too many pennies—you hitched up the buggy and trundled three or four miles downstream and an equal distance back up to Main Street.

Campbell Switch Bridge was surprisingly short. The river narrows here, as if anticipating the canyon-squeeze of the lower Gunnison; one span of twelve elegantly lean steel trusses reached across nicely. Completion of the bridge was celebrated by the usual all-night dance—orchestra on one end, refreshments at the other, couples whirling over the brand new planking under starlight and lanterns strung from truss to truss. The river not only narrows at Campbell Switch, but

"Modern" ferry crossing the Gunnison in 1891, carrying team and wagon. Earlier ferries towed wagons like boats, and made teams swim along behind. Courtesy of Delta County Historical Society.

also it lunges this way and that, as if seeking an easier way to the sea than through that canyon up ahead. One spring it looped off, leaving the bridge high and dry. The county commissioners met and decided to wait a year or two before moving the bridge, to see if the river wouldn't change its mind and come back.

In 1924, the highway department bridged the Gunnison River with a 608-foot steel structure having four arched spans, linking North Delta to Main Street at last—as well as to New York City and Los Angeles via scarcely-graveled roads. That bridge served for more than half a century, carrying everything U.S. Highway 50 funneled onto it. But as traffic thickened and vehicles widened it became hazardous—one observer noted that two semi-trucks meeting midway barely cleared their coats of paint. It was replaced with two double-lane concrete bridges so much like a continuation of the highway itself that you must look closely and quickly to see that you are crossing a beautiful river.

The power of water to produce and sustain life on the planet far exceeds its moving force, though that can brush away bridges, move mountains into the sea, and drive monstrous turbines. Confluence homesteads were sage-cactus worthless until settlers rigged ways to tap that greater power of water and spread the two life-giving rivers over the land. It was the first of many projects in which they wrested profit from an asset by changing it before they let go of it.

First-comers almost instantly staked all the low land bordering the rivers and about as instantly put both kinds of water power to use: with their waterwheels they powered the river to lift itself up onto dry land, thus putting the water-power of life into dry seeds.

Costing about two hundred dollars, the wheels were some twenty-five feet high and four feet wide. Axled on substantial piers, they had wooden buckets or scoops every two feet around the rim, each lifting several gallons of water. The massive structure was powered by the river's pushing against wide paddles. The flood of 1884 got them all.

Compared to digging miles of irrigation ditches, the waterwheel was a quick, cheap way to get water up out of the river and onto the land, so immediately after the Big Flood of '84, the town's two hardware stores had a run on spikes and bolts, as waterwheels were replaced. Some wheels promptly went out again in the high floods of 1885 (stratospheric dirt from the Krakatoa eruption affected weather for two years). You can still see an old wooden irrigation waterwheel at Dominguez, half buried in mud and willows. And the sluice box for one of the earliest waterwheels rests among river cottonwoods on the Roy Long farm, under the bluff that doctors dub Pill Hill because so many physicians live on it.

Waterwheels are fine if your farm borders the river, but ditches deliver more water to ground that lies higher and farther from the waterway. Only a few weeks after the first covered wagons pulled to a stop where the rivers meet, all the bottomland had been staked out. Next-comers eyed the surrounding mesa benches, estimating the cost and labor involved in bringing water up there.

Though W. O. Stephens still had time to restake bottomland after selling his homestead to the city, he chose land on Garnet Mesa, overlooking the confluence on the east. It was considered an unwise move; to get enough fall to run water that much higher, the ditch would have to tap the Uncompahgre five miles upriver. Folks thought W. O. was just too busy with other things—he built the first Methodist church, served two hitches as Delta postmaster, helped organize the building and loan company, and was a shareholder in the Delta Bridge Company, among other things—to realize what he was getting into with that Garnet Ditch and Reservoir Company. But as it turned out, the reddish mesa soil was softer and took water better. Folks began saying that W. O. always landed standing up.

On the Gunnison, the first diversion dam was two miles above the confluence, just high enough to carry water to North Delta farms. Hartland Ditch, at the original level, proved inadequate for North Delta farms; so another cooperative, the North Delta Canal, was organized, taking water out of the river near the mouth of Black Canyon and ditching it fourteen miles through adobe badlands—and decades of trouble.

"Irrigation ditches are being taken out of the Uncompahgre and Gunnison rivers in every direction. Before summer is over water will be on all the mesas surrounding Delta," the *Delta Chief* announced in May, 1883, seventeen months after the first settler came.

Surveyors with professional equipment and do-it-yourselfers using levels made of six-foot stoppered glass pipes marked precise lines of fall. Threading back into coves and out around points, mile after mile, they maintained elevation through the tumbled country that rises above the flat valleys and lower mesa benches. Men with plows and horse-drawn scrapers transformed the staked lines into controlled brooks.

Cushman Ditch was put in by the Farmington Colony to water country between the Uncompahgre River and Roubideau Creek—the wide bench land known as California Mesa. This was the first of several "colonies" organized back east to settle *en masse* on western land chosen by their leaders. Some, like Nucla west of the Uncompahgre Plateau, were communes. Most were stock companies, in which the amount a shareholder paid was the amount it would take to bring water to his homestead plus the promoter's profit. A few were scams, luring would-be homesteaders to put up money for irrigation projects the company made only a token effort, or no effort at all, to implement.

Perhaps unjustly, Peach Valley was viewed as being in the latter category. Named by the company, the grayish, bleak expanse was extravagantly promoted nationwide in the 1890s as a paradise for growing fruit. Thousands of fruit trees were planted in ten- to forty-acre tracts. One double row of pear trees was a mile long. If you were an absentee owner (as most owners were, having bought by mail), the company would plant and tend your tract. The project failed, apparently not because of dishonest dealings but because, unknown to the company or anyone else, a layer of caliche shale under the topsoil prevented the plants from developing the deep roots they needed to survive. As it turned out, almost anything *but* fruit trees thrives in Peach Valley, given irrigation water and drainage ditches to keep alkali from forming like snow across the landscape. One crop flourished so well that it attracted the sheriff's attention more than once—marijuana, grown in corn-camouflaged patches.

The horses the pioneers brought with them were playing out from overwork. Straining and heaving, horses drag-scraped those miles of canal; heaving and trembling, horses drag-cleared and furrowed those thousands of acres of root-tangled, rocky, tough, 'dobe earth. They'd been in poor shape to start with, worn down by pulling heavy-loaded wagons across plains and over mountains, their rest and feeding time skimped on because of the drivers' urge to "get there first." Some horses had suffered crippling strains, some were sick, some died. And there was no nearby replacement supply; all of western Colorado was strapped for horses.

Newt and Herb Castle saw the situation as an opportunity. Their kinsman, Dr. G. W. States, wrote of them: "The Castle brothers were young, wide awake, and impatient as the wind to be doing worthwhile and profitable things." They knew where lots of horses were—on the new Indian reservation over in Utah. Those Utes had driven hundreds of horses when they left. Pooling resources to raise cash, the boys packed up and headed for Utah.

Having arrived, the Castles didn't hurry, and they didn't try to cheat or drive hard bargains with the Utes, who by this time had had several generations to learn tricks of their own in horse-trading with whites. The two young men spent several weeks riding the reservation, looking the horses over, and gaining the confidence of the Ute leaders, especially Chief Ouray's widow, Chipeta, who, though a woman, was very powerful in tribal decisions.

As one means of gaining trust, they approached an Indian woman, handed her a pocketbook containing money, and asked if she would keep it for them while they rode out. When they returned several days later, the woman brought out the wallet intact, just as it had been left.

The brothers came home with half a hundred horses. These were broncs, tough and hardy, and supplied the community's need for some time. Crossbreeding these imports with the settlers' steeds produced a durable new equine strain.

Beginning with that business trip, a lifelong friendship developed between the Castles and the Utes. Whenever the Tabeguache Utes camped at the confluence on their way to visit tribesmen on the Southern Ute reservation, they would get together with Newt Castle (Herb by then was busy establishing the Eckert store), either at Newt's place or at theirs—the camp of tipis and wagons clustered at the Council Tree.

Newt's daughter, Winifred Castle Schmidt, remembered some of those get-togethers when she was a child: "Every year when Chipeta came, Father would get out the Stanley Steamer and go down to the campground below Delta to meet her and bring her and her people home for dinner to our house on Meeker Street." Whether sitting in a saddle, on the ground with feet tucked under her, or at a table set with the best linen and silver in her honor, Chipeta was self-assured and queenly. "She was gracious and composed at dinner, knew all about knives and forks. She spoke remarkably warm and flexible English." Winifred Castle Schmidt

Chipeta, widow of Chief Ouray, camped with other women of the Tabeguache tribe near the confluence on their trek to visit Southern Utes in 1912. Photograph by druggist John W. Nickson; used courtesy of his son, Dudley Nickson.

had a good basis for comparison; after graduating from college, she taught in Indian reservation schools for most of her life.

Another house on Meeker Street that Chipeta and other Ute tribal leaders visited each year was the Pace home. Before he brought his family to Delta, Charlie Pace had been employed with the government on the new reservation in Utah.

During his last year there, 1906, Ute Indian Jim Capota's woman gave birth to twins. The Pace's twelve-year-old daughter, Margretta, heard about the event, went to see the babies, and cuddled and cooed over them so lovingly that the new parents gave her one, the girl, as a gift. Just tied a flour sack around its middle, wrapped it in a blanket, and handed it over.

When Mrs. Pace unwrapped the "gift," she knew what it meant—not that the Capotas didn't love this baby, but that they couldn't keep both papooses. Though in the old nomadic days bearing twins had posed a threat to tribal survival, that was no longer the case on the reservation. Even so, the traditional taboo was still in force. One of any set of twins—the female if they were of different sexes, the weaker if they were the same—simply disappeared. No white person ever knew what happened to them. Saving the tiny papoose by giving her away was the strongest possible evidence of her parents' love.

But Mr. and Mrs. Pace had no supplies to clothe or feed a newborn, and, besides, they were moving to Delta soon. Though they quickly became attached to the baby they called Audry, they knew they couldn't take her with them. Utes at the Indian Agency would not allow it, because their tribal law prohibited a white man's raising an Indian child.

The Utes took care of that. They provided infant necessities at the time, and, when the Pace family wagon was packed and moving out, they took care of the legalities. A brave held the wagon up while the assembled tribe went into a pow-wow. When the brave came back, he announced: "White man not raise Indian baby. Charlie Pace all same Indian now. We adopt him at powwow. Little girl Indian have Indian papa."

Jim Capota visited his daughter at the Pace home on the annual trek to the Southern Ute Reservation. When she was six, he bought a new suit and paid a photographer to take a picture of little Audry Capota with her "two papas."

One Deltan's memories of Utes went back even farther. As a child, Eveline Nutter lived in Ouray before the Uncompahgre Valley was taken from the Utes. She saw Chief Ouray frequently. It is said that no one is gone, so long as someone remembers the individual. That means not mere data—birth, death, successes—but someone's memories of little happenings that reveal what that person was like. This is Eveline's recollection of Chief Ouray:

> Ouray had gone to Washington, and when he came back, he had a
> Prince Albert coat and silk dresses for his wife Chipeta and for some of
> the other squaws. And little black umbrellas, about the size of a plate, all
> covered with ruffles, and hinged so they could be tipped to shield the face
> from any angle.

The government gave him a surrey and harness, and the Indians hitched some wild horses to it and stood holding them while Chief Ouray and Chipeta and the other women—all in their finery—settled themselves in the surrey. Then they turned the horses loose and they went racing in crazy circles through the sagebrush. Ouray, standing up to drive, kept them in control and the buggy on its wheels until the horses wore themselves out.

What had drawn settlers to the Uncompahgre Valley was 175,000 acres of free farmland. What they seem not to have checked out was the fact that the Uncompahgre River could water less than a tenth of that amount.

Two main ditches, diverting water miles above Montrose, watered either side of the valley. Each ditch company claimed rights to all of the water in the Uncompahgre, if that was how much it took to fill its canal. Lower California Mesa, below Cushman Ditch, began drying up even before the canal banks had settled properly, mainly because new people kept coming in, taking up new land below the ditch, and claiming a share of its water. Loutzenheizer Canal (a project of the man who had escaped being killed for food by cannibal Alferd Packer) was supposed to come all the way down to Peach Valley. Not a drop of its water ever reached the development; this was one of the reasons that ambitious project failed.

Crops began to wither in June and by July were dead.

A scarcity of water can cause one man to kill another—or at least clap a lawsuit on him. As the water situation grew graver, shootings occurred at headgates where farmers "stole" water by opening the gate out of turn to save their dying crops. Ditch meetings ended in fist-fights, even knifings. Toes were chopped off by shovels stomped down to emphasize warnings. Ditch riders went armed. Lawyers prospered.

An example of how things stood as water became scarcer was reported in the *Delta Independent* of June 19, 1903:

> Late Sunday afternoon W. O. Stephens drove up to the headgate of the Garnet Mesa Ditch to see how it was standing the high water. When about five miles above town he stopped where R. M. Logan and others were attempting to prevent the waters of the Uncompahgre from overflowing some land belonging to Jeremiah Cornelius. Cornelius saw Mr. Stephens when he drove up and asked Mr. Logan for his pitchfork. As he said it in a very quiet manner he was given the fork.
>
> He walked out to where Mr. Stephens was tying his horse, having just got out of his buggy, and almost immediately assaulted him with the

pitchfork. Mr. Stephens partially caught the blow with his hand, but was jabbed in the neck with one prong and in the jaw with the other. The one in the neck came near severing the windpipe. The other prong passed through the jaw into and under the tongue and made a very painful wound.

Mr. Stephens fell but retained his hold on the fork, but being somewhat stunned by the blow, Cornelius finally wrenched it away from him, and in the opinion of those who witnessed the affair was bent upon killing him and would have done so had he not been prevented by Roy Welch who seized and disarmed him. . . . The trouble grew out of the breaking up of the Bonny Reservoir sometime since when Cornelius' crop was more or less damaged.

The Bonny Reservoir was built by the Garnet Ditch and Reservoir Company on tributary Dry Creek in an effort to eke out a water supply when the Uncompahgre was sucked dry. The dam was built of good tight adobe clay that, tamped into place, would hold just about anything. But no test drilling had been done. The men driving the scraper teams did not know that they were tamping clay over a buried rift of gravel deposited by some prehistoric stream or glacier during the Ice Age. When dammed up water found that rift, it first trickled, then flowed, and then burst, flooding the Uncompahgre Valley bluff to bluff. The railroad waived damages for washed-out track, and, except for Cornelius with his pitchfork and Cash Sampson with the law, most of the citizens hurt by the flood limited their wrath to cussing. Quiet, careful Cash Sampson sued for damages for his twenty-two drowned cows and won $605. Without preaching about it, Cash Sampson believed in justice, an attitude that got him appointed state stock inspector, set him to tracking down horse thieves and cattle rustlers, and put him fatally at odds with Ben Lowe. Besides, Sampson needed the money; he was helping to put his nieces through college. The tense irrigation situation lured yet another law firm to town, Anderson and Plumb, which specialized in water cases. To give themselves an edge in legal fights, the partners uncrated and shelved five hundred law books in their offices on Palmer Street. Offices that, though they didn't know it, were temptingly close to the new Delta County Bank.

As the fields dried up, the town suffered an equally devastating financial drought. It was the custom for farmers to charge their purchases all year long—groceries, hardware, dry goods, new wagons, everything—and pay up in the fall when the crops came in, at which time businessmen settled up with *their* suppliers. But what if the crops dried up?

In July 1901, E. B. Anderson pulled the cultivator out of his cornfield on Garnet Mesa. "Knee-high by the Fourth of July" is the ancient corn growth gauge. This withered stuff was lucky to have stayed alive that long. He looked east at the black wall that lay between him and enough water to make an Eden of the whole Uncompahgre Valley. A black wall so close and so tall that it made the sun come up late for everybody on this side of town. He was no engineer, but he would bet that the Gunnison River in the canyon slot on the other side of the wall wasn't much lower than his head ditch. If you were to go upstream just a few miles and blast through that wall—

The Black Canyon of the Gunnison, which forms the eastern wall of the confluence, is a weird piece of geography. It is perhaps the only place on earth where a river runs right down the middle of a long mountain. Fly-over geologists (those who say a little about this region and a lot about the Rockies in general) do not agree on how Black Canyon came to be. They differ about which came first— the crack that water found and deepened; or the stream that, after scraping down to granite under the soft shales it had been eroding, just went right on digging, creating, by water power alone, a crevice two thousand feet deep.

But in his 1978 graduate thesis for Purdue University, Scott Sinnock focused solely on the Uncompahgre Plateau and the valleys of the confluence. If we dare reduce his book-length study to a paragraph, this is the picture that emerges. Everything around the confluence was a mile deep in layers of shale and clays. Grand Mesa's height, protected by its lava roof, shows how deep underground this spot sat at one time. Over to the west, the Uncompahgre Uplift was rising and gradually shucking those shales off, going down to the Dakota Sandstone that presently roofs it and that deeply underlies Delta and Grand Mesa. During four ice ages, the Uplift eroded vast quantities of glacier washout; it is these that make California and Ash Mesa soils such rich farmlands.

Over to the east, buried thousands of feet deep under all that shaley stuff, a thirty-mile-long bulge of molten rock tried to force its way to the surface. This action was part of the West Elks vulcan upheaval that pushed Mount Lamborn into the sky and cooked low-grade coal into anthracite. The long bulge shoved up so hard that it bent all the covering strata and stood the lowest layer—the Dakota Sandstone—almost on end along its western side. (If you read this to mean that Delta lies on the confluence of geological down-tilts—a syncline—you are right.) Whether from heat or subsequent cooling, the long black bulge cracked full-length down its middle, like a loaf of French bread. The strata above the bulge had been weakened by the upthrust. When runoff streams found easy-going down that shaken-up place, they converged and stayed with it right down through shales and sandstone and into that weakened French-bread crack in the hard rock, cutting as much as two thousand feet deep in granite. While water was deepening that crack, it was eroding the country around it, so now you can stand on the western rim-crust of this French loaf, look down into the canyon, and turn and look down into the valley that is almost as deep, running parallel alongside.

Why didn't the river take the easy way out through Cimarron Gap and down the valley? On a contour map it looks so easy, until you realize that Cimarron Gap didn't exist at the time the Gunnison River got locked into its black granite gully.

E. B. Anderson wasn't alone in wanting that water. For almost a decade, there had been wishful talk of taking water out of Black Canyon. Perhaps up at that fault-crack where Cimarron cuts through . . . Then maybe wriggling around Squaw Hill, maybe squeezing past Poverty Mesa. Some way, somehow, by ditch or by gosh . . .

The most persistent talker was a French-Canadian, Francis Lauzon, who held meetings in churches and schools, waving his arms and rolling his *R*s like a revivalist, as he explained his scheme of flumes and pipes that would bring the water up and over the wall—with farmers themselves doing all the work and paying for it by local vote. Nothing came of it. Two civil engineers surveyed his route and reported that it would not work. Then they surveyed out the idea of cutting a hole through the wall. Nothing came of that either.

But those engineers had not explored the entire canyon, merely the easily accessible sites near Cimarron. Beyond that point, the water, after gaining power in a fast, confined drop, raged over and under and around boulders the size of houses, crashed down rock-riddled falls, spewed through heaped driftwood, and squeezed past narrows. In one place, the whole mass of the river rammed through a twenty-eight-foot slot. From the rim you could see why no one had ever dared navigate it.

Anderson dared. He talked four others into taking the trip—surveyor J. A. Curtis of Delta, Montrose electrician W. W. Torrence, M. G. Hovey, and J. E. Pelton. They fitted out two flat-bottomed wood boats with supplies for thirty days. They were sufficiently impressed with the dangers that they held a prayer meeting in Cimarron the night before they left, enlisting God as a crew member.

They needed Him. The flat-bottomed boats had "good navigation" for about 140 feet, according to the band of anxious family and friends that scrambled along the ins and outs of the rim more than a thousand feet overhead, trying to keep the men in range of their spyglasses. After that first ten yards, all hell broke loose. They poled and teetered through rapids and dragged the boats up over drifts and around blocking boulders. At one place, the river vanished under a tumble of immense rocks, roaring underfoot as they struggled to get the boats up and over the blockage. They lost one boat and half their supplies. They disappeared. After five days they were given up for lost, and a wire net was rigged down at the mouth of the canyon to catch their bodies. But at a sag in the rim, watchers got a better

Black Canyon of the Gunnison, like a crack in a loaf of French bread. The upthrust mountain is sliced lengthwise by the turbulent Gunnison River. Photograph 1987 by Muriel Marshall.

view. The party had come to the place where the river drives through that gap where a drop of twenty-eight feet is called the Falls of Sorrow. Impossible to get boat through that and come out alive. Impossible, too, to return the way they came. They gave up. After twenty-one days and fourteen miles—about half the total distance—they found a vertical crevice in the sheer wall and began inching their way up, hanging onto toe- and fingerholds. Without any kind of climbing gear, all five made it to the top.

For all their risks and struggles, what did they learn? Nothing. Not one thing about how or where to tap that water. But the drama of their trip galvanized the valley into action.

Rep. Mead Hammond of Paonia began another kind of canyon run—steering a bill through the cavernous halls of the state legislature to appropriate twenty-five thousand dollars toward mapping the valley, surveying ditch lines, and filing on Gunnison River water. He was backwatered until he teamed up with another politician, Rep, C. T. Rawalt, who was trying unsuccessfully to put through a bill to establish a college in Gunnison. This kind of mutual-nudge navigating, called logrolling, generally is not held in high regard, but in this case it produced two splendid contributions to the Western Slope.

The U.S. Bureau of Reclamation got into the act; Gunnison Tunnel was that new agency's second project in the West. Bureau Engineer A. L. Fellows, along with W. W. Torrence, made the full thirty-mile run of the canyon, including the power-squeeze at the Falls of Sorrow.

Once the tunnel site was chosen, under the rim area called Vernal Mesa, the actual work began in January 1905. Blasting and digging through 5.8 miles of granite that wouldn't move—and shales that didn't want to do anything else, once they were disturbed. It was slow and dangerous work. Several lives were lost to trapped blasting gasses, cave-ins, and other accidents.

Four years and four million dollars later, the gate that would release a thousand cubic feet per second to valley farms was officially inaugurated by U.S. President William Howard Taft, who was accompanied in the Grand Parade celebration by the Utes' Chipeta.

Because of Black Canyon's unusual structure, water enters the tunnel at river-bottom level and is propelled by gravity straight through the wall. No dammed-up water swallows the beauty or obscures the unique geology of the canyon, and none ever will, thanks to its designation as a National Monument. Legal difficulties, first encountered in getting landowners with prior claims to pool their rights so that the Gunnison Tunnel could be built, did not end when water started flowing under the wall. Their content merely changed. Attorney A. Allen Brown was too young to be involved in pretunnel legal disputes—he was the first student to enroll in brand new Mesa College in Grand Junction—but after getting his law degree, he became so active and so knowledgeable about water rights legislation that he headed the Colorado River Water Conservation District.

The water supply was further augmented and stabilized, as the Colorado River Storage Project led to construction of large dams on the upper Gunnison—Blue Mesa, Morrow Point, and Crystal. These dams not only make water available during dry years, but they also help prevent destructive floods like the one that washed all the bridges out in 1884.

Black Canyon has other fascinations besides the water it channels. Its geology opens like a book at the canyon mouth, where the pushed-up layers of Dakota Sandstone on either side illustrate what happened. These two matching humps are called Smith Mountain, after hermit John B. "Canyon" Smith, who for thirty-five years placered gold in the river between them. If you take the "Ute Trail" to the rim via the strange, rutted formation that Dorre Stogner labeled the "Roman Chariot Racetrack," you will pass—on your way down into the canyon—the remains of another gold prospector's cave and cabin.

Beside the river, a mile or so above the canyon's mouth, a geyser similar to Yellowstone National Park's "Old Faithful" for decades gushed at regular intervals. Its mineralized water was tapped in 1919, when G. A. Billstrom was drilling for oil and struck water under pressure from carbon dioxide gas. Making do with what came, Billstrom used the gas to manufacture dry ice. A little farther up the canyon is a deposit of almost pure sulfur that from time to time has been mined and shipped; around the bend near the east rim are lime deposits still marked by the laid-stone kilns Elmer Rice built many years ago for burning lime for plaster.

Even soft Dakota Sandstone was changed by the heat that formed this canyon-riven mountain, becoming rock that rings like iron to hammer blows. During the Depression, Civilian Conservation Corps camp leaders recognized the enduring quality of such metamorphosed rock and set crews to drilling and blasting it for bridging stone. Some of the holes they drilled but didn't get around to stuffing with dynamite still may be seen north of the Chariot Racetrack.

6

Funneling Profits Attract Gang Robbers

Brand new land, virgin soil free of pests, pure snow water. All this newness was like a shot of adrenaline to the pioneers from the war-weary South and East. The variety of crops, industries, and businesses they ventured into is amazing. They tried everything. Preacher L. C. Aley set out ten thousand berry grafts in one year; Dr. H. K. Braisted invented an irrigation pump; blacksmith J. J. Barker invented a churn to make butter from warm milk; George Duke patented a railroad-car coupler.

Besides the usual farm crops—corn, wheat, oats, alfalfa—the settlers grew fields of asparagus (which got out of hand, to the delight of townsfolk, who to this day wander irrigation ditch banks in spring to gather it), beans, melons, molasses sorghum, onions, peanuts, peas, potatoes, pumpkins, rutabagas, sugar beets, sweet potatoes, tomatoes, and turnips. Sam Wade grew artichokes. Rev. George States not only grew broom corn but also made brooms and gave away seed to insure that his broom machine would have raw material. Lewis Thomas and John Young raised tobacco with such success that the confluence got its own cigar factory run by E. E. Ryan.

Nobody seems to have tried bananas, though D&RG ads, attempting to lure Europeans to populate the railroad's new towns, called this valley "The Banana Belt of the Rockies."

The big thing was orchards. From the narrows of the North Fork above Paonia and the narrows of the Uncompahgre above Montrose down to the narrows of the

Gunnison below Delta, all the bottomlands and irrigated mesas were furred with fruit trees.

The area grew the best fruit in the nation. At the 1910 National Horticultural Congress at Council Bluffs, Iowa, Delta County fruit won thirty-six out of forty-three awards. When Colorado was the Apple Capital of the nation, a third of the state's apple trees were in Delta County.

Many of the settlers brought stands of bees with them and captured wild swarms later. Bees were necessary for pollinating the orchards, and honey was a crop that required very little work or cash outlay. In the first decade, some orchardists had as many as three hundred stands of bees and shipped honey by the carload. Honey harvesting continues. One of the larger producers is Rick Cooley, who got into it after an accident cost him his right hand. He moves his stands to where the nectar is, from the mountain flowers on Columbine Pass to blossoming orchards down along the rivers.

During a "back-to-nature" enthusiasm at the turn of the century, it was in vogue for ladies to own orchards and work them, climbing up the picking ladders, petticoats and all. Newspaper headlines in 1912 documented the following: "Denver society woman toils in Delta orchard" and "Miss Inez Ridgway of Chicago, daughter of A. D. Ridgway, president and general manager of Rock Island RR, arrives to direct harvest of apples near Delta."

The harvest was immense. At picking time, North Fork orchards produced so much fruit that the loaded, four-horse wagons wending their way toward railroad cars at the confluence raised a continuous plume of dust from Paonia to the Delta depot. Lee Wise recalls his father's recollections: "Drivers not only tied bandannas over their own faces to keep the dust out, but they also fastened damp cloths over the horses' nostrils to prevent damage to their lungs. The trip took two days. All wagons laid over at Dad Baird's Halfway House at the mouth of Black Canyon, drivers camping out when rooms in the two-story stone hotel were full."

Bucking all that traffic, Hank Hammond's drivers somehow managed to keep the North Fork Stage operating more or less on schedule even during fruit harvest. The paper noted: "The North Fork Stage goes out loaded to the guards every day." Furthermore, "owing to increased travel up the North Fork, Hank Hammond has put on a new stage. Larger, having three seats, which makes it much more convenient for the public." A three-seat stagecoach would hold at least nine passengers.

Until State Bridge was built in the canyon mouth, the river was crossed by ferry. The ferryman—called "Ark" Hall because J. R. Hall was a character and came from Arkansas—charged twenty-five cents for one span and wagon, fifteen cents for a saddle horse, ten cents per pack horse, and three cents each for sheep and swine. Ark loved his ferry, and, when he married Miss Howard, he staged the service right there and wrote the marriage lines himself, including some of Longfellow's poem "Hiawatha":

> *As unto the bow the cord is,*
> *so unto man is woman:*
> *though she bends him, she obeys him,*
> *though she draws him, she follows;*
> *useless each without the other.*

Among the earliest settlers was Joseph Rollins. He homesteaded in North Delta and bought rights to forty acres of a coal vein halfway up the mountainside behind his house. That piece of ground turned out to be one of the most dramatic acreages anywhere around. A great bare cliff-cove, it is bounded by creamy sandstone pillars at each end and roofed with a steep slant of red rock above. The coal vein lies under the red layer (prehistoric burning of the coal turned the layer red) and is an outcropping of the sheet of coal that runs straight through Grand Mesa like filling between cake layers, reappearing in mines at Cameo and Redstone on its other sides. Because the outcrop looms like a signboard and because Joe filed early, that pale layer, wherever found, is called Rollins Sandstone.

Rollins Mine caught fire twice. Once, it is said, a disgruntled employee piled oil-soaked logs on a mine car, struck a match, and gave the car a shove down the tunnel slant. That 1904 fire was put out, and mining resumed. Another fire, however, retreated into the mountain out of reach and may still be burning. It broke to the surface several times. One outbreak ignited a spectacular forest fire that took a week to extinguish. More than one cowboy's horse got singed hooves from sloughing off into a soft pit undermined by the fire.

In 1913, at Rollins Mine, gold was discovered that assayed three to twelve dollars a ton. The town went wild. People—including the newspaper editor—scrambled the seven almost straight-up miles to stake out mining claims. The Dugger women, whose family by this time owned Rollins Mine, served meals to the lawyers, doctors, and other big-shot prospectors. Abruptly the paper ceased writing excited stories about the strike. Nothing was heard of it again, but that wasn't the first or last time that gold was found on Grand Mesa. It is there, but not in quantities rich enough to tempt any but placer buffs such as Red Davis, who panned it, retorted it, and cast it into little gold patties that he gave to his friends.

Joe Rollins' coal heated the city power plant, Mundry Foundry, and just about every roofed structure in town—at a cost of three dollars a ton, delivered; two if you drove up to the mine and hauled your own.

Mining coal wasn't enough for Joseph Rollins. In keeping with the town's emerging policy of making a product pay twice before turning loose of it, he converted coal and 'dobe clay into brick, setting up the area's first brickyard on his homestead across from the confluence. The yellowish gray brick that adobe clay produced when mixed, molded, and fired didn't please Joe. Bricks are supposed to be red, right? He found out how the Indians made red pottery and used the same ochre earths to dye his brick.

For several years, North Delta brick was used in the construction of almost everything in the town that was not wooden: the AnnaDora Opera House, schools, churches, stores, homes. But except where refaced with harder brick, none of the North Delta Brick structures remain because the brick was very soft. Perhaps the problem was the clay, but more likely it was the coal. Veins at the west end of the coal field don't burn as hot as those farther up the North Fork of the Gunnison.

After the D&RG North Fork branch line was laid, putting hotter coal within profitable reach, five men, headed by J. E. Farmer, started Delta Brick and Tile. The five had absolutely no experience in making brick, but they had some money, and they recognized the perfect spot for the plant—west of town, with the railroad on one side, an eighty-foot bluff of fine clay on the other, and the Uncompahgre River flowing plenty of water between. That first summer (yard-dried brick could be made only in above-freezing temperatures), the twenty-five employees turned out almost two million bricks, plus uncounted feet of drainage tile. DB&T brick was superb—a natural creamy beige and so hard it rings like stone to a hammer blow. Soon railroad cars were hauling it to towns on both sides of the Continental Divide. Even in Grand Junction, where brickyards used the same clays and coal, post-office construction stipulated DB&T brick.

Making brick required a lot of hand labor. Jack Dempsey, at seventeen, was among the score or so hefting brick from drying yard to kiln and out again.

The plant didn't keep up with the rest of the world. Long after other plants were mechanized, DB&T was still using hand labor. Owing partly to this inability to compete with the mechanized plants and partly to labor's dissatisfaction with the pay the company could afford and still stay in business, the heirs of J. E. Farmer decided in 1958 to close down.

When the town was four or five years old, Peter Mundry set up an iron foundry at the corner of Third and Palmer streets. Mundry made buggies, wagons, and farm machinery. *Made* them. From scratch. His plant included a woodworking shop for shaping wagon beds, spokes, and tongues; metal lathes for turning iron and steel to make wagon kingbolts and curlicues for buggy lamps; shapers creating wooden patterns from which sand molds could be formed to pour such things as a replacement for a broken cookstove leg. Then there was the foundry itself, melting iron and pouring it into molds.

Mundry Foundry was the only thing of its kind in the western half of the state. If you needed something done in iron that a blacksmith couldn't handle, you had to go to Mundry or send back east. Yet Mundry must have operated in an environmentally responsible manner. His plant was one street over from the main intersection, but there is no record of complaints about noise or smoke from the editor who so heatedly objected to the braying of burros all over town. And Charles Fulghum, who grew up in the house next door to the foundry, had only good memories of making sand castles with the strange green sand left from the iron-casting molds.

Peter Mundry invented a while-you-wait method of tightening buggy and wagon tires. In the dry climate at the confluence, wagon and buggy spokes dried out and shrank away from the wooden felloe segments, leaving the steel tire unsupported. The tire could simply roll off; neglected too long, the wheel fell apart. There were two do-it-yourself ways to tighten the spokes: take the wheel off and soak it in the horse trough, or pound wooden wedges into the cracks where the spokes came together at the hub, forcing the spokes outward to tighten into the felloe sockets again. Quite evidently, Mundry's invention was quicker and better, but what it was, no one knows. Charles Fulghum, who worked for Mundry during his high-school days and who recorded his memories for the Delta County Historical Society, did not explain the process.

Another Mundry invention anticipated progress by at least fifty years: an automatic beet-digging and -pulping machine. He was perfecting that machine when he died.

The gold and silver mines and mills up at the source of the Uncompahgre River had from the start trickled money down into the economy of the area at the confluence. The mining operations bought farm and ranch produce and paid wages to local residents who worked in the mines part of the year. The Castle brothers plowed their pack-train money into homestead improvements. George H. Smith bought river bottomland and race horses with money he made at the tricky job of packing iron bottles of mercury to mine mills. But a big share of the money that helped the town boom was itself gold and silver from the San Juan mines.

Andy Meldrum, a blacksmith at the Sheridan Mine in 1881, grubstaked three prospectors who stumbled over an unusually heavy rock that turned out to be weighted with galena and silver. The four of them staked out four mining claims, and Andy's became the fabulous Yankee Girl.

With thirty-two thousand dollars in cash, he came down to Delta, bought land at the tip of the confluence wedge, set up a ranch with blooded horses and Galloway cattle from Scotland, built a brick house (said to have been the first brick house at the confluence), and looked around.

Across the Gunnison River was a pretty girl who also was looking around—for a man with money. She was Polly Bond, daughter of Joe Bond, who had been a saloonkeeper in Leadville. She married Andy Meldrum and, in the process of the divorce (which ended up in the Colorado Supreme Court), admitted that she had married him for his money and was in love with prizefighter Charley Mitchell, whom she had met in Leadville. The divorce proceedings dragged on for a long time, kept Andy from sharing in the eventual Yankee Girl bonanza, and left him with nothing to show for it but a few gold nuggets set into the watch chain he thenceforth wore across his middle like a rueful rosary. Polly and her lawyers got it all—the ranch, a Denver home he'd bought, and all the cash from his share of Yankee Girl. She liquidated everything and set out for California, where Charley Mitchell was. The Yankee Girl went on to make other shareholders very very rich indeed.

The story of J. Frank Sanders and his bonanza money is about as different from Meldrum's as could be. When he and his prospector partners struck it rich, finding the vein that became the legendary Bachelor Mine, he was already married to a sturdy little woman who took in washing in Ouray to support them while her man was off prying at rocks. It is said that, coming home after the lucky strike, he took an ax to the wooden washtub she was using down by the creek and he said, "By God, you'll never do that again!" and she said, "Frank, you're drunk again!" Bringing her to Delta in 1895, he built her a splendid house on Dodge Street, completing it with "one of the most elegant fireplaces that could be purchased in Denver."

"Bachelor Mine is making its three owners rich," the newspaper reported. "The mine is so easily worked that only 40 men are needed. Geo. Hurlburt bought into the Bank of Ouray, Armstrong is the main man in Mascette Power Co., and Sanders is backing the Stable Enterprise and building a big cannery in Delta—Armstrong is the only bachelor of the trio."

Sanders started the cannery in February and finished it in August. He bought controlling interest in Gillette's Grocery. He and McKinley bought out Rollins Brickyard. Sanders and Ray Simpson created the AnnaDora Opera House on the second floor of the hardware building they erected on the corner of Third and Main. Later, when the aftermath of tragedy caused Simpson to move, Sanders bought Ray's interest in the opera house, as well as Simpson's hardware store. He bought George Stephens' interest in the Farmers and Merchants Bank.

New Farmers and Merchants Bank, built by J. F. Sanders in 1897, had polished marble floor, mahogany cabinet-work and elaborate brass grill-work to deter robber set on jumping the counter, gun in hand, as happened in the old F&B Bank. Courtesy of Delta County Historical Society.

All that in 1895, and Sanders wasn't through yet. In 1896 he bought the two-story county courthouse (which had replaced that weevily log cabin and which itself already had been outgrown), cut the building in half and made two tall, gingerbread-bedecked dwellings of it. A fire gutted one, but the other still flaunts its wooden lace on Dodge Street. Getting into cattle, Sanders secured range that included the Uncompahgre Plateau's Columbine Pass. The cow camp he established there later became Columbine Ranger Station.

J. Frank Sanders left town as dramatically as he came. Walking down Main Street one winter day, he was stricken with apoplexy and died right there.

Gunnison City druggist Trew Blachly didn't move down to the confluence right away. First he had to endure a lot of bad luck.

Gold and silver were being mined on all sides of Gunnison City. New veins were discovered almost daily, and soon it would all be filed on. And then there was that wonderful land over in the Uncompahgre and Gunnison valleys. You had to act fast, or the best would be taken up. The only way not to miss out, if you were tied down by business and family, was to finance prospectors who were not.

And to do that, you had to borrow money—but gold and land, they were sure things. You couldn't lose.

You could if the entire town folded. Lou Blachly, one of Trew's sons, wrote many years later: "The frantic boom of Gunnison had busted. Prospectors and miners and their hangers-on had left town by the hundreds . . . the fancy four-story La Veta Hotel closed up; stores up and down Main street went out of business. Among those which crashed was the once-flourishing wholesale and retail drug business of A. T. Blachly."

Trew Blachly lost not only his business, but the house, the furniture, and even Dellie's piano, joy of her life, that she had bought on time by giving music lessons and cleared with another loan from her mother in Siam. One day a lawyer handed Dellie a note in Trew's handwriting: "Let Mr. A. have the piano."

The only thing left was the 160 acres that he had bought, sight unseen, on Oak Creek, a day's ride north of the confluence. The land was available only because it was too shale-tight to grow anything but chico brush, which thrived, announcing the property's poor quality to any homesteader in the know. Dellie and their four small sons lived there for several years, wretchedly. A horrified member of her well-to-do family (which was always trying to get past her pride and help her) wrote: "She is about to be confined of her fifth child and is living in direst poverty and privation. In a tent in the open air and they know not whence their food and clothing is to come."

Dellie and the little boys did most of the work on the homestead, digging and planting the garden, ditching water to it, taking care of the cow and the burros, putting up hay, putting up fences, putting the hay up on the roof out of reach of the burros. Trew was in Delta most of the time, trying to recoup his fortune. And he managed to do so. Five years and three more sons later, he had acquired good land on Garnet Mesa, built a two-story house on it, and was co-owner of a bank.

There is no record of how he accomplished so much so quickly. One supposition might be that the town and county were growing so fast that all a man had to do was ride the tide. But not many succeeded that well that fast. Part of it was his personality, as Lou Blachly pointed out. Trew was honest, so honest it showed, and so bubbling with hope and confidence that he infected people. Anyone he approached was eager to lend him money to put to work. In a wry turn of fate, his persuasiveness was his doom.

Trew and Daniel Baldwin opened the Farmers and Merchants Bank on Main in Delta, in a small wood building constructed by the Methodist preacher, Rev. L. C. Aley, also a carpenter, who was an atypically silent member of the firm.

Reading the papers of the time, you might wonder how the Reverend Aley had any time left over to preach. In the spring of 1884, he was planting strawberry, cranberry, and currant plants by the thousands on his Gunnison River homestead. Undaunted when, a few weeks later, the Big Flood removed much of his farm and tried for the house, he merely transferred his fruit operations out of reach—to the top of Garnet Mesa. Evidently he attempted to take up this land without relinquishing the other, because Senator Teller wrote informing him that the new preemption law did not allow two claims of 320 acres, but only one. Aley opened a combination furniture store–lumberyard business, shipping in doors and windows by the carload (mute evidence of how fast the town was growing). He set his wife up in a millinery business; he invented Aley Lime to get rid of bedbugs; and he went to California, where he did some preaching in San Diego. Upon his return, he bought out Bigelow and Sons grocery store, advertising that he would sell below all competitors—for instance, he sold sugar at $6.95 the fifty-pound sack. In between, he was an active member of the all-male Croquet Club.

Two years after Trew Blachly and Daniel Baldwin established the Farmers and Merchants Bank, the government rejected "free coinage of silver," throwing the nation into a depression and Colorado into a panic. The silver mines that had created Colorado's boom times closed down. Silver stock that had made men fabulously rich wasn't worth the paper it was fancy-printed on. Twenty thousand miners lost their jobs. Banks began to close. Banker Trew Blachly was on the West Coast when he got word of the Colorado bank failures, along with the news that his own bank was in trouble. He had gone to the Northwest with the idea that, if he liked the area, he might move the family there. Racing home as fast as rails would take him, he sped right on through town to Montrose, where he borrowed enough money to stave off the threatened run on the Farmers and Merchants Bank. If he hadn't succeeded in doing that, if the bank's doors had been padlocked on September 7, 1893, Trew Blachly might have lived to be an old man.

The McCarty Gang—brothers Tom and Bill and their brother-in-law Matt Warner—had been shot at many times in their careers as cattle rustlers and bank and train robbers, but they never had been hit. They had come to feel that they were bullet-proof. Part of their luck stemmed from careful planning and fast horses. With his first outlaw "profits," Tom McCarty, the oldest and the leader of the gang, had gone east and bought the fastest horses he could find, paying a thousand dollars each. They trained those high-strung horses to stand stock still under gunfire and locomotive blasts. Prior to a strike, they scouted site layout, getaway routes, and positioning of fresh relay horses.

Preparing for the Telluride bank robbery, four years earlier, the newest McCarty Gang member, Butch Cassidy, spent some weeks getting to know the lay of the town and training one of Tom's horses to stand while he made a run-

ning jump into the saddle. At Cortez, Tom and Matt Warner likewise were training horses and making leather bags to carry gold loot inside the legs of their
pants.

Successful at Telluride, the gang escaped to Washington State, where lucrative
holdups on banks and businesses put the law on their trail. Riding southwest again,
they holed up in Robber's Roost between the Uncompahgre Plateau and
Hanksville, Utah, and planned their next job. They had intended to hit Telluride
again because of the mine payroll, but changed their aim upon learning that Telluride officers had been alerted.

A string of "if-only"s make the Delta bank robbery particularly poignant. If
only Butch Cassidy had been with the gang, they might not have selected small-
town, two-bank Delta, and almost certainly no one would have been killed. Though
he was a dead draw-shot, Cassidy staged holdups for a quarter of a century without getting himself into a spot where he had to kill somebody. But Butch Cassidy
and Matt Warner were off talking their way out of cattlemen's courts in Wyo-
ming. Taking their places in the gang were Tom's brother Bill McCarty and Bill's
eighteen-year-old son Fred. (A holdup team usually consisted of at least three
people: two to pull guns and back each other up, and a third stationed outside,
holding the getaway horses at the ready.)

The only hands-on "outlaw" experience that teenager Fred McCarty had had
was once being entrusted to hold a gun on a sleuthing sheriff whom Tom and Bill
already had disarmed. The boy longed to get in on the action and begged for a part
in the next holdup. Tom was skeptical, but Fred insisted, and Bill sided with his son.

Apparently they trailed down off the Uncompahgre Plateau, hitting the
Gunnison about where Palmer Gulch cuts a gap in the red canyon wall. They
were camped there—three men with a pack mule and eight exceptionally fine
horses—when R. S. Mow's stepdaughter Mabel Dennison came by looking for
cows. One fellow was about fifty, another somewhat younger, and a third a kid in
his late teens. They said they were the Bradley brothers and a nephew. Asked by
"the kid" about the road to Delta, she described it: up past the Mow peach orchards at the mouth of Escalante Creek (this was decades before the Gunnison
was bridged at Escalante), up the canyon, up the looping ledges of Big Hill, then
out across the tumbled 'dobe barrancas along the south side of the river. It isn't
known if they took that route, but if they did, we can presume they resolved sure
as hell not to leave town that way! Likely they didn't. Mountain riders used to the
torn-up Robber's Roost country would have had no trouble finding a ford across
the August-low Gunnison. At any rate, when everything else was ready for the
strike, they stationed their relay horses on the other side, down on Pinion Mesa,
along with their rifles and part of their cartridges.

During the week or so they camped in the area, they probably came to town several times, sizing things up from saloon and livery stable. No one remembered seeing them except Ruby Hutchinson. Ruby had an eye for fine horses and daredevil riders, as she later proved by becoming Ben Lowe's bride. In old age, she remembered the McCartys' racing stunts up and down the Gunnison River road past her father's potato farm, and how they tipped their hats to her as they streaked by.

People did remember having seen the three in town on September 6, because of what happened the next day. They tied their horses to the hitch rack in front of the Central House, clomped across the boardwalk to eat supper, registering as James G. and Clarence Bradley. After supper "the three of them asked for lodgings of Mrs. Sprolls, Mrs. Edwards, Mrs. Sparr and Mrs. Collins down by the Gunnison" but didn't sleep at any of those boardinghouse-inns. No one knew where they spent the night, but the next morning they breakfasted at the Central and did a little shopping after the stores opened and before the bank did—a pair of shoes, a bottle of whiskey. Nobody paid any attention to them—ordinary cowboys like you saw every day passing through. If they showed particular interest in the little wooden Farmers and Merchants Bank building between Third and Fourth on Main, nobody noticed it.

The town began to stir, store doors were propped open, racks and barrels of products wheeled out onto the boardwalks. The North Fork stage left the Delta House and early-bird fruit wagons began to straggle in, kicking up Main Street dust. Across from the bank, Ray Simpson opened his hardware store.

Simpson had had a bad night. He dreamed that his store was robbed. The dream was so vivid that the first thing he did after getting the store squared away for the day was pick up his .44-caliber Sharps and clean, oil, and reload it. His favorite Sharps wasn't the only weapon around; the store stocked guns. Guns were part of the frontier way of life. Everybody had guns, loaded and usually close at hand; slept with them under their pillows (as did Judge King); wore them on their bodies. Many cowmen donned gunbelts along with their pants in the morning. But guns were especially natural to Ray Simpson. Growing up in Kentucky, as a boy practicing on wink-quick squirrels, he had learned to shoot a rifle accurately from the hip without shoulder-aiming.

When Newt Castle came in, Simpson didn't tell him the dream, he just handed him a gun to crack and clean.

Nobody noticed when three exceptionally fine horses were ridden into the alley between Third and Fourth streets east of Main, or when two of the riders dismounted and, leaving one behind with the horses, passed along the narrow boardwalk that ran between buildings to the bank's front door.

Cashier Trew Blachly and his assistant, H. H. Wolbert, had come to the bank early to get in some work before opening time—letters, ledger catch-up, open the safe, check its contents. Attorney W. R. Robertson, who rented office space in the back of the bank, was already at work.

Trew's spirits were high. He'd saved the bank, and if things kept on looking up . . . As his son Lou wrote a quarter of a century later:

> The fall of 1893 offered the best prospects Trew and Dellie had ever had in the sixteen years since their marriage. Trew was a leading citizen in the county—banker, justice of the peace, large land owner, elder of the Presbyterian Church . . . The trip to the West had greatly improved his health. Business was slack all over the United States but he got a substantial sum from the Montrose bank and had adequate funds to forestall any run on his bank.

Perhaps the McCarty Gang, nosing around, had smelled that money.

Ten o'clock. After unlocking the door, the bankers began the paper work, Wolbert at the ledger on his desk, Trew at his typewriter. The latch clicked open, then the lock snapped home, but Trew Blachly didn't hear that. He rose to serve the two customers who had entered and were standing on the other side of the cashier window. Then he saw the guns.

Bill McCarty said, "Put your hands up and don't make a sound."

One of the bankers made a move that Kid McCarty, young, tensed-up, and trigger-eager, took to be reaching for a weapon. He started to come piling over the partition. That's when Trew Blachly yelled and grabbed for the gun under the counter. One of Fred's bullets hit the floor, the other angled down Trew's bent head.

Two shots and that yell blew the holdup; the town would be on them in seconds. The McCartys rushed out the back, the boy taking time only to grab a sack of gold coins from the open safe.

Hearing shooting inside, Tom McCarty, who had been holding lawyer Robertson at gunpoint at the back, whirled and hit the saddle. Grabbing leather, Fred dropped the sack but managed to mount with Bill right behind, and the three took off, crouching like Indians in the protection of their mounts' bodies.

Across the street, Ray Simpson heard the shots, knew what they meant, and was instantly outside, rifle in hand. Bill raised up to spot pursuit, just enough. Ray's rifle bullet tore off the top of his head.

Buildings got in the way, and Simpson raced toward Second. They'd have to swing onto Main to cross the bridge, and when they did, they'd raise up to look, and—

Fred raised to look back, saw what had happened to his father, and seemed about to turn back to help him, but Tom yelled him on. Ray's second bullet got the kid in the head. By then Tom McCarty was out of range, nearly to the bridge. Ray's third shot missed.

Men with guns had appeared everywhere. One horse was killed, and the other, covered with its rider's blood, was caught and tied. Sheriff Giradet, who had been in the newspaper office, joined Simpson, Newt Castle, the druggist McMurray, and several others in pursuit. But Tom had a head start and a faster horse.

They did find Tom's getaway horse, spur gashed and ridden to exhaustion. By loosing and following the kid's horse, Sheriff Gheen was led to the relay mounts the dead robbers were to have used, and brought the splendid animals back to town.

Tom McCarty was never found, but that wasn't the last of him in Ray Simpson's life. Soon after the killing, Ray received the first of several threatening letters from McCarty, altogether so disturbing that Ray eventually sold the business and left the state.

Perhaps the publicity, as much as the deaths, embittered Tom McCarty. The two dead robbers were buried immediately—a necessity in a time when no chilled morgues existed. They were exhumed for official identification by state authorities who wanted to make sure which McCarty got away (first reports were wrong). If the dead man was Tom, then Ray Simpson would receive the ten-thousand-dollar reward that had been on Tom McCarty's head ever since he held up the Denver First National Bank four years earlier. The dead man, officials decreed, was Bill, not Tom. Reburied, the bodies were re-exhumed to be propped against a wall and photographed by young Ben Laycock, using a camera from his father's photography shop. Those pathetically ghastly pictures appeared everywhere.

Mementos of the holdup were darkening splashes of blood on the boards of Hank Hammond's yard fence, where Simpson got the boy. And the guns. The McCartys' six-shooters and Ray Simpson's rifle were displayed on the bank wall and went with the bank through several changes in ownership, until they were donated by the Colorado Bank and Trust to the Delta County Museum. No one knows what happened to the handmade leather sack, empty and unused, fastened inside Kid McCarty's pants leg.

The shock of the murder almost killed Dellie and did kill their unborn ninth child. On what she feared was her deathbed, despairing over what would become of her sons, she called them around her and made them responsible for each other. That is, each boy would have as his "son" for life the boy next younger, in his sole trust, to care for, raise, and train.

It didn't work out quite as rigidly as that, because of differences in their health and temperaments. The oldest was not strong, so the second son, Fred, at age thirteen became the man of the farm, assigning the duties of irrigating, fencing, milking, etc., to the younger boys. But over time, the arrangement worked. Each boy was responsible for his "son" in every way, from seeing that he was scrubbed and dressed for grammar school to writing "fatherly" notes of advice (and sending money) when he was in college.

Dellie lived and for a time spared her sons the facts: Banker Blachly left no money except the dollar or two in his pocket; he was indeed a "large land owner," but all of the land was deeply mortgaged. Only by selling three pieces could Dellie clear one for her family.

It has been said that the widow Blachly worked and sent all her eight sons through college. She did better than that; she gave them the drive to put themselves through college, earn doctorates, and pursue notable careers. Proudly her sons would say later in life: "Our mother never worked!" They meant merely that she never took in washing or cleaned house for other people—the standard definition of women's work in those days. Work she did, like a horse. That slight woman and her eight children put in field crops and orchards, built the roof over their heads, and still found time to study the classics together. She had help. Her music lessons brought in a little. There was the annual "missionary barrel" of clothing from her folks (all she would accept). Oh, yes—some help came from Colorado bankers. Soon after the killing, Dr. Braisted circulated a letter among them, citing Trew's heroic defense of the bank's money and his widow's plight. They sent a total of sixty dollars.

7

Land with Character
Draws Characters

There were two ways to become a lawyer in those days: go to college and get a law degree; or, lacking college money, apprentice yourself to a practicing lawyer and "read" under him until you had transferred enough law from his books to your head to pass the state bar exam. In his home town of Peoria, Illinois, Albert Eldridge Amsbary did the latter.

Stuffed in mind and body—he was an immensely wide man, according to his daughter, Katharine Amsbary Hedgcock—Amsbary brought his bride, Margaret Wilson, to Delta, took up a homestead on California Mesa southwest of town, built just enough house to pass homesteading regulations, and commuted the three miles to the office every morning by shanks mare. In soggy weather, it was Amsbary's practice to carry a shovel to lift and scrape Main Street's duckboard crosswalks—mired out of sight in 'dobe mud by yesterday's wagon traffic—so that ladies could get from one side to the other without sinking to the eighth button of their French kid-leather shoes.

Connoisseur of life in general, Amsbary never let ambition cinch him into one narrow goal-track. He practiced law just well enough to make a good living for his family (for whom he soon built a fine home in town) and held one judicial position just long enough to be called Judge Amsbary for the rest of his life.

Typically, the homesite Amsbary chose was on the corner of First and Main, crux of all the confluences—the rivers, railways, and turnpikes. Any rig or rider headed for the North Fork, Grand Mesa, North Delta, Grand Junction, the Con-

tinental Divide, or California passed Judge Amsbary's windows. From his upstairs bedroom, he could look down and see what the rivers were up to in the way
of flood or waterfowl. When, in 1902, the D&RG ran a spur track up the North
Fork to the coal mines at Somerset and all towns between, the cars passed so close
that they trembled excitement through the timbers of the judge's house, and he
could see and return the engineer's wave. When the city built its first light plant
on the riverbank kitty-corner from his house, the judge could guess when the
lights would come on by how soon before sundown operator Shue had arrived to
fire up the steam engine that generated electric light for street lamps and parlors
until bedtime. But, for the judge, the best confluence of all was the Delta House
across the street.

There were other hotels—the Avenue, the Commercial, Ziegler's, and Mrs.
Abel's, and ubiquitous boardinghouses where newly arriving families lived while
finding or building a home. All these came and went. But the Delta House stayed,
and stayed current—soon a little steam plant was installed behind the building to
provide guests with hot water more handily than having it carried upstairs in a
pitcher by the chambermaid.

Streams of traveling salesmen brought the world to this lobby confluence. Delta
House maintained sample rooms for them—luxurious, equipped with bar, counter,
and ice chest—where they set up displays for town merchants to view and order
from. They preferred the Delta House to hotels in other towns and adjusted their
schedules to be there for Sunday layover. After hours, these professional rovers
loved to talk about where they'd been and what they'd seen on the face of the
globe.

But salesmen were the least of it. Every notable or interesting person who came
to town stayed at the Delta House: governors, senators, and politicians trying to
become governors and senators; lawyers, bankers, mine owners, and cattle bar-
ons; teachers, musicians, and show people—the casts of traveling drama companies putting on a minstrel show or "East Lynne" at the AnnaDora Opera House.
Governor Pinchot stayed at the Delta house often during the process of creating
the United States Forest Service, which started with the mountains in view from
the Delta House verandah. Doc Shores stayed there while sleuthing down the
Wild Bunch suspected of the train robbery between Delta and Grand Junction.
Geologist Willis T. Lee stayed there in 1912 when not out with his crew mapping
the coal under Grand Mesa and the West Elk Mountains—a solid sheet that he
assessed at eleven billion tons. Thomas Keirns of New York City, who was playing in Broadway productions of Gilbert and Sullivan operettas when tuberculosis
drove him west, stayed for a time at the Delta House. In fact, the only notable
visitors who didn't stop at the Delta House were those who had their own private

railroad cars and spoke to crowds from a rear platform—Jay Gould when the D&RG North Fork Branch line was opened, President Taft when the Gunnison Tunnel opened.

Judge A. E. Amsbary visited with them all, attired to meet a prince if any turned up among the many remittance men being exported by the English nobility to England's former colony.

One such was Grand Mesa resort and fish-hatchery developer William Radcliffe. His daughter remembered:

> Papa dressed in style, wearing white shirts with stiffly starched fronts and white linen bat-wing collars, all of which had to be sent to Denver to be laundered. Greatly overweight for his height, he had his suits tailored in Denver. Each evening, after supper and his daily bath, he would don his good suit and, swinging his cane, depart for an evening at the Delta House where, quite frequently, VIPs in politics or government would be staying overnight on their rounds across the state by train.

In this boardwalk and hitchrack frontier town, where paths dwindled off into sagebrush a stone's throw in every direction, Radcliffe, Judge Amsbary, and the plumed and corseted ladies were not alone in transcending the milieu. Edith Castle Parker described one Delta House proprietor: "Bill Shaver was one of the most picturesque, irrepressible characters that ever entertained hotel guests—full of highly colored stories, laced with a bit of profanity. Visiting his friends in stores, he walked daily up Main Street dressed to the hilt—white starched shirt, striped gray trousers, long dress coat, always wearing gray spats over his shoes, and twirling his favorite cane."

Apparently Judge Amsbary did not use any of the Delta House guest contacts to further his career. Nor did he use the churches. The judge never joined a church, but he attended them all. Rather, he *listened* to them all—the Baptists, whose Colporteur Father Clark had established eleven churches on the Western Slope; the Methodists, whose Reverend Aley had established almost that many businesses; the Catholic Mass at the monastery or the mission; a Jewish rabbi from Denver; Greek Orthodox rituals; the Rev. George States, who laid his life on which Day was Sabbath; the lively messages of Sister Clara, the lady preacher at the Pentecostal Church.

Altogether it was as if he were gathering up pieces to fill out a jigsaw puzzle in his mind, a puzzle without borders, free to expand in any direction. But there were two rigid boundaries to the life-puzzle in Amsbary's head: in addition to being fastidious, he was a teetotaler.

In this matter, Judge Amsbary was not alone. Town by town, the west was going "dry" by local option. The trend represented community reaction to the lifestyle prevalent in mining towns and cowboy hangouts. There were nightly disturbances, mounted drunks "hurrahing" Main by shooting out streetlights on purpose and store windows by accident; fatal gun fights; knifings; enforced dancing to bullets; wife and child beatings; families half-starved because the paycheck was spent on liquor rather than food.

Near the Oasis Saloon, the teenage Bass boys, in an argument over baseball with another kid not much older, disarmed him of his gun by stabbing him to death. Cowmen Blair and Ward, trundling up Main Street, discovered Bert Enore in town—where, according to their lights at the moment, he had no right to be, especially not sitting like that on the boardwalk with his legs hanging over. So they put a few shots in the vicinity of his bottom and invited him to get up and dance, then kept the dance going for quite a while with shots just short of his feet. Ben Lowe flashed his gun in saloon, restaurant, or street so frequently that the newspaper gave up counting. Ben never hurt anybody, he usually was just in high spirits because one of his superfast horses had won a race again.

Ouray and Norwood, being miner and cowboy centers respectively, never voted dry. Montrose local opters tried; Judge Grey, finding in favor of Mrs. Fist's saloon, took his feelings out on the WCTU, calling the women "yellow-skinned, hollow-eyed, hollow-chested, knock-kneed ladies of ancient beauty." Grand Junction went dry. When Delta first put booze to the ballot, the "wets" won, and, because Judge Amsbary had been in the dry forefront, they demonstrated on his lawn, setting off bomblike firecrackers and flinging street manure onto his porch, while the four little girls huddled around their unperturbed papa upstairs.

When the town did vote dry in 1891, it remained noticeably damp. All they did was close the saloons. Liquor was available surreptitiously from bootleggers' stills out in the canyons that long had been underselling regular suppliers by evading the revenue tax. After local option cut off legal competition, these stills greatly increased in number and production. Eda Musser remembered, "As we bought up ranch after ranch in Escalante Canyon, we would find a still hidden out on almost every one."

Or liquor could be obtained openly by doctor's prescription at the drugstore. Liquor long been had a part of the pharmacopoeia; a *United States Dispensatory* published before the Civil War prescribes wine for typhus, tetanus, and recovery from fever, among other uses. In the days before controlled testing of medicines, the efficacy of a drug was judged by its apparent effect. Opium or laudanum made babies quit crying and go to sleep, so it must be helping whatever was hurting. Brandy revived ladies subject to frequent fainting spells (a prevalent ailment caused by too-tight corsets). Whiskey disinfected wounds and slightly anesthetized the wounded. And then, of course, there was always snakebite remedy. All of these drugs could be bought over the counter like a package of Tums until the town voted dry. After that, to get tight legally, you had to have a doctor's prescription.

Conveniently, most drugstores were owned by doctors. Delta's first doctor, V. L. Albers, had his office in the town's first drugstore building, R. M. McMurray's, and at one time he probably owned it. The connection was natural, for physicians knew the available pharmaceuticals, and they needed the income.

Doctor's fees were low, usually a dollar or two per call; sometimes these were paid in eggs, butter, or chickens, and often not at all. Before the coming of public relief and medical insurance, all doctors donated many free hours to those who had no money. Even well-to-do patients might never be billed. Mrs. Judge King remembers: "Dr. Hick never sent a bill for his services. Father sent him a check when the spirit moved."

This was the norm. Doctor's bills could run on for years, a small payment being made from time to time. And practicing medicine was so time-consuming that it cut the profits. For the most part, doctors went to where the patient was. Surgery was performed on the nearest flat surface, usually the family table. With few real cures at his disposal, the physician might spend long hours sitting beside a critically ill patient, giving the only thing he had, the strength of his presence. Making a house call (and most patients were seen at home) could involve long hours of travel time, especially if the patient was in the country—and most of them were, since more people lived in the country than in town and country dwellers were more accident-prone. Even though the doctor's buggy—tiny and light, with high, spidery wheels—and horse were chosen for speed, he could get in only a few calls in his twenty-four-hour day.

Many people avoided doctors, relying on folk medicine. Mrs. Judge King, for instance, believed that Epson salts would cure any ailment of the abdomen, and when her son Edward developed acute appendicitis, she was certain that a good dose of the salts would cure him. When Dr. Lawrence A. Hick forbade it and called another doctor to come by train from Salida to assist with the operation on the Kings' dining room table, King maintained that the whole horrible ordeal could have been avoided if salts had been given soon enough.

Not every doctor had the added income of owning a drugstore—there weren't that many drugstores. Some doctors lacked the money to set one up, and some preferred not to. Usually the doctor's office was in the same building as his drugstore. You got your prescription and went downstairs to have it filled.

When the town voted Populist—and dry—drugstores immediately took over the liquor business. After listing the stern provisions of the ordinance, the newspaper opined that liquor sold at drugstores would have to be labeled "Microbe Killer" and later noted that Edward Stone was again dispensing "Worm Killer" at McMurray's.

Right through the local-option brouhahas, McMurray's maintained its dignity as *the* place to have a soda with your friends on Sunday afternoon. While discreetly advertising its "prime medicinal liquors" in newspaper ads, it insured its supply by posting a sign, "Delta Drugstore," out in the wilds of Escalante Canyon, advertising not only where to buy drugs in town, but also where to sell "bootleg." That sign stayed there right through the comings and goings of local options and through national Prohibition and Repeal. Nobody took it down or shot it to pieces, it being considered a secret joke too good to spoil.

The newspaper editorialized: "The principal objection to the closing of the saloons is that it will give the drugstores full swing without receiving any license money. Rather strange thought that a drugstore cannot be controlled as well as a saloon." The alert state revenue department fixed that by clapping a $25 liquor license on the drugstores, just as if they were saloons. One of them virtually was.

Dr. H. K. Braisted sold so much liquor by prescription in his drugstore that he was arrested more than once on liquor violations. One of the cases went to the State Supreme Court, where it was decided against him. Apparently you could prescribe liquor for some ailment or other, or you could fill such a prescription, but you couldn't do both. The *Delta County Laborer* wrote a limerick about the town's loudest Populist:

> *A versatile pharmacist named Braisted,*
> *lots of his good substance wasted;*
> *to better his condition*
> *he got prohibition,*
> *and now by the law he is basted.*

Braisted sold his drugstore to Dr. E. K. McComber. Then it was Dr. and Mrs. McComber—Mrs. Doctor being co-owner—whose names were in the paper for liquor violations.

While he was still in the drug business, Dr. Braisted was the cause of a change in the town building code. Most pioneer towns—built of siding, shingles, tar paper, and other inflammables—were nearly wiped out by fire at one time or another. These blazes usually were caused by a lamp upset in a riotous brothel or saloon. Delta's historic fire began as an explosion, when Dr. Braisted came in the back door of his drugstore at night and lit the kerosene lamp, igniting ether that had filled the room from a leaking bottle. The fire destroyed or damaged several other businesses and resulted in the town's ruling that only brick or stone could be used for commercial walls in downtown Delta.

Leaking ether was not the only peril for physicians in the early days. Dr. Fairfield disappeared. They found his clothing neatly folded beside the Gunnison River at the mouth of Black Canyon but discovered no body downstream or anywhere. Three years later, he contacted his family, explaining that he had taken a plunge bath in the river and the water had been so cold that apparently it had knocked him unconscious, because the next thing he knew, he was on a steamer headed for Alaska. After unreported adventures there, Fairfield received a blow on the head—and restored memory.

When the bicycle was invented and came to town in the early 1890s, doctors were the first to use the machine; they could jump on a bike and get to a house call and back in half the time previously required. The paper noted: "Dr. Braisted is riding a bicycle when the bicycle doesn't ride him. He has an inclination toward ditches." Dr. McComber went Braisted one better by making house calls on a bike with one wheel. But Police Magistrate S. L. Fairlamb was called on to slap his wrists for riding it on the sidewalk. It would seem that Dr. McComber might more appropriately have been given a medal for staying on top of a monocycle on a rickety, decades-old boardwalk.

Doctors L. A. and L. L. Hick, father and son, practiced medicine with such warm, efficient success that they are remembered not in terms of details and incidents, but with a nebulous glow of love. Third-generation Dr. Joe Hick, inducted into the Armed Forces during World War II, first practiced medicine on soldiers. As a result, Dr. Joe had an abrupt, off-hand bedside manner that the town never got used to. Perhaps Joe's wife Lauri (a breeder of Icelandic horses) never got used to it, either; or perhaps Dr. Joe never got used to his wife's bedside manner. There's that story she tells about the Sunday morning he didn't rise early enough for a planned family outing. After repeatedly calling him, without results, Lauri led one of her horses clomping into the bedroom to nudge him awake. Anyhow, all three—Dr. Joe, his wife, and the town—got divorced from each other, and Dr. Joe went back to practicing medicine in the military.

Another doctor, R. C. Underwood, had unusually strong feelings about the rights of the babies he launched into life. On at least one occasion, he took it upon himself to rename an infant he had just delivered. Billi-Bob, or something like that, the parents dubbed him. Cupped in his palm, Dr. Underwood saw a very male person, who, given the right start, could become anything—a general, a president, a scientist. With a girl-baby, pet-puppy name like Billi-Bob, such an outcome was unlikely. So the doctor wrote "William" on the birth certificate. Let them call him Billi-Bob while he was tiny; still, he'd have that masculine William when he needed it. The indignant parents had to pay good money to get the certified name changed back their way. Probably Dr. Underwood wasn't around when Mr. and Mrs. Rule named their daughter and son Golden and Slide.

Underwood is remembered as being well out on the cutting edge of science and a free-thinker about medical vogues. He was the first to bring the miracle drug penicillin to town; and in the thirties and forties when it was medically *de rigeur* to put the delivering mother to sleep with ether and hasten things by surgical episiotomy, Dr. Underwood was practicing natural childbirth.

When medical instruments and chemicals were so few and simple that almost everything a physician or surgeon had to work with could be contained in a small black bag, "hospitals" were wherever the doctor was. Delta's first hospitals were patients' bedrooms, the first emergency rooms were the doctors' offices that usually included a side room with cot, the first operating rooms were kitchen tables. The monastery, a sanatorium for tubercular neophyte priests, was a hospital of sorts but was not open to the public.

When Judge A. R. King and his family moved to Denver, their home "Garnethurst" was left empty. Two sisters from the Denver Mercy Hospital took over the house, caring for patients there for several years before the building officially became a hospital in 1915. Soon the town's needs outgrew its capacity of five or six beds.

Western Slope Memorial Hospital Association was incorporated by private citizens, one of whom, H. E. Perkins, donated the big house he had bought from Captain Bragg at Seventh and Grand. By splitting parlor and dining room, they made its two floors into a thirteen-bed hospital, beds going for twenty-five dollars a week, care included. The superintendent drew exactly that same amount. If any ailing were bedded up on the third floor, where Captain Bragg used to keep tabs on the town through his round peep window, nobody remembers it.

When, in the mid-1940s, town and medical requirements outgrew Captain Bragg's old walls, the town debated expansion while dreaming of a brand new structure. But World War II made building materials scarce, and the postwar transition made money even scarcer.

Reorganized and renamed—focusing closer to home, the Western Slope Memorial Hospital Association became the Delta Memorial Hospital Association—the organization accepted Allison Vanderpool's gift of ten lots and started raising cash to construct a building on the lots. In small towns, as elsewhere, money to benefit the public is raised by first approaching the ready givers—everybody knows who they are, they make the world go around. Then the reluctantly generous: "Subscribe, it will make your name (business, profession) look good." And then the ungenerous: "What will it do to your name (business, profession) if the line after it remains blank?" Different committee members home in on the kind of giver each works best. Gordon Hodgin smiles his way into the pocketbooks of all three kinds.

The new facility bedded twenty-nine in rooms, and halls were wide enough to screen off surplus patients. The hospital superintendent was June Musser, R.N., a graduate of both the cattle range in Escalante Canyon and Massachusetts General Hospital. June never let her position keep her from doing whatever had to be done. When the cook was sick, it was June who prepared meals for patients and staff, using whatever was in the storeroom. You never knew what that might be— much of the food was farm produce brought by people who lacked cash and paid their hospital bills in potatoes, eggs, apples, or other staples.

Too few beds is no longer the only thing that makes a hospital obsolete. As medical science advances, hospitals must install newly invented equipment, both to save patients from dying and to keep doctors from moving away. The loss of physicians in small towns and rural areas is not because doctors dislike living in such heavenly places, but because, wanting to bring their patients the latest in scientific treatment, they tend to practice where it is available.

Delta's newest hospital, also financed by subscription, was built in 1975. It expands to meet the community's needs, at present housing forty-nine beds, as well as equipment sufficiently advanced to meet most of the requirements of the physicians who practice in the area.

Increased transportation speed—the helicopter and the racing ambulance— makes it unnecessary for small hospitals to buy extremely expensive equipment they might use only once a year. The trend is for one large institution to equip itself to handle rare cases for a widening cluster of smaller hospitals. There is scarcely a contraption for poking at, peeking into, subtracting from, or adding to the human body that is not available at Saint Mary's Hospital in Grand Junction, less than an hour by car from the confluence.

For some time, Dr. Winfield Scott Cleland had been disturbed at the large number of infections he was treating, especially among boys and usually in summer. This was before penicillin was developed; infections could kill. After observation, study, and questioning patients, he concluded that the infection followed swimming in the river.

There was nothing he could do about it. All towns dumped untreated sewage into rivers, serenely sure that, within a half-mile of flow, the water completely purified itself. It was an innate property of water: if it moved, it got clean. The cited distance could be somewhat less if the circumstances demanded. Anyhow there was then no such thing as sewage treatment. Even if towns upriver somehow did sanitize sewage, there still remained all the farm backhouses built over irrigation ditches (where available) in order to have automatic flushing.

And you couldn't stop kids from swimming. One of the powers of water is the attraction it holds for boys small and large. The confluence wedge was surrounded on all sides by enticing rivers never the same for twenty feet or two days. Rivers with mysterious holes under cottonwood roots to hold your breath and dive into and explore; with sandy shoals that bare feet ached to feel the suction of; with islands that you would bet your life, literally, you could swim the current to reach.

Fadely's cattail swamp stretched a mile or so along the rivers across the northwestern side of town. In the swamp were whistling redwing blackbirds with nests to rob if you could wade out that far, fry-legged frogs to lunge to your armpits after, fascinatingly hideous water dogs to seine and take home to scare your sister with.

And there were the irrigation canals, flowing smooth and innocent between grassy banks. But water does not like to flow straight. Below the surface, it rolls and pushes and sucks. More children were drowned in smooth-looking irrigation ditches than in any other water in this land.

Down by the depot is a swimming hole and channel that every generation of boys discovers, without realizing that it is the old mill pond and mill race. At one time, the pool and empty railroad station were dominated by boys known as the Depot Gang. They claimed the pond, but the seven boys of the nearby Armour family disputed their right. It was a very stylized war. The youngest Armour tot would go down and paddle around in the pool, and the smallest of the Depot Gang would tackle him. Whoever came out the loser would run home and get the next larger, and so on, up to the oldest Armour boy and the biggest member of the Depot Gang. They would fight it out to a finish—for the time being.

Paul Edwards, who also swam there, observed later, "It would happen over and over again, like a game with rules. As if they had some kind of unspoken system to teach the younger ones on each side how to take care of themselves."

All the Armour boys survived those "gang" wars and the impurities of the water, but it is significant that the first grave in the cemetery at the confluence of waters was that of a person who had drowned. That was the first of many drownings. If illness and death by infection were Dr. Cleland's concern, the threat of death by drowning tormented the mothers.

Children needed a safe park to play in and a clean, supervised swimming pool. Together, Dr. Cleland and the Delta Federated Woman's Club—with the help of just about everybody in town—achieved both.

Organized early in the town's history, the Woman's Club already had several large achievements to its credit when it tackled the park. Members chose a site—seven acres at the southeastern end of town—that, because it was unused, swampy, and would have to be filled in, ought to be cheap or even free.

This marsh, running all the way along the base of the bluff of Garnet Mesa, had been a prehistoric channel for the Uncompahgre River. During the eons after the river changed course, the old channel had partially filled with erosion from the bluff, becoming a long seep-grass meadow. Two enterprising boys, Ted Wigram and Harry Lane, worked up a business commuting town cows. Mounted on pony and burro they herded milkers to this seep-land pasture every morning, returned them to their individual barns up and down the town's alleys after school, and once a month collected their pay—one dollar per cow.

The marshland wasn't free, but after the club had raised eighteen hundred dollars by putting on dinners and bake sales, the four owners conceded the rest of their asking price, and the land was deeded to the city. The city council appointed Dr. Cleland president of the project and set aside seventy-five dollars a month to hire a man to make a park of the swamp, noting, "That ought to attract a pretty good man."

The good man was right there waiting. Clarence Riley, aged twenty, of Illinois had been told to go west for his asthma. With his wife Edna and small son, he had traveled the intervening dirt trails in his Model-T Ford and was holed up in what someday would become the firehouse, doing odd jobs while waiting for something steady to turn up. That park job was it. He and the job were so well suited to each other that he never would have another. Of course, the city raised his salary from time to time.

Clarence Riley planned, executed, and maintained the place that was named Cleland Park. With the help of equipment and labor donated by the Lion's Club and other civic-minded young organizations, he got the seep-land filled, smoothed, and planted; and installed curbs, drainage, and sprinklers. He brought in blue spruce and water cedars from Ouray. He scrounged up mulberry, plum, and willow trees. He made flower beds of the wealth of donations pouring in from garden clubs and individuals—peonies, roses, iris, cannas, spirea.

He kept inventing new things to make the park better—benches in this or that lounging nook when this or that flower bed was in seasonal glory, swings for the children, horseshoe pegs for after-supper play when the men came home from work.

Inspired by children's interest in two golden pheasants he had at home, Riley created a zoo in the park, building it himself, obtaining the animals, and providing their food. Most of the creatures were natives—raccoon, deer, elk, coyote, a bear or two—that children could love and learn from as they watched the animals raise their families. There was a lion, of course, in honor of the Delta Lions Club, cosponsor of the zoo. Riley's Zoo, it was named; and the street where he lived was named Riley Lane for him.

In the 1960s, when public places began to be dangerous, park shrubbery every-where too often became the den of lurking attackers. The shrubs in Cleland Park were thinned out and the evergreen trees trimmed up like ladies lifting their skirts for fear of mice.

After the death of both of his sons in World War II, Riley's concern for Delta's children was even more marked. He knew them all. Every evening before leaving the park, he would gather the things they had lost or forgotten—bikes, coats, mittens—and return them to their owners, to save them from possible scoldings.

In appointing Dr. Cleland city health officer, the town gave him a corner of the park for his pool but warned him there wasn't a cent in the city strongbox to con-struct it. Cleland floated the Delta Swim Pool Stock Company, issuing a hundred shares at a hundred dollars each. The Delta Woman's Club went into its bake sale–big dinner–ice cream social routine and raised another two thousand. Wear Brothers got the contract. The firm dug, poured, and prettied up the pool in forty-five days. Asked to make a speech at the grand opening, Dr. Cleland stood on the edge and orated: "Here's your pool. Jump in."

The city manager in 1962 was Paul Shields of Michigan. An engineer, Shields had been involved in building a sliding roof over a swimming pool there. He did the same for the Cleland Pool, making it a year-round facility. That's the way it was for thirty years—summer swimming in sunshine under leafy trees, and then, when the great roof had been shoved into place along its track, swimming all win-ter long in misty warmth, no matter how much snow lay on the ground outside.

8

Industry on the Hoof

Waters are not the only tributaries that converge at the foot of these valleys.

Wagon-train streams of wealth, the produce of mine and field and orchard, came creaking down the Uncompahgre and North Fork roads to the depot. Cattle trailed a thousand paths to the railroad, where they were scared senseless but not voiceless in the process of being jammed into stock cars.

The cattle wealth came first.

Unlike breaking new land to the plow—which involved clearing cottonwoods and brush, leveling fields, stone-boating tons of rocks, digging miles of irrigation ditch—the cattle industry arrived full-blown, its profits immediate. The raw material (grass) was already there, the processor (cow) arrived under its own power, and, because you didn't own the factory site (the range), you didn't have to do anything to it—not even pay taxes on it. The seasons and the surrounding mile-high mountains were like a gigantic conveyor pulling the cattle up the slopes as spring sprouted grass ahead of them, feeding them all summer on rain-rich plateaus, driving them back down in fall with the threat of snow, and leaving them to winter on valley grass that had grown lush in their absence. Perfect.

Cattlemen already were running herds in the mountains before the Utes left. When little Nellie Stephens enjoyed beef cooked in a wash boiler on Black Mesa, she was a guest at an established cow camp. On the Uncompahgre Plateau, Ed Wetzel, manager of Johnson & Johnson Surgical Supply Company cattle outfit, had been grazing reservation land for some time. His trespassing was overlooked because he operated from a base just over the reservation line in the San Juans, supplying off-reservation mine-town butchers. But he may have been the fall guy (literally) in that variously attributed account of a grim Ute joke: Some Tabeguache Utes came upon a cattleman they repeatedly had told to keep off their lands. At gunpoint they ordered him to get down on hands and knees and eat some of that grass, since he liked it so much.

Bringing in two hundred blooded horses and countless cattle, the Roberts outfit trailed onto the Uncompahgre mountainside before the scenic highlights had been earmarked—except for Indian descriptive names which were largely ignored. The Roberts brothers tacked labels on the geography they "owned" to direct cowboy and wrangler to the job, and the labels stuck. Of the dozen or so slender mesas that ribbon down the Uncompahgre mountainside, Roberts Mesa was so named because home base was there; Briggs, Potter, and Monitor mesas were named for three Kentucky racing studs that ruled separate harems on the respective plateaus; and 25 Mesa was named after their cattle brand. Only incidentally is 25 Mesa precisely that many miles from town.

Among the horse trainers whom the Robertses brought with them was Missouri-born Ben Lowe. Handsome, suave, a daredevil, Lowe would have been a natural for the movies if he had been born later or hadn't got himself shot so soon. Everyone loved Ben, except when he left town. Along about 2 A.M. every week or so, he would come bursting out of a saloon, flip onto his horse, and pound up and down the dark, silent streets shooting his guns empty. Woke everybody straight cussing up! Especially the consumptives in their health-tents who had come to the pure, quiet West to be cured. Ben wasn't the only one, of course. On occasion, any cowboy might feel called upon to leave town noticeably like that, but Ben did it oftener and louder.

Ben's homeward route usually took him at full gallop (the Law thundering close behind) up the west draw past Sylvester Huffington's upstairs bedroom. And one night Sylvester, with awesome faith in his aim at a hat bobbing in the moonlight, put a bullet through the brim, just to advise Ben to take another route next time.

Ben's escapades weren't limited to nighttime, however. Once he and Shorty Gibson dared each other to do their shopping on horseback. The Boardwalk Saloon that Ben crashed is gone, but you can still see the iron horseshoe gouges that Shorty Gibson's horse made on the oak floor of Davis Clothing's store.

If you think the Ben Lowe cowboy types went out with the hitching rack, think again. Not too long ago, trader-farmer Geezer was driving his dump truck loaded with culls on his way to the landfill. On the near side of town, he stopped at a bar for a bit of refreshment, during the course of which he took a dare. Beezer went out, climbed into the cab, engaged the truckbed lift, and proceeded to pave Delta's Main Street, end to end, with very imperfect onions.

For almost a decade, the cattle business prospered without hindrance, expanding enormously. Vast leggy herds came in by trail and train, mainly from Texas and Mexico. The enhanced product—range-fattened steers—went east by the trainload. Cattlemen became so rich, lorded over such expanses of range, that they were called "cattle kings." Some built townhouses to suit the title.

"Killian's Castle" was impressively towered, bay-windowed, and frosted with wooden lace; its curving verandahs looked down upon the town from the crest of Garnet Mesa. The main stairway to the upper floors divided on either side of a stagelike landing, where the lady of the house could pause (incidentally displaying her gown) to greet callers her maid had shown into the drawing room, before descending to mingle with them. The floors of the "castle" were of parquetry inlaid by Harry Snyder, a German immigrant and the sole artisan in this craft west of the Rockies.

Killian Pasture, as it was called, ran in a swath miles wide up the mountainside, from the Bar I home ranch to Grand Mesa, where cattle ranged open land to the far rims overlooking the Colorado River. Their cow camps hosted members of the English nobility; the American equivalent—President Teddy Roosevelt—was a Killian guest while hunting bear over in Coyote Basin.

In the Silver Panic, Jack Killian went bankrupt and sold the Bar I to banker-businessmen, who changed the base of operations. Instead of letting cows amble winter range, picking and choosing salad items, they penned and stuffed them with corn and alfalfa grown on vast tracts of converted lower range. To store the products closer to bovine stomachs, they built a huge hayloft barn and three octagonal silos "woven" of squared logs that loomed like immense baskets towering above the trees. They also profitably "penned up" some of the Killian range by subdividing a fragment to form the town of Cedaredge.

Cattleman Alex Calhoun, of Canada and points southwest, bought the Killian townhouse to winter his family in during school months. The castle was never again the same prissy place it had been.

Calhoun was on his second or third fortune. The first had come when he bought a string of pack mules at a sheriff's sale for fifty cents each and then, after working them for a while, sold a hundred of them to railroad builder Otto Mears for one hundred dollars each plus a contract to wrangle them. With the pack-train profits, he bought a cattle outfit in the San Juans; he parlayed that into partnership in a chain of butcher shops in four mining towns, with himself as the beef-producing partner. In the Silver Panic he lost it all, but he collected on a bad debt by taking over the Telluride Meat Market, then snowballed that into enough assets to buy the Johnson & Johnson Club outfit and later the upper end of Escalante Canyon, where he built a family summer home.

By the time Alex got around to marrying Rhea Leeka, he was over half a century old. Rhea was never very well, but they managed to parent a daughter and five sons of such energy and inventive mischief that one of the hired hands was heard to say that he had feared the children would kill one another and later feared they wouldn't! Left pretty much to themselves—their pranks made it difficult to keep a housekeeper—the Calhoun kids treated the ornate hearth in the Killian house like a cow camp fire pit to cook on and the divided stairs as a racing hurdle. When they had grown (their drive and creativity pushed them into notable careers), Killian's Castle became Sunshine School for the handicapped.

All the stockmen with children in school had winter homes in town. School terms were shorter in the days when children worked alongside parents to make store or farm or ranch successful, and a big part of education was learning at first hand how a living was made. Even Ben Lowe had a townhouse on Dodge Street, after he had acquired ranch property and married and settled down—if it can be said that Ben ever settled down or that the girl he chose ever wanted him to. In town during the winter half of the year, Ruby Lowe mothered their children and hotly supported Ben's escapades in letters to the newspaper taunting the authorities for their inability to catch Ben when he didn't want to be caught.

At the confluence as elsewhere in the West, sheepmen challenged the cattlemen's "God-given" sole right to harvest the range through animal digestive systems. From the start, large nomadic flocks of sheep grazed the mesa benches along the river valleys, passing from Utah to summer range on the Uncompahgre Plateau or in the West Elk Mountains. At marketing time, sheep by the thousands converged on the D&RG stockyards, adding their frantic sopranos to the mad bellowing of bullocks.

Charles Nutter was a sheepman—among other things. With his wife and daughters, Nutter came to Ouray by ox-drawn wagon soon after the Utes were treated out of their rights to the gold and silver wealth that town is nested in. Co-owner of a livery stable there, he had helped to finance the Beaumont Hotel and the Otto Mears Toll Road that later became the Million Dollar Highway.

One autumn he attended the Delta County Fair as a guest of his mining friend, Andy Meldrum. In those days, the fairground was in the crotch of the confluence, not far from the place Andy bought when he got rich on Yankee Girl silver. Nutter liked the look of the land, bought some, drew up house plans on the spot—"brick, three verandas and a bay window"—and went back to get his large family of women. Among his other concerns—such as purebred Holstein cows, Hamiltonian race horses, and an interest in the Bar I Ranch—Nutter got into sheep, so effectively that by 1894 he was appointed the state sheep inspector. About this time, scab disease began scourging sheep herds. (Another scourge was cowboys who plagued sheep by running them over cliffs, stabbing them with knives, and shooting them with bullets.) Furthermore, the Silver Panic depressed prices, and a tariff reform raised the tax per head. Under such adverse conditions, treating scab wasn't worth the expense, and many growers let the disease spread untreated. Nutter killed his sick sheep, sold his ranch, and moved to California—for good.

A year later he was back and buying the monastery.

The monastery building had been empty for two years. Unable to finance the combination school-health facility by establishing a Servite parish in Delta, and with several cross-marked graves to prove that the climate was not quite the tuberculosis cure it was touted as being, the remaining priests and their acolytes returned east, and the building was sold to the Delta school board. The board couldn't decide how to use it, so Nutter bought it for a third less than cost, clearing the deal by stipulating a special election to give the public a voice in the personally profitable transaction. He then engaged a Denver decorator to make the monastery into a home. The refectory was converted into a formal dining room, the chapel became the living room, the chancel a library where Charles Nutter would read the classics to his daughters every night. The cells occupied by the priests were very small, but there were many of them, so each member of the family had two rooms, one to sleep in and one in which to study, play games, or store things, according to the memory of Eveline, the youngest. Only five of the six Nutter daughters lived in the monastery; Stella already had married Delta lawyer Millard Fairlamb.

The vast, unused attic was a mysterious place, but nothing compared to the subbasement, where, standing on tiptoe in the furnace room, you could look out across a series of earth mounds that filled the space under the building. Eveline, who had enough imagination to get her fiction published in *McCall's* magazine when she grew up, would bring her little friends down to view the mounds and scare them half to shivering death with tales about hypothetical nuns secretly living up there with the monks and burying the resulting babies down here. Because of those tales, one whole generation couldn't quite dismiss the monastery mounds— not, in fact, until John Calhoun bought the building from Eveline in her old age and, while converting the monastery into apartments, uncovered nothing but dirt in those mounds when he put in new plumbing. In 1966, Lawrence and Doris Schwartz turned the monastery into a nursing home. Later, the historic building was razed to build a condominium.

Having no sons to compare next-generation imperfections with, Charles P. Nutter's standard for sons-in-law was so high that at least two of his lovely and financially well-endowed daughters never married. To the end of her life, Eveline wore the ruby engagement ring given to her by the man her father had failed to approve.

The demands of large-scale stock raising produced managerial skills in both men and women. While the men worked range and cattle to produce profit, their wives, often in sole charge of the paperwork, had better knowledge of ranch finances, deciding when and what to buy or sell, when and how much to borrow. The community availed itself of these skills. Robert and Wilson Rockwell, father and son, served in the Colorado Senate, and Robert was a U.S. Congressman. Kelso and Jack Musser, father and son, played leading roles in the National Cattlemen's Association and the Bureau of Land Management (BLM). Josephine Beach Gore served as county clerk for decades. Enos Hotchkiss was certified to the Cowboy Hall of Fame for, among other things, founding the town bearing his name. J. D. Dillard, Jr., was a grazing consultant for the BLM.

A cattleman managing range for the BLM? Dillard was perhaps the last person on both sides in a government-cattleman conflict that splits the two interests farther apart every year. He fended off clashes by telling jokes, like the one about how rugged the cattleman's life is: "Move camp twice a year. Every blame thing you're going to need for the next six months—bed, grub, duds, cookstove—heaved onto pack horses. My folks didn't believe in coddling their tykes, the horses had too much to pack, anybody with legs had to walk. Twenty or thirty miles up the side of the mountain from Fat Man's Misery Canyon. Barefoot to save our boots for school. Even made me lug my own bed roll on my back." J. D. waits for the wince of sympathy or outrage at such child abuse, then finishes: "Worst of it was, I was only six weeks old!"

And then there was Fred "Kelly" Calhoun, who distinguished himself as a college athlete and served flamboyantly in an open PC boat with the U.S. Navy in World War II. Later he became a one-of-a-kind district judge without blunting one iota the prankish Calhoun wit that made him a risky delight over coffee at Comet Drug. When Kelly died, his friends thought that a moribund funeral service with organ music and sermon would be an absurdly inappropriate farewell for this man. Since ex-cowboy Judge Calhoun always had liked to hang around the corrals and barns down at the sales yard, some of his friends arranged a "roast" for Kelly in the auction barn. Mel Renfrow and Don Lane arranged it, spreading the word that mourners were to dig up their favorite "Kelly story" and share it with the crowd. The barn was packed, tear-wet faces roaring with laughter as tale after tale unfolded.

This was Dr. Gerald Burgess' contribution.

Kelly was to have some dental work done, difficult extractions. We'd grown up together, so I knew how high-strung and intense he was. I thought things might go better if he had pre-medication to calm him down beforehand. I wrote the prescription and handed it to him. "Don't drive after you take this," I cautioned.

"Okay if I fly, Doc?"

He sounded so flippant I thought he might disregard it, so I grabbed the prescription, turned it over and wrote on the back, "Don't drive. Don't fly. Don't even ride a horse!"

Well, Kelly obeyed orders.

When his appointment time came, the town ambulance backed across my lawn right to the office door, lights flashing, siren screaming. Passersby gathered, gawking. The undertaker's assistant got out and opened the door, and Kelly stepped down.

"This okay, Doc?"

The focus of all those cow trails meandering down the mountains on four sides, and of valley feed-lot beef factories, was the railroad stockyards at the confluence. There were two, extensive yards at the Delta depot and even larger ones at nearby Roubideau Switch. The latter was almost a town, with a saloon at one end and a school at the other, decently separated by a half-dozen houses.

Cattle by the trainload—many trainloads a day in the fall—were packed into cars at these yards. Stock bound for Denver, Kansas, or California must be unloaded, fed, watered, and reloaded at regular intervals along the line, or they would lose weight and, consequently, profit. The owner or manager often went along (riding in the caboose if the brakie was friendly), not only to finalize the sale at the other end, but also to see to it that station feeding crews were thorough and honest. Such an overseer received a free return pass by passenger coach.

Not all the cows left town alive. Delta had a meat-packing plant and later a company that rented freezer-lockers to those who did their own butchering, whether cows, sheep, deer, or elk.

Three disasters hit the livestock industry in one five-year span. First, cattlemen lost their winter range, as farmers finished fencing the valleys into plowed squares. Second, the price of beef plummeted when the Panic of 1893 hit the country after the government went off the silver standard. Third and worst of all, the grass played out.

Competing with each other in using the range, early ranchers overgrazed. A newspaper item, anticipating profitable use of Delta railroad facilities, estimated the cattle population of the White River range alone at three hundred thousand head. Seeing the grass being chewed and hooved to dust, it was the cattlemen themselves, some of them at least, who instigated government control, petitioning for the creation of national forests with limited grazing permits. In response,

Battlement Mesa National Forest, later renamed Grand Mesa National Forest, was established in 1892; Uncompahgre National Forest was designated not long after. But for most of the range—the part below scrub-oak altitude—it was too late; the damage was permanent.

Early settlers were unanimous in saying that, except for the steepest 'dobe slopes, the grass when they came was stirrup-high. Nothing approaching that abundance has been seen by anyone now alive.

To celebrate the first Earth Day, a Girl Scout Troop attempted a project to see if the range could be restored. Buying varieties of grass seed native to the area, they sowed some of the mesa benches west of town. The experiment failed. A BLM official explained why:

> For grass seed to sprout and grow in conditions at this altitude and annual rainfall, there must be a mulch to keep the ground moist until roots are established. Formerly this was provided by centuries of decay resulting in a mat of natural compost around each plant. The mat not only helped new grass get started but allowed old grass to grow thicker and taller because it slowed water-loss by evaporation. The lusher grasses then produced still thicker mat that in turn . . . It was a natural cycle broken when overgrazing and trampling destroyed that ancient mat forever.

Cattlemen coped with the triple calamities of the 1890s in various inventive ways. Having to run fewer cows as the range grew sparser, they bred up the reduced herds to produce better, higher-priced beef. Some turned to raising sheep that could survive on short range by eating the grass closer (or so their disapproving compatriots accused). To take the place of the lost valley-range, some cowmen, turning farmer, grew large acreages of alfalfa, while others bought ready-grown alfalfa hay. Their winter feedlots, formerly empty during summer months, were converted into the valley's present year-long beef-fattening industry.

When the price of beef fell below the cost of producing it, cattlemen borrowed to keep operating; and when banks began to fail in Delta, Montrose, Grand Junction, everywhere, many cattle companies went broke or changed hands.

The third-party Populists were blamed for the hard times, for not getting their presidential candidate elected on a free-silver platform. Founded by discontented farmers in the Northwest and South, the Populist party demanded unlimited coinage of silver, government ownership of railroads, and repossession of land that had been given to railroad companies to induce them to lay rails. These issues deeply affected western Colorado because of the area's silver mining and because railroads owned so much land. In 1893, the party swept the

Western Slope, in Delta County taking "every office except Sheriff Stell."

In the middle of the Silver Panic, the Methodist Epworth League threw a "hard-times party" to raise money, announcing: "All people who are struggling with Poverty invited. People who are not dressed in accord with the theme will be fined. The fines—new woolen dress 10 cents, old woolen dress 5 cents, new calico dress 3 cents, new suit of clothes 10 cents, mustache waxed 10 cents, mustache not waxed 5 cents, watch gold 15 cents, watch silver 10 cents." But the really heavy fines, 50 cents, were for the corsage you gave your girlfriend or for a Waterbury watch.

The town's mine-rich men were not affected when the mines closed—Sanders had invested most of his silver profits in area businesses, and Meldrum's wife had beat the Panic in relieving him of his.

Though it was the cause of his death, Ben Lowe played no sustained role in the cattle-sheep "war" that began with the first settlers and ended with the truce still sustained: cattle have their assigned areas, and sheep for the most part do their summer feeding up where the country is too rough and rocky for the larger beasts.

Ben Lowe homesteaded south of town, running cattle, of course, buying the property in Escalante Canyon that, though he stayed there only a few years and many lived there after him, will forever be known as "the Lowe Place." He had a run-in with the Delta city council on opening a livery stable on Main Street, appealed the case, lost, and moved his stable over to Dodge, where he had built a two-story house for his family. For an office he rented the public reading room and changed its character completely from the quiet retreat established by the town's intellectuals to a jolly place full of people who loved to be around Ben Lowe.

He married the perfect wife for him—Ruby Hutchinson, the girl who noted and remembered the horsemanship displayed by riders who turned out to be the McCarty Gang. The daughter of "Spud Hutch," a well-to-do potato grower just downriver from town, Ruby was spunky and pretty (Ben's nickname for her was "Chiquita," a Spanish shortcut for saying a whole lot: "My Pretty Little Girl One"). The only child of money, she could have had any man in town, but it was dashing, show-off, kind-hearted Ben Lowe she adored. She would drop everything to watch him perform at racetrack or home corral; his favorite trick was to target-shoot at a dead run, aiming from under the horse's neck. She cheerfully cooked and cared for the homeless he brought in—Old Batch Castle, the orphan kid Claude Marsh— and defended Ben hotly, accusing the law of chasing him on "trumped-up charges." When one of the charges was serious enough to make Ben build a "stoop-door" hideout cabin in upper Roubideau Canyon, Ruby rode in with saddlebags of food, outwitting the nose-to-trail law enforcement officers, and taught her little boys how to do it. Ben Lowe had adventures on both sides of the law, helping the sheriff track horse thieves and himself being accused of "sleepering"—putting a nearly invisible mark on the ear of somebody else's suckling calf, so that, when weaned, with no identifying mother giving tit, it could be claimed by the mark and branded to match. However, as Ruby maintained, this and many similar deeds may have been committed by others and blamed on him because the law needed someone to hang things on and he was so visible and reckless.

Bad blood between Ben Lowe and stock inspector Cash Sampson climaxed when the pair happened to eat the midday meal together in Musser headquarters at Escalante Forks. Because Eda Musser was in town, Kelso was cooking for himself and hired-hand Shorty Gibson and whoever else might drop in. In old-time cattle country, if you happened on any kind of an occupied kitchen within two hours each side of mealtime, you stopped. Anything else was considered discourteous, maybe even suspicious. Cash Sampson arrived first, an officer wearing a gun, chatting while waiting for the steak to fry. Next Ben Lowe and his two sons—Robert, age eleven, and William, age nine—rode into the yard. All three wore guns, the children's in belt holsters and Ben's in a shoulder holster, as his gunbelt was at a harness-maker's, being mended. That may have been important—he was used to drawing from the hip. Seeing Cash Sampson's horse tied to the hitching rack, Ben could have ridden on, avoiding the confrontation. It is impossible that he didn't recognize the Sampson horse; all cattlemen knew every horse in the country at sight, who it belonged to, who it had belonged to before that, and whether it toed in or out.

The six made polite talk as they fed. Sampson was the first to leave; Ben and the boys followed, after he was out of sight in the cedars.

From that point on, nothing is known except what the boys remembered. The three Lowes overtook Sampson; perhaps he had dallied purposely. Ben sent the boys on ahead, saying that he had business to discuss. When they had gone a short distance down the road, they heard shots and raced back. Sampson was dead, and Ben Lowe died as his sons reached him.

The tracks showed that Ben had spun his horse to shoot under the neck from the far side of the animal's body, but, perhaps because he was slow in drawing from the shoulder holster, his first shot did not hit the mark. One of the other four bullets to leave his gun found Cash Sampson's brain. The one shot Cash got off traveled the full length of Ben Lowe's spine.

9

Eddies of Talent

The settlers pouring into the confluence brought a wealth of technical and social skills in their individual heads—and brought or created organizations to implement them. A surprising number of settlers were college graduates, in an era when it was uncommon even to finish high school; of those graduates, a surprising number were from Ohio's Oberlin College.

Oberlin in the 1880s was far ahead of its time. Co-educational and interracial, it focused not so much on how to make a living with your learning as on how to use knowledge to enrich your own life and that of others. Though qualified to issue doctorates in science, the college stressed music and the accumulated human wisdom embodied in literature. In the explosive cross-country migration after the Civil War, Oberlin College specialized in preparing ministers and school teachers for the West.

When an Oberlin man, Professor Philip Condit, stepped off the train, neither he nor the town knew that he would set the tone for education at the confluence for all time; they just thought of him as the high-school teacher they'd been doing without. The high school itself was tiny, only one room. The first graduating class was small, only two seniors. Ada McMurray, under Condit's tutelage, was able to go directly from high school into teaching; and Jacob Cowan was accepted at Cornell University, where he did so well that he was named to the faculty, although he was stricken with tuberculosis before he could begin working.

The first grammar school had been even smaller—half a room. Teacher Ada Carr had partitioned her cabin to create space for the class, drawing children indoors from excited exploration of their new world—thickety woods along unexpected streams, echo-haunted canyons, weird adobe domes layered with seashells.

When the Methodists built their first little church, they rented it out as a school on weekdays; but with new families trailing in daily, the child population quickly outgrew these rooms, so Jennie Ash (Perdy) took up the slack by holding classes in a log-adobe shack in the shadow of the Uncompahgre House.

In 1895, a real schoolhouse was built on Schoolhouse Square. Actually, this block had been platted as "Courthouse Square," but the drayman made a mistake. After he had loaded the huge foundation slabs of Escalante Canyon sandstone off the railroad cars and onto his wagon, and then off his wagon onto the ground, the city fathers decided that it was easier to switch names on the map than to load and unload all that rock again. Schoolhouse Square which became Courthouse Square had been sited on the west side of town because most of the people lived over there—the east side was largely marsh—and children would not need to cross Main Street, where they might get hurt. Runaway teams were frequent, wagon traffic to the depot was heavy—nose-to-tailgate during harvest time—and herds being moved through town often included bulls.

Central High School, as it was called although it also accommodated grade-school classes, was two stories high, with tall slender windows, fancy gingerbread on the portico roof, and a bell tower. The lower floor held two classrooms, and the entire upper floor was a gymnasium. This was during a health and body-building craze in the 1890s, comparable to our own today. Every modern school with at least two classrooms included a gymnasium.

Behind the schoolhouse were wooden privies and a shed with hay mangers for horses ridden in by country children and for the teams that pulled the canvas-covered school bus, called the Kid Wagon. For one brief period, the Kid Wagon hauled nobody but Dempseys, when that family lived out on California Mesa. Jack's big brothers kept other children off the wagon and cowed the driver into keeping eyes focused on the horses' ears while they "rode the school bus like they owned it."

Central School was made of Rollins brick, dyed red and so soft that one of the playground rules was: "Don't dig at the schoolhouse with your fingernails." That it stood for half a century was owing to additions propping it up like buttresses. By the time Lincoln School came along, Delta Brick and Tile was producing a product so uniquely enduring that specimen bricks (with the defunct company's name impressed) now are considered collectibles.

Not designed merely to house students and desks as economically as possible, Lincoln School classrooms had *class*. The impressive façade, with its arched stone-work and stepped gables, reminded the entering student of the importance and the luxury of getting an education. High ceilings, wide stairs, carved frames, hard-wood floors, and wainscoting lent an air of elegance. Just as elocution classes helped

"Kid Wagon" school bus, with Thomas Griffith, wrangler, at Central School, 1909. Jack Dempsey rode to school in this wagon for a time. Courtesy of Delta County Historical Society.

students become leaders in public life, the building was designed to help them feel at home in a gracious surrounding and to motivate them to achieve their own generation's version of it.

It takes more than enduring brick to make a building immortal. Eight decades later, Lincoln School was dated and shabby, though still sound. It needed refurbishing—new wiring, plumbing, and heating. One group, who apparently had managed to have nothing but bad memories of attending school there, wanted it torn down. Blast it out of sight! Out of mind! It looked dowdy, didn't it? Those lofty ceilings, those wide stairs, that domineering bell tower—ugh! Another group argued to keep it, noting that, in history-rich Europe, old buildings are not demolished simply for being out-of-date, but instead are inconspicuously piped, wired, and kept in use. Perhaps Lincoln could become an office building, or City Hall.

Lincoln School was sold and demolished. Before the protest group got organized, it had become a parking lot. The loss, however, triggered more alert action from the history-minded, who since have helped the town keep several important landmarks.

Schoolhouses sprang up all over the countryside, up tributary streams in the mountains, wherever land provided livelihood for families. The sites were spaced so that no child would have to walk more than three miles each way, or ride horseback more than five. Because each school was financed out of taxes within its district, they were not equally well funded. Town schools, supported by business and suburban tax bases, were well off. But a school district up on a mountain creek might afford the barest minimum of space and equipment—a wall map, a blackboard, a hand bell, homemade benches and desks. Wood for the heating stove was cut, hauled, and corded by fathers or big-boy students. Part of the teacher's pay was board and room, furnished by families in turn. Even so, funding often ran out before spring, cutting the school year short. The quality of teaching often was poor—done by eighth-grade graduates with a single year of training, or rejects from elsewhere. Instructors good enough to get better teaching jobs did so.

Even country schools were far from equal. If the district's tax base included rich orchards, sugar beet fields, or large sections of railroad-owned land, then the school might equal or exceed town schools in quality of facilities and number of instructors per student.

There were two ways to equalize educational opportunity: leveling and consolidation. Leveling would pool all county school funds and apportion them among the districts equally, in which case the poorest schools would become richer and better, the richer schools would become poorer and worse. Consolidation would bus all the country kids to the five towns in the county, which then could afford to build bigger and better schools to receive them.

Motorized school buses had been around for a long time before the word *consolidation* was spoken aloud. Country schools fought it hardest. The best of these schools would lose their per-student advantage. The poorest country schools protested because the little schoolhouse, however minimal, was a center of community activities and pride. On Sundays, it was the church house; on Wednesday evenings, it was the place of prayer; on Saturday nights, it was the dance hall. It housed women's clubs, ditch meetings, box suppers, potluck picnics, speaking programs, and debates both serious and comic:

Resolved: The government should own all railroads.
Resolved: Commodore Dewey should get the heck out of Cuba.

A community would lose its self, its soul, if it lost its school.

After the consolidation of grade schools was achieved, consolidation of all four high schools into one super education facility at the confluence was proposed. No way! If the little old schoolhouse was the soul of the community, the high school, with its sports, music, drama, and teenage togetherness, was the life of the small town. Without a high school, a town died. When the smoke cleared, the decision was: there would still be four high schools, all bigger and better than before.

The pioneer seeding of highly educated people from Oberlin, Harvard, and other famous schools consistently produced excellence in various fields of scholastic accomplishment at the confluence. Consequently when the nation's schools, spurred by Russia's Sputnik, put a sudden new priority on scientific education, Delta already had students doing advanced work in those areas.

The schools' capacity to prepare students for top fields was demonstrated by two of them in a very high field indeed—the Apollo moon flight. Ludie G. Richards received an Exceptional Service medal for his work on the Saturn V Rocket that launched the flight, and Dr. Tom Osborn, III, designed the soil-sampling potassium bromide probe that the astronauts thrust with such difficulty six feet into the moon's hard surface. Osborn himself tested some of the fragments of moon-stuff the flight brought back, searching for chemical clues to the moon's history.

Harry Brauneis brought the fascination of space study to even younger children. An amateur astronomer, Brauneis came to the Uncompahgre Valley to escape Boulder's glaring city lights, which spoiled his stargazing. He installed his ten-inch telescope and observatory on California Mesa and invited youngsters in small groups to come take a look at what was out there. "In Boulder," he told teachers and parents, "I saw an interest in astronomy giving orientation to kids who were problems to themselves and to others." Through Brauneis, the school system received a telescope and roll-roof observatory of its own, the antique (but tops for its size) scope that Dr. Beard of Fruita, Colorado had mounted in an octagonal observatory on the roof of his home at the turn of the century.

At the beginning of the 1990s, the school system took a step that was to bring local education to international attention. Centers of Applied Learning were set up, in which students work in teams on such subjects as robotics, electronics, math, video, technology, music, and desktop publishing. Evenings and Saturdays. At their own instigation. And in addition to the regular curriculum. The idea was to change the way instruction is delivered, to make education relevant to the student, and to give students more responsibility for their own learning.

The success of the program drew thousands of visitors from all over the world. Five hundred high schools in this nation adopted the idea. In 1992, Delta was the only American school district invited to attend a thirty-eight-nation world technology conference in Germany.

The first sound of church music at the confluence came from McMurray's tent drugstore. Families of the several denominations sat on crates and cottonwood stumps, singing the same hymn together.

Soon the group diversified. Petitioned by Rev. L. C. Aley and George McGranahan, the Uncompahgre Town Company deeded five plots of several lots each, just off Main Street, to the five churches then represented in town: Methodist, Presbyterian, Baptist, Episcopal, and Catholic. This was a sizable underestimation of the town's potential religious variety; at one time, there were twenty-nine denominations.

M. A. Clark, a Colporteur missionary, founded the Baptist church with a congregation of five. A Colporteur missionary is a traveling salesman of religious books, but Clark expanded this role into something more. Father Clark, as he was known, founded eleven Baptist churches in western Colorado just months after the reservation was opened, and did it very economically. Not owning a horse, he walked hundreds of miles between far-flung communities in the territory he served on both sides of the Continental Divide—from Pueblo to Eckert and everything between. He walked barefoot, carrying his shoes tied over his shoulder to save them for Sunday. Typical of Father Clark's make-do style, the steeple of his Eckert church was crowned with a homemade skyward-pointing wooden hand instead of a cross.

Five adults and five children formed the nucleus of the Methodist Church, under the leadership of farmer-minister L. C. Aley. Although Reverend Aley later became one of the town's foremost businessmen, he is remembered as preaching in a shirt without a collar and with holes in his shoes.

Known as Methodist Brethren, Aley's group built a log church on the back of its assigned lots—visualizing the fine church it was leaving room for—and promptly rented the building out to the District 1 School. Methodist sisters (the Mite Society) took the lead in raising money whenever the congregation outgrew its church and had to build a bigger one. Their *modus operandi* was to ask for donated food and then charge people to eat it, at banquets, dinners, and ice-cream socials costing fifty cents a place. Mrs. Amsbary recalled baking twenty-one squash pies in one day, while a friend turned out twenty-eight apple pies for the same event—both using rolling pins and wood-fired ovens! For ice-cream socials, gallons of donated cream, eggs, and sugar were coaxed into freezing by hammer-crushed ice, salt, and hand cranking.

Those dinners, plus cash contributions, financed first a white frame building with a slender steeple, then a red brick building with real stained glass, and finally the Reverend J. A. Johnson's dream church.

Reverend Johnson already had built several churches back in Illinois, and he resolved that this one—for a congregation obviously on the increase—would be bigger and better. Sandstone for moldings on the brick structure was quarried at Escalante by church members. Andrew Carnegie contributed half the cost of the pipe organ, the other half paid for by Ladies Aid and Mite Society dinner money.

The building, its bell tower adorned with battlements, is described in the National Register of Historic Places as "Victorian Tudor." In 1993 the building caught fire, destroying the interior, the stained glass windows, and the pipe organ. The brick walls and tower stand firm, however, and the building has been restored.

Speaking of organs, the Episcopalians for a time had two, one in the church and one in the vicar's home. Father A. Blanchard Boyer was in the process of building his own organ when he arrived in town. Towering organ pipes and an uncased console completely filled the manse living room, and rows of pipes overflowed onto a bench on the sunporch. Boyer shaped the pipes himself of sheet zinc, a slow "tuning" process that apparently had lasted through stays at several parishes. Perhaps his interest in music exceeded his interest in his parishioners, accounting for his frequent moves. At any rate, to stand in the middle of the vicar's pipe organ while he performed Bach was an extraordinary experience.

The Presbyterians had an organ before they had a church. The trunk-sized folding reed organ sported carrying handles, a lid that flipped open to reveal the keyboard, a pop-up music rack, and drop-down pump pedals. Between that portable instrument and the eventual fine pipe organ, the congregation sang to the music of an ornate reed organ pumped by a little boy wedged out of sight behind it. Dr. Lawrence Hick remembered, "One Sunday when I was ten, I fell asleep during a long sermon and when the organist tried to play the final hymn, no sound came out."

The noted pioneer and author, Rev. George M. Darley, pastored confluence Presbyterians several years after conquering the San Juan peaks to bring religion to both sides of that skyscraping hump. In 1876, he had built a church (he was also a carpenter) on the edge of the Hell's Acre saloon and red-light district in the Lake City mining camp. Then he built a church in Ouray and pastored them both regularly, crossing the intervening eleven-thousand-foot passes on foot, even in waist-deep snows.

When early automobiles made the top of Grand Mesa accessible in one afternoon instead of two days, several churches joined to create a youth camp there. The "Institute" (only half an hour's drive in today's cars) still provides week-long retreats for young people of all denominations. Activities include programs, studies, boating, and hiking along spine-of-the-earth Crag Crest Trail. Campfire services and daybreak meditations are especially poignant beside the still waters of lakes two miles in the sky. Thousands of teenagers have found life-direction during these camp weeks.

One might expect that Catholics would have worshipped in the monastery chapel, which was open to everyone, but that chapel belonged to the Servite Order, and the people wanted and achieved a church of their own. At the dedication, Caballo's orchestra came over from Denver to perform Haydn's "Imperial Mass in D." The church was little and homey, with sweet and gentle figures the people loved. When modern art trickled into the confluence, the figures were replaced by featureless Marys and Jesuses. After much protest, the people got their beloved statues and paintings back.

Historians have noted that it was the men who wanted to pioneer the West and that most women came because their men came. Diaries and memoirs of confluence pioneer women, many of whom came from lush eastern homesites, record their dismay at what they saw when they stepped down from wagon or railroad car: sagebrush and greasewood surrounded by steep badlands of ash-gray adobe clay.

A surprising number of the college graduates who helped to get things started at the confluence were women, many of them young wives and mothers. For women of culture and courage, with young families to raise in this raw environment, there was only one option—improve things as fast as possible, so that their children would not be handicapped culturally when the time came for them to function in the world outside.

While still in tents and cabins, these women organized reading, dramatic, and debating societies—Lyceum and Chautauqua in their time. The Shakespeare Club was introduced by the Nutter women when they moved down from Ouray, where Shakespearean readings, male and female, had been one of the influences that kept that rowdy mining town from popping off the map. In Delta, the Shakespeare Club was among the early educational clubs that endured longest; and, in a coincidence the members loved, one of its later presidents was Mrs. Verna Shakespeare. The women put on musicals in public rooms and in their homes. Several, like Letitia Obert and Dellie Blachly, who had been schooled at the Oberlin Conservatory of Music, were professional musicians. They gave music lessons and sent their children to dancing school.

The women petitioned the town council for a Reading Room, won a place for it upstairs over a store, and donated their own books and time. Well patronized, it provided a quiet alternative to the ubiquitous saloons for travelers, ranchers, and cowboys staying overnight in town. The Reading Room evolved into a Community Room, with space for socials and dances.

Where pioneer women saw stretches of adobe badlands, and pioneer men saw future fertile fields, modern scientists see pre-history in fossil seashells and dinosaur bones. Photo by Muriel Marshall.

Tapping outside strength, the ladies organized a local chapter of the Federated Woman's Club. Before the days of service clubs—Kiwanis, Rotary, Lions, and Jaycees—the Federated Woman's Club was the generative force in many towns. The club began small, working first to get a school drinking fountain. Every child in school used the same cup. (This wasn't unusual. The communal cup was ubiquitous. Persnickety people carried their own folding cup in pocket or purse, made of metal rings that telescoped flat.) The children would come in sweaty from recess to slosh water down their gullets and then pass the cup along. This at a time when childhood death from summer complaint was so prevalent that some infants were simply called "Babe" until, by surviving one summer, they had established a grip on life; and when almost every passenger train deposited a disease-wasted tubercular patient in desperate search of a cure, some with families of children.

After the women got the drinking fountain, they tackled the streets. Street cleaning—that is, grubbing out sagebrush, picking up rocks, and shoveling manure—usually was accomplished by putting prisoners to work, but they were few (cowboy ruckuses aside, crime wasn't rampant), and they were slow, being hampered by ball and chain. Windblown weeds accumulated against buildings and under boardwalks. The Woman's Club got trash kegs placed along the streets and saw to it that the kegs were dumped regularly. In those innocent out-of-sight, out-of-mind days, dumping simply meant hauling trash into the adobe hills and tossing it out. The group also succeeded in getting the boggiest streets graveled over. During spring thaw, a loaded wagon could sink to the hubs right there on Main Street.

Next the ladies tackled those boardwalks. They were a rattling nuisance, catching heels, snagging petticoats, and giving a baby in a perambulator a mighty rough ride. If you stepped on the end of a loose board, the other end could fly up and wham you where you weren't looking. Club members approached businessmen and town officials about it—approach is all they could do, not yet having the vote—and were patiently told that the matter would be taken care of in good time, but cement sidewalks cost a lot of money, and the town had other, more urgent needs, and . . .

Though voteless, the women were not without power. Remarking that these businessmen and town officials were their husbands, the Woman's Club conspired: no more fine evening dinners would be served, only a sandwich, until sidewalk action was taken. The Main Street sidewalks were paved almost at once. Serendipitously, cement walks created a brand new recreation for children, roller skating.

But the town hadn't heard the last from the ladies about sidewalks. There was all that *spit*. Chewing tobacco and snuff were so prevalent that every structure with a roof and floor had at least one spittoon, but anyplace outside was an open target. The sticky brown splotches were too ubiquitous to avoid; the ruffles of the ladies' petticoats dragged through the stuff and brought it home. And there was all that hacking and spitting by people with catarrh and tuberculosis.

In response to female pressure, the brickyard scored bricks with the words "Don't Spit" to be set into the sidewalks as wanted, and one enterprise laid out a more personal message: "If you spit on the floor at home, go home and spit."

The crowning achievement of the Woman's Club was the library. The Reading Room was all well and good, but it stocked only donated materials; the club dreamed of a full facility with funds to stay abreast of the publishing world.

At that time, rags-to-riches millionaire Andrew Carnegie was helping towns all over the country establish libraries. The Woman's Club applied for Carnegie money and launched a drive to raise the required start-up minimum, thirty-four hundred dollars. They managed to do it in about three months by solicitation and feeding folks, mainly at oyster suppers. The raw oysters (a food fad at the time) came from the Atlantic by the barrel in iced railroad cars. If we compare the price of a loaf of bread then and now and apply that ratio, the amount raised was equivalent to nearly a hundred thousand today. Moreover, these women also were members of one church or another and were busy putting on fund-raising dinners to build the town's first real churches. How they managed to cook so much food is as big a mystery as how a town that tiny could ingest it all.

Andrew Carnegie was a shrewd benefactor whose gifts were designed to make towns help themselves. He asked for population figures and upon them based his terms. The Delta library was to cost not less than ten thousand dollars; was to be built of pressed brick or stone on land donated by the city, not far from the main section; and was to be financed with matching funds from the town itself, with an assessment levied on property to maintain the building, supply books, and pay the salary of a competent librarian. But Carnegie was not adamant; when the town came up short of its share after exhausting all possibilities, he provided the remainder of the construction money himself.

With Professor Condit, alderman Starr Nelson, and lawyer Millard Fairlamb, club members petitioned the city for land and got a corner of Courthouse Square. The "neoclassical" building was constructed in 1911 of cream-yellow DB&T brick and Escalante red sandstone.

Nutter women, first to last, ran the library, maintaining a quality of reading material to match the beauty of the building. Anna Nutter was succeeded by little sister Eveline, each serving into advanced age. The present head is their grandniece, Lali (Ethel) Fairlamb Jackson.

In 1969, times were hard. The city ran short of funds and was faced with closing something down. One possibility was to close the library. Esther Stephens, who had worked for lawyers so long that folks said she knew nearly as much law as her employers, confronted the City Council, provisions of the Carnegie contract in hand. They *could not* close the library, not even if they closed down everything else in town! As a result, a special library district was created, with its own tax base, to fund the facility.

Some sixty years later, the population of Delta, upon which Andrew Carnegie had based the original library specifications, had more than doubled; demands on the facility far exceeded its capacity. The library board started raising money to enlarge the building.

But times had changed. This was 1980. Those people in the community who had the will and energy to raise money by putting on big dinners, cake sales, and box suppers were working at full-time jobs and had little enough time left over to care for their families. Anyway, few people attended such events anymore; the workplace and television fulfilled their social and entertainment needs. The way to raise money in 1980 was to get a "grant engineer" to locate and tap funding sources, just as a civil engineer might locate ditches to tap irrigation streams.

Lali Jackson tapped three rich streams: the Delta County Capitol Improvement Fund, the Energy Impact Assistance Committee, and Colorado State Library Services. Lali had four goals: the addition must at least double the original area, it must have a children's story and reading room, it must contain adequate office space, and it must not destroy the Carnegie Gothic architectural style. She achieved them all.

The Ute Council Tree was endangered.

Immemorial landmark, the place where intertribal decisions were made when the Utes were free, the Tree remained the clans' gathering point for the spring Bear Dance. Here unrelated young people could meet, fall in love, and mate, after the manner of teenager *Aapa-vu-ci* of the Old Ones, who started it all by marrying *Maamakwiya*, the She-Bear. After the Utes were split into separate reservations hundreds of miles and a mountain range apart, the Tree continued to mark the cherished campsite to which they traveled to visit with one another. Its Ute name is unknown, being perhaps too sacred to be divulged to whites.

But now the Tree was ancient and rotten, its massive branches threatening the homes that had sprung up around it. A cottonwood branch two feet in diameter, water-logged as all cottonwoods are, can crush a house. And the Tree was untidy. A big cottonwood creates half an acre of continuous litter—leaves, twigs, fluff, and chartreuse caterpillars. The neighbors who had to cope with it wanted it down. Utes in pickups, whizzing down the highway between Uinta and Ignacio, ignored it and anyway couldn't have found room under it to pitch a tipi, even if they still had one. Someone proposed cutting it into dollar-size chips to sell to tourists.

It was the niece of a man killed by Indians—Capt. John Gunnison, slain by Paiutes in 1853—who founded the Delta group that saved the Tree. The Capt. John Gunnison Chapter of the Daughters of the American Revolution (DAR) was organized by Julie Gunnison Porter, an artist schooled at the Julian Academy in Paris.

After Fred Wilder was induced to deed to the historical society the land upon which the Tree grows, the DAR called a tree surgeon to strengthen it with cement implants, shoot it full of vitamins, and take a tree-ring specimen to see if it actually was old enough to be as monumentally historic as it was claimed to be. It was. But the Tree is not eternal, although the Delta Tree Board is attempting to make it so by cloning it—that is, by snipping off cuttings to be rooted and planted.

The Tree hasn't quit dropping tree-sized branches. The latest to fall (in autumn of 1992) was presented to the Utes, who sent tribal leader Alden Naranjo to bless it by chanting and burning sweetgrass. Sectioned and hollowed out, the wood was covered with hides to make drums for the spring Bear Dance.

The John Gunnison Chapter of the DAR is no more, but Julie Gunnison Porter left Delta other mementos of herself. Deeply interested in Egyptian art and history, she laid out a garden beside her home in the shape of a sacred Egyptian scarab. A fountain pool formed the head of the gigantic insect, while cement walkways and shaped flower beds outlined the body. This scarab garden still exists at what is now the Fairlamb place. Julie also deeply admired the music of Wagner, but the paintings she made on the walls around her Steinway piano, depicting tumultuous operatic scenes, are gone, perhaps papered over by later owners with staider tastes.

In this place where rivers meet, where things and people tend to settle and take root, three generations living in old-style houses with generous attics accumulated ordinary things that with passing time became rare treasures. Things like Stella Nutter Fairlamb's side-saddle and Mrs. McClanahan's riding habit, fashioned long on one side so that the hem would hang gracefully straight across the bottom when her right knee was crooked up over the horn. But the treasures in the old homes were disappearing—discarded when sons and daughters came home from far away with only a few days to attend Mother's funeral and prepare the house for sale.

Eleven people organized the Delta County Historical Society to provide a place where the treasures could be saved and seen. Having petitioned the county for space, they were assigned one room in the courthouse basement. It was as if a dam had broken. Treasures poured in, as people and businesses brought their keepsakes. The Co-op's first telephone exchange board and its tall slender stool. Guns used in the McCarty Gang bank robbery. And something that isn't there anymore, the swaddled mummy of a prehistoric infant discovered in a Roubideau Canyon cave. Displayed by the museum for many years, the babe was relinquished in deference to the new (and equally historic) sensitivity to racial rights.

No one knew how to run a museum, but Esther Stephens and Katharine Hedgcock went to Denver to learn about cataloging and records in training sessions of the Colorado State Historical Society. They returned able to do the job and teach it. Esther gave—literally, that is; she accepted no monetary recompense—thirty years of her life as curator.

Historical annals are exceptionally available in this town, because so many of the old families have remained. These documents are stored in museum files, on microfiche, in taped memories, and in the total-recall and instant-retrieval head of Esther Stephens.

Every few years, the museum would outgrow its space and be assigned larger quarters—in the courthouse annex, then back to the basement, finally in the firehouse. With Urban Renewal funds, the firehouse was remodeled and enlarged to form an unusual building with a Southwest-hogan motif. The outer walls are alcoved to frame two sandstone urns that once stood on either side of the home of pioneer silver king J. Frank Sanders. The carved urns, it is said, were special-ordered to fancy up the Sanders mansion when President Taft was expected to stop there for tea on his way to dedicate the Gunnison River Tunnel. Maybe. There's no evidence, except that the door of the house indeed was remodeled extra-wide, as it would have had to be to let that massive man pass gracefully through.

10

Keeping Current with Progress

The story of getting water into the Delta kitchen sinks goes back before there were any. Groundwater lies so near the surface there that a man could dig a well in his back yard in a day, platform the hole, and install a hand pump the next morning. A public pump stood at the intersection of Third and Main, offering a trough for horses and a tin cup for people. Then irrigation of farms on surrounding mesas ruined the lowland groundwater. Salts and alkali, seeping down through ocean-laid Mancos Shale formations, made the water undrinkable, then unusable—too hard to lather even with homemade lye soap.

People turned to river water. Driving his wagon out into the shallows, a man hoisted water by bucket into wooden barrels, floated boards to diminish slop-loss and headed home. One enterprising fellow ran a water wagon up and down the streets, filling rainbarrels from his tank at twenty-five cents a refill. So they started digging wells again, but deeper. After all, the town was surrounded by deep springs—the warm sulfur spring at the foot of Main Street; the icy spring nearby, where Mrs. Fadely cooled dairy milk; and another, almost in the center of town, around which a lawyer and two businessmen built the Model Block—a square of identical pointy-roofed houses, with the spring spurting from an ornate structure in the middle of an alley they christened Fountain Avenue.

With that many springs, there had to be artesian water, if you drilled deep enough. Charles Nutter erected a wooden derrick on his property down by the depot. The *Delta Chief* reported the progress: "Well at depot down 175 feet." "Well still drilling in shale." "Artesian well down 500 feet, drill broke. Unusually hard formation struck in artesian well, will require a diamond drill, which is coming." The cliffs cut by Escalante Creek reveal the stuff Nutter was drilling through—

Mancos Shale, Dakota Sandstone, Morrison, Wingate. "Down 600 feet." That was the last word. Newspapers in up-and-coming towns seldom report dry holes.

The town hadn't waited. A steam pump located on a river island pushed water to the top of Garnet Mesa, from where gravity propelled it to every house with a tap. But the pipeline from the island ran under a marsh; eventually it rusted through, and people were incidentally drinking the invisible creatures that inhabited the swamp. Dr. L. A. Hick, the town's medical official, declared the water dangerously contaminated, and the plant was closed.

That was when people began looking at the mountain streams falling from mile-high Grand Mesa north of town. The water in those streams was pure as the driven snow it came from, but the names had to be cleaned up. Doughspoon Creek wasn't so bad, though it faintly suggested dishwater. But Nigger Creek and Dirty George Creek? The city bought the water rights, renamed these streams Negro Creek and George Creek (George was a perpetually unbathed man, the first homesteader on the creek), then snaked a pipeline down the mountainside past the pioneer black man's old stone cabin, past the ancient Ute racetrack, across the river, and into town.

To buy the water rights, the city had to buy the farms that had been irrigated by the creeks, just as Los Angeles bought and dried up Owens' Valley a little later.

Water from Grand Mesa streams was clear and legally clean but not always uninhabited. Not infrequently, residents discovered that what had been stopping up the faucet was pieces of dead water dog.

The drama of the city water supply came to an end when the town joined the government's valleywide Project Seven. This meant that mountain streams were released to grow food again.

The fire department is crucial in a town built almost entirely of wood, lit by precarious kerosene lamps, and warmed by coal stoves subject to overheating.

Until that river pump and mesa-top water tank were installed, the Delta Fire Department consisted of everybody and every bucket in town, lined up from the river to wherever the fire was. The pump's lift power was gauged not on the basis of how many taps it would serve, but on whether the pressure would jet water from a fire hose to the top of a two-story house.

Once the town had water pressure and fire hydrants, it could build a Fire House on the lot Governor Crawford gave them. The structure was a small one-story wooden building, just big enough to hold the hose cart, with a two-story stacklike structure for hanging the wet hose to dry.

Being a volunteer fireman was not something you volunteered for; you achieved it. Firemen had to be the fastest men in town, so races were held regularly to

Harvesting ice at Tucker's Ice House on the Gunnison River about 1895. Man at left saws blocks of river that are hauled up the ramp by horse-powered chain conveyor. Private collection of author.

establish who could best man the hose cart in emergency. It wasn't enough to be fastest man in town, though. A fellow strove to be on the fastest fire crew this side of the Continental Divide. Town vied with town at county fairs and Fourth of July festivities. With spectators out-yelling each other in support of their teams, the competing fire crews rushed to their respective carts, grabbed the ropes, and raced to the imaginary fire.

The town outgrew the sound-range of the fire bell that had called up the bucket brigade. In 1898, a committee was appointed to buy a new bell. Before electronic amplification, loudness came by the pound, as far as bells were concerned—the heavier, the louder. The committee—J. Frank Sanders, Newt Castle, and Millard Fairlamb—was instructed to buy not less than half a ton of bell.

That bell moved around town following expanding fire facilities. For a while, after being on top of the hose house, it had a steel tower of its own on Main Street; then it moved to Meeker Street, when a multi-truck firehouse was built there. It sat on the ground in the alley for a year or so, while City Hall was deciding where to move itself (by this time, sirens had replaced bells in sounding disaster). Mayor Bill Heddles tried to give it to the Honor Camp (Colorado Correction Facility), but Warden Pat Marah said it was too much bell for them, and anyhow they already had the old bell salvaged from Central School. Finally Earl Hawkins welded a steel rack-tower for it and hoisted it into a niche on top of the new Fire Station on what had been Schoolhouse Square before the razing craze. When the town turned one hundred years old, Amy Fults of the Episcopal Church promised to ring that bell every day at 4 P.M. for the entire centennial year. Amy didn't do it herself, of course; it takes two men to ring that bell, pulling on two ropes.

When electricity came to town, not everybody favored it. The city held an election in the summer of 1897 to decide whether to grant W. R. Gale a franchise to build a power plant and wire invisible forces up and down the streets and into people's houses. The vote was forty in favor and twenty-seven against.

Gale built the plant at the foot of Main, down by the railroad track handy to coal, and assured his future customers that, by the time nights began to get long, they would be able to blow out their kerosene lamps for the last time. At dusk each day, the steam engine was fired up, and it shut down at ten, when folks were supposed to be in bed.

Having trouble keeping up with demand, the town franchised to a power company for a couple of decades and then decided to resume producing its own energy. Fairbanks-Morse sent its man, William C. ("Buster") Daily, to build the light plant and install machinery. Before the project was off the paper, the town's demand for current had outgrown the planned supply.

"The overload wasn't a miscalculation," plant superintendent Daily explained thirty-eight years later, on the day he retired.

> It was owing to increased use of electricity during planning, and legal procedures before the city-owned plant could take over.
>
> We would have to go down to the Delta Flour Mill for extra power. Every evening when the street lights were due to come on, I'd go down to the flour mill and turn the water from the mill ditch into the penstock and activate an old synchronous motor they had down there. About two hours later, when the load eased, I'd go down and turn it off.

As people found new ways to use electricity—from feed grinders to toasters— more generators were added and larger spaces to house them. The fuel changed from coal to oil and then to gas. The use of this latter fuel, more economical and locally available, is the reason the Delta plant remains one of the few town-owned plants not taken over by the big electric companies.

As initially constructed, the Municipal Light plant was the most beautiful building in town. Its arched glass facades to east and west, under the simplicity of a bridge-span roof, displayed the magic machinery within like props on a stage. With increased demands for electricity, the building had to be expanded. The east facade was removed to make way for tall, boxlike structures that obscure the view of the original building from Highway 50. You can still glimpse a portion of the beautiful west facade by walking across the railroad track beyond Palmer Street, though.

In the early days of the telephone, two companies organized to bring in local service. In 1901, the Colorado Telephone Company, a statewide business with long-distance connections through Denver, set up a magneto-powered switchboard over a store building on Main. "Magneto-powered" meant that, to reach the operator, you generated your own electricity by cranking vigorously. When the initial fifty subscribers grew to almost four hundred, the company changed to battery power and then joined six other states to form the Mountain States Telephone and Telegraph Company.

The Colorado Telephone Company was interested only in servicing towns— profitable clots of customers with fewer costly miles of telephone line between them. That left the state's rural areas with no quicker means of communication than a fearless boy on a fast horse, a critical dilemma if big brother had fallen while greasing the windmill, and the nearest doctor was fifteen miles away. But up in Crawford, a country doctor already had organized a telephone company, very frugally using barbed wire fences and trees for lines and poles where available and putting ten people on a line.

Dr. William Follansbee's Delta County Co-op Telephone Company was owned by its users. The money a user paid to have the phone installed automatically bought a share in the company.

Co-op bested Colorado Telephone Company and held out against the world monopoly, American Telephone and Telegraph, for nearly half a century. Co-op and Ma Bell operated side by side, unlinked. On Co-op, you could not call outside the county or receive calls from loved ones elsewhere; on Bell, you could not call your country cousin down by the creek. Every business and office had to have two separate phones. Anyone who owned both phones constantly had to receive and pass on messages between them.

But Co-op was a homey phone. The writer, coming from Los Angeles, was surprised, when calling Eveline Nutter, to be advised by the operator, "Why don't you try again in about fifteen minutes? I saw Eveline and Stella Fairlamb walk by here a few minutes ago on their way home from Terrill's Cafe. They'll probably be there in a quarter of an hour." In 1948, the rival companies made a deal, completed a decade later: the Co-op Telephone Company purchased all of Bell's country phones north of the Gunnison River, and Bell bought all the Co-op phones south of the river. The two sets of phones were linked under two directories. The county joined the wired world at last. It wasn't easy. So many Co-op shareholders had died, moved away, or misplaced their share certificates that Co-op had been unable for decades to hold an annual meeting, for lack of a quorum. The purchasing company went through agonizing financial contortions to ferret out enough shares to make the transaction official. The old Co-op now is Delta County Tele-Comm Inc., providing the latest in equipment and a number of cable television channels.

Just after the turn of the century, there was a rash of schemes to put electric railway lines between towns on the Western Slope, side-stepping the D&RG railroad monopoly and accessing areas the D&RG couldn't be bothered with. The move began one especially muddy spring, when wagons couldn't get to the coal mines on the side of Grand Mesa. Customers and mine owners felt like hostages to the D&RG branch line bringing coal from the North Fork.

At first the movement was surreptitious. When Mudge Ziegler slanted a new road up to his Fairview mine at a shallow grade obviously intended for rails, he explained that it was for traction engines—steam-powered tractors with huge spiked iron wheels that could pull a train of wagons over any kind of road. But later, when it seemed that everybody was floating stock to start a railroad, he organized the Fairview and Intermountain Railway, to go from his mine to Delta and on to California Mesa.

Among other projected lines were the Fruit Belt Railroad, with spurs like a splayed hand to coal mines and orchards; and the Colorado and Red Canyon Railroad, to tap gypsum kilns on Black Canyon rim, through a now-vanished town called Appleton or Saxton (depending on whether a fruit grower or a railroad man was talking). The most ambitious planned line was the Uncompahgre and Gunnison Valley Railroad, which, when the bubble burst, actually had engineers surveying its extensive route south to Montrose and north to the top of Grand Mesa.

What put an end to these schemes was the advent of the gasoline motor. Soon Ziegler and Watson of Fairview Mine bought "an auto truck with monster wide tires that would haul three and a half tons at a time." The railroad no longer was needed.

With the coming of the automobile, the town entered an era of safer transportation. No matter how you figure traffic accident rates—by population or by number of vehicles—the car is safer. And if you figure according to miles traveled per accident, horse power was astronomically more dangerous.

Scarcely two issues of Delta's weekly newspaper went to press without reporting a runaway accident in the little community. And those were only the ones that happened in town or resulted in death, injury, or a joke: "Norton and Clark had their monthly runaway yesterday. It is perfectly safe to ride with them the rest of October."

Ruby Lowe, Ben's widow, lost an arm when her team bolted while hauling a wagonload of water barrels up Brickyard Hill. Trying to control the horses, she was thrown out. The steel tire of the rear wheel severed her arm.

Mrs. James Young was not so lucky. When the buggy's kingbolt broke, startling the horse, she was killed.

Judge King, Annie, and baby Fred were driving their buggy in the country when the horses took off. "Throw the baby out and jump!" he yelled. She did. He stayed with the buggy as the team leaped a fence and crashed in a ditch.

If "Throw the baby out!" sounds like child abuse, consider that in those days the roadsides were furry with grass and weeds, that babies were padded by layers of blankets, and that almost anything was safer than riding it out in the buggy. Built for speed, light and with high wheels, they turned over easily and ripped apart even more easily. In addition, buggy horses were bred for speed and spirit, which made them nervous. They would shy and bolt at the flutter of a store awning, a flying bit of paper, a suddenly raised umbrella. And the brakes were inadequate. Six or so inches of wood rubbing on two iron tires might lock the wheels if you had the muscle to pull the rope that hard, but locked wheels wouldn't even slow a fear-crazed horse.

Not everybody in Delta saw the automobile as an improvement. One prominent citizen tried to have horseless carriages legislated off the streets, according to Dr. L. A. Hick, who bought the second automobile in town. The official speed limit was ten miles in town, seven at intersections.

Starr Nelson bought the first home-owned automobile to chug its way across the bridge at the confluence. It was a Locomobile. Other makes bought that year (1910) were Ray Stanford's Reo and Joe McGraw's Stoddard-Dayton. Sheriff J. L. Sprung owned a Dort, which, to his embarrassment, he somehow allowed to be stolen, and he was forced to do his sheriffing on horseback until the auto was found over in Cortez.

Safer the automobiles might be, but trouble-free they were not. You started them with a crank that was supposed to disengage the instant the motor caught, but it didn't always do so. If your thumb was on the opposite side of the handle from your fingers, it got sprained. If you didn't get your arm away in time, it

This 1911 two-cylinder horseless carriage, complete with kerosene headlights and whip socket, chugged newlyweds Mr. and Mrs. Oosterhous over the Continental Divide. Private collection of author.

got broken on the back stroke. Miss Genevieve Hartig, owner and operator of her own cattle and sheep ranch, fractured her wrist while cranking her car.

And if the car happened to be in gear when cranked, it came at you. Facing this situation (literally), Eugene Hanlon was pinned to the wall, Ed Hanson got run over, and H. R. Elliot "wisely stepped aside and let his car ram into the Hillman building store window. Again!" the paper reported.

The automobile created new businesses and industries. Ed Hanson, who summered at "Hanson Castle" on Leroux Creek and wintered in town, opened an Oakland dealership in Hotchkiss. P. H. Miller bought the old town hall for $750 and converted it into a garage. The Laycock family opened a garage and dealership selling Star cars, proudly reporting buyers by name in the paper.

The first garage was designed to cater to both old and new forms of transportation. In 1910, Dr. McConnell proposed to build a two-story fireproof cement building on Main Street to house both a garage and a livery stable. The city fathers refused the permit. They already had exiled livery stables from Main, and they weren't about to allow something even smellier on the main drag.

Ten Deltans in four cars set out for Denver in the summer of 1911. The trip took seven days, over roads so bad that in places they had to latch onto trees with block and tackle to get through. George and Helen Stephan were driving a Winton Six, Walter and Letitia Hillman a Flanders 20, Ruel and Ethel Johnson a Mitchel, Will and Alice Mathers and sons rode in an EMF 30. The group took a lot of pictures, and in almost every shot somebody is fixing something on a car.

The coming of the automobile sparked inventiveness in several local people. A Hotchkiss boy, Ernest Webb, invented and patented a car lock. "It is attached to the controlling lever and works like the combination on a safe. When leaving the car, the driver turns the combination off, locking the lever."

The bane of the new form of transportation was tire trouble; you could expect at least one flat on every trip. The tire had to be wedged off the rim, the hole located by dabbing spit, and the rubber mended with goo and flame, rewedged, and pumped full of air at very high pressure—altogether an excruciating exercise in muscle and temper control. Auto pioneers Hal and Mary Reid set out for the West Coast with tires encased in metal protectors so unprotective that they were abandoned a few miles out.

William Darling designed, patented, and instigated the manufacture of an all-metal wheel that would bypass rubber altogether. The *Tribune* for August 2, 1912, described it:

> Made of hard saw steel with a thick steel tread that forms the framework and casing for a number of steel springs that are fastened to a hub supplied with steel bearings. The axle of the car goes through an opening in the steel casing at the back of the wheel and enough room is allowed so that it has free play when the springs receive the shocks from the rough road. In other words, the axle is attached to a series of steel springs that by their resiliency break all the jars of traveling.

Springs instead of spokes? Ten local men financed the project, tested it in Denver, and set up production in Britton, Oklahoma.

Poor rubber was only part of the tire problem, however. Worse were the rocky wagon ruts the wheels had to bounce over. Before the automobile, roads had been maintained merely to be wagon-safe—bogs filled, washouts fixed, with no effort at smoothing. The work had been supported by a road tax, three dollars annually or the equivalent in man-hours of labor.

That situation had to change. The new Delta County Auto Club and a similar Grand Junction club proclaimed Good Roads Day in May 1914. Starting at the county line, scores of volunteers worked back toward home, pitching rocks and smoothing forty miles of ruts with shovel and rake.

For use by motorists in trouble, the Delta Automobile Club mounted a phone on a pole on Alkali Flat some miles in the desert northwest of town. The Grand Junction Club put up a similar phone near Indian Creek.

Those phones were noted in the *Midland Trail Tour Guide 1916* that included Delta that year. In 1916, crossing the continent from Washington, D.C., to San Francisco by automobile on the "Midland Trail" was an adventure. Not only was the trail unmarked and unpaved, it wasn't even graded and graveled. Just ruts. The guide listed every blessed bend in the road from sea to sea and told you exactly where you were, to a tenth of a mile. It had to, as there were no road signs, no service station maps, and very few service stations.

Noting that Delta's south boundary was precisely 327.3 miles from Broadway and Colfax Avenue in Denver, the guide continued:

> DELTA: One block to (327.4) Ford Station on right; gasoline, oil, expert mechanics. Ahead to New Perkins Restaurant; fine meals and excellent service.
>
> Fill water bags. Turn left from Main St. at Telephone building on far left. 327.7 cross railroad track; 327.8 bridge over Uncompahgre River; 327.9 curve to right upgrade.

(This route passed Sylvester Huffington's house, though the book didn't know it.) The account goes on, tallying by tenths of a mile every crook and hump—including the Alkali Flats telephone and what the motorist must do before leaving Grand Junction to tackle the Utah desert: "Go over all equipment, filling water bags (one 4-gallon or two 2-gallon), inspecting chains, block and tackle, and shovel. Check up gas and oil supply. Portable telephone may be taken from Grand Junction or Mack for use in emergency on line of the Midland Telephone Company across desert from Mack west."

There is a story that, in the days before stoplights stretched across the thoroughfare, some early aviator landed on Main Street, waved at goggle-eyed pedestrians, and took off again, in the best local Geezer–Ben Lowe tradition. Research hasn't been able to pin the story to a name.

However, the confluence doesn't really need that stunt to be notable aviationally—it has Starr Nelson.

Starr Nelson was a railroad engineer on the Salida run. Tall, dashing, impressive, he was the epitome of what made little boys worship engineers. He bought a ranch out beyond the Horn, made big plans for watering everything between Delta and Grand Junction by bringing water from the North Fork through a hundred or so miles of ditch, and went into aviation about as soon as it came along.

A group of men organized the Delta Flying Club in 1940. The thirteen charter members were young men—all but one. Starr Nelson was 78. A month after the club was organized, J. T. McBride, its president, brought in the club's first plane, a Piper Cub that he flew from Lockhaven, Pennsylvania. Two thousand miles in twenty-four hours, with eight refueling stops. The group had hardly had the Cub long enough for a change of oil when Starr Nelson crashed it. The other members kicked him out of the club. They really hadn't wanted him in it; after all, he'd been almost middle-aged when the Wright brothers were trying to get off the ground. Starr Nelson acquired the wreckage, repaired it, and then kicked them out of the club, becoming sole member and owner.

As far as is known, he never had another wreck, though he flew all over and all the time. He built a landing strip at his ranch beyond the Horn and another one on upper Garnet Mesa.

Starr Nelson Airport, on a flat-topped mesa east of town, stands among the surging adobe hummocks rather like an anchored aircraft carrier in a tossing sea. Nelson built a hangar on the mesa, scraped the boulders off the runway, and used it for commuting to his ranch, to Denver, or any other place accessible by small aircraft.

When passenger air routes were being established in the area, Starr Nelson offered to donate his airport to the county, to be one of the regular stops. The county declined. And with good reason, says Ira Edwards, former manager of Torrance Airport in California. Edwards landed there frequently to visit his mother, Leta, before himself moving to Delta. "At times there's an invisible airflow down off the edge of that mesa. The wind sock doesn't show it. Makes it tricky to land."

As Starr Nelson was nearing his nineties and it could be assumed that heart attack or stroke might be only a breath away, his license renewal carried the provision that he have a licensed pilot as a passenger at all times.

But an air crash didn't get him. He died even more dramatically. One of the frequent events honoring him as the "oldest licensed pilot in America" was a Denver banquet. He flew himself to the banquet, listened to the laudatory introduction, rose to speak, and keeled over dead.

The mountains that surround the confluence sometimes create an aerial barrier. Ira Edwards notes that, when conditions are right, a great push of smooth, strong wind like a giant sea wave surges up over the entire hundred-mile length of the Uncompahgre Plateau and falls downward on the lee side. A small plane headed west simply lacks the power to buck through or surmount that wave and is pushed down onto the ground, unless the pilot can turn back and get out from under in time.

Apparently the Continental Divide at times is subject to a similar air surge, which caused problems for even the "big" planes of an earlier day. The *Delta County Independent* noted on November 15, 1929: "More than 4,000 people attended the opening of Delta airport on Thanksgiving. The Douglas bomber couldn't make it from Denver over the passes in three tries because of high winds. The first plane to land carried the first shipment of mail to leave the Delta Post Office by air."

The official airport is Blake Field, located on a flat of 'dobe moonscape still called Orchard Mesa because of what grew there before the town appropriated water from George and Doughspoon creeks to fill city water mains. Lighted and manned, the port is used by crop dusters, small-plane devotees who fly for pleasure, and commuters whose work is in Denver but who prefer to live at this confluence of quiet rivers and quiet lifestyles.

At intervals all through the year of 1922, the *Delta County Tribune* ran a series of articles on how to make and install your own radio, using such technical terms as *air gap*, *lightning switches*, and *counterpoise aerials*. Carl Himes took the articles to heart. In 1933, he secured his amateur license and launched W9MST.

Eph Towne and his family set up radio station KDTA in a small building under a thready steel tower in North Delta. While Eph did the book work and daytime broadcasting, Mrs. Eph solicited advertisers. Eph started broadcasting before any rules were established and is most vividly remembered as being hotly and lopsidedly loyal to the home team when airing local sports—"That was a foul! That blankety-blank referee, he's a liar or he can't see his nose—Foul! You dumb-ox referee, can't you tell a foul when you see one!"

A disadvantage of living cuddled in mountains is that straight-line broadcast signals can't find you. AM radio goes up to the stratosphere and bounces back down like falling rain; you can catch it anywhere, in a receiver no bigger than a cup. But FM radio and television travel straight—"line-of-sight." When a TV broadcast hits the side of a mountain, most of it stops right there.

The Twilight Zone had been around for quite a while before it brightened any screens at the confluence of rivers, although several sets—purchased in anticipation—sat in their own kind of twilight zone, darkly waiting.

Then Cecil Whitchurch relayed East Slope television over the Rockies with a series of steel towers—booster stations—on mountain peaks: Badger Mountain, Monarch Pass, Storm King Mountain, and Brickyard Hill west of Delta. Whitchurch's project wasn't easy, and it wasn't cheap. Each tower cost a thousand dollars, plus the electronic equipment housed at its base. Where Cecil economized was in the housing—old farm backhouses. The two-hole seat made a convenient shelf for the equipment; padlocks on the doors discouraged the curious mountain hiker. A backhouse, as anybody knows who has used one in winter, does not keep out blizzards, and on Storm King Mountain and the other peaks there is plenty of driving snow. Cecil got the idea of using old refrigerators on every peak, one for each network he was boosting. At the confluence, ABC and NBC, housed in white porcelain enamel, stood back-to-back under their tower on Brickyard Hill.

Cable television improved reception greatly, and the satellite dish snags it down even in remote, deep-walled places like Coal Creek Canyon, but a large enough population continues to subscribe to boosted television to keep Whitchurch's successor in business.

11

Make It Pay Twice Before It Flows On

There is no dam at the confluence. The streams of water, natural and artificially diverted, reconverge and move on past. And so have the products those streams have made possible. Beef, wheat, apricots—the merest fraction of products have remained as steak and loaf on local shelves, as jam bubbling on kitchen stoves. The bulk of raw commodities have flowed in freight lines to the outer world.

Beef enters cattle cars under its own power, grains are mechanically lifted and poured from elevators. Of products that have to be handled, the biggest shipper was Delta Fruit and Produce Company (DF&P). Its warehouse was the destination of most of those fruit wagons.

The DF&P in turn pulled in tributary enterprises, one being a supplier of barrels for all those apples. Ellis of Surface Creek made barrel staves of aspen wood that were then coopered into curves at the plant.

In the 1920s, the DF&P hired a young clerk, R. W. Stephens, who before long would become its owner. Injured in a mine accident that left him crutch-dependent at the age of twenty-one, he turned to work he could do sitting down—paperwork. He was a genius at it. His office was close to the railroad track. Very close. The loading spur ran between buildings through a slot so narrow that, if R. W. threw up the sash, he could shake hands with the engineer inching out with a trainload of his produce.

Across from R. W.'s desk was a shoulder-high brick fireplace, crackling with a cedar wood fire. You can still see that office fireplace if you come to Schall Chemical for weed killer, but the rails and ties that floored the spur slot are gone, spurs no longer being needed. The D&RG's mile-long trains of North Fork coal now clickety-clack straight through town.

On R. W.'s desk were two phones: the local Co-op phone that connected him with his suppliers, farmers and orchardists up the two valleys that come to a V near his warehouses (and with nobody else on the planet); and the Bell phone that connected him with New York, London, Quebec, and other worldwide markets. R. W. made a lot of money—so much that folks believed he had a direct line to Wall Street. That wasn't true, nor was the idea that he drove the same car all his life, though he came near doing so. Once a year, he disassembled his automobile to the last bolt and nut, painted the undersides of the fenders to prevent rust, cleaned, oiled, and reassembled everything again. The car always ran. Dependable. Quiet. Comfortable. He saw little reason trade it in on an unknown other.

All that produce flowing down to and out of the confluence incited commercial creativity. If you could do something to a product as it passed through town on its way to the world—refine it, convert it—you'd wring another profit out of it.

Wheat as a crop was profitable, but you could make it pay again by purifying it into flour. The Delta Flouring Mill Company diverted a millstream from the Uncompahgre River to power its waterwheel and turn its burrmill. "Unrivaled" proclaimed the brand name on barrels and cloth sacks of the bleached white powder resulting when bran and wheat germ were efficiently removed.

Wheat is wheat wherever it sprouts, but when the superiority of area fruit began attracting world attention and prices to match, so much grain acreage permanently was converted to orchard that flouring profits sagged. Also there were power shortages when the millstream dried up because more homesteaders were diverting water from the finite Uncompahgre. Delta Flouring limped from one bankruptcy to another until Aden Crabill acquired it. By feeding hogs on the deleted "impurities"—bran and wheat germ—Crabill produced yet another profitable refinement of the confluence inflow—carloads of ham and bacon on the hoof.

The Delta Flouring Mill burned to the ground in a typically explosive fire, barely outlasting mills at Montrose, Hotchkiss, and Austin, which burned earlier. None was rebuilt; the powder-charged air that fills a flouring mill is so explosive and mills are so prone to burn that fire insurance was virtually unobtainable.

But millers were not through trying to profitably detour raw material headed for outbound railroad cars. Farmers Milling and Produce Vegetable Mill made flour of pumpkins and potatoes by first cooking and then rolling them into thin sheets to be dried and flaked. Pumpkin flour was not an unqualified success. Esther

Stephens' mother, chosen to give it the home kitchen test, commented, "It made a fine-tasting pie if you ate it with your eyes shut, but if you saw the gray-blue dirty-looking stuff you were putting in your mouth, you sure lost your appetite."

Wheat can be held in a granary or elevator for months or years without damage, waiting for the right price. But if the crop is fruit, its salable life can be days. One way to prolong the profit-life of peach, cherry, or tomato is to keep it chilled. Harvesting the "cold" itself was a big industry on the waters of the confluence.

Ice had to be put up fast—a summer's worth in about three winter weeks. Cutting began in mid-December, as soon as the ice got thick enough to support horse teams, and continued furiously until the January thaw.

Men with ice saws cut solidified river water into blocks. Horses powering elevator inclines hoisted the ice into vast, barnlike ice houses where the blocks were stacked and insulated with sawdust to last all summer. Hauling sawdust from mountain sawmills was yet another enterprise at the confluence. Grocers George and Ike Conklin built a commercial ice house, and ran a wagon up and down the streets selling cold.

The biggest ice customer was the D&RG railroad. That river of fruit rolling down the North Fork each fall had to be shipped in iced cars. In 1907, the D&RG, icing fifty cars a day, fell short of the demand and projected enlarged facilities at the confluence, to include "a new depot, a five-stall engine roundhouse, siding for 125 cars, and an ice house capable of icing more than a thousand cars."

The proposed D&RG facilities never materialized. Fruit production declined because of overproduction, competition from other areas, and because of changes in land conditions—the invasion of pests and declining fertility of the no-longer-virgin land. Annual harvest of river ice ended with the advent of machinery to make ice without the help of God-deployed sub-zero weather. Delta Dressed Meat Company's (DDMC) equipment manufactured ice from scratch—any time of the year and as much as ten tons a day.

This meat company was another enterprise that shunted raw materials off-trail long enough profitably to work them over. The town always had had butchers "refining" steers into steaks for local trade, but DDMC shipped counter-ready meat by the (refrigerated) carload.

After Billstrom's oil well in Black Canyon turned out to be a water geyser emitting carbon dioxide gas, the Quik-Kold Company of Denver leased it and brought in a dynamo compressor capable of producing fifty tons of dry ice a day. Quik-Kold had problems. The first was not enough capital (this was during the Depression), and the second was too much CO_2—the gas kept erupting around the edges where it wasn't supposed to.

When the Depression eased, refrigerators gradually replaced ice boxes. The yellow cards propped in windows to waylay the iceman disappeared.

Another way to hold perishable products in a state of suspended life long enough to get them sold is with heat. They can be cooked, as in the case of pumpkin flour. But canning is better.

Silver king, J. Frank Sanders, built a cannery down by the railroad track on a corner of his ranch. The long two-story building housed boiler and engine to power pulpers, seeders, and kraut cutters. Redwood vats held cleaning and steam-cooking processes.

He got the tin cans next door. Tinsmith Nick Arch heard about the cannery and the local orchards (by this time, confluence products were taking prizes all over the apple-eating earth). Bringing his equipment to town, he hooked into the cannery diversion of the produce flow and had his noisy shop in full production when the first tomato was canned, capped, and sealed with a drop of molten lead in the hole left for that final operation.

Contracting acreage, the cannery operated profitably until locked down tight by the Depression. The unemployed took it over until good times returned. With government help, the workers set up Colorado Cooperative, providing work for many jobless and an outlet for farm produce that otherwise would have rotted in the fields for lack of anyone with a dime to buy a bushel of tomatoes.

Still another way to hold off the natural course of decay is to put the cold inside the product rather than merely around it, freezing it solid from the inside out.

Skyland set up its frozen foods plant at this confluence of rivers and railroads to process "the finest fruit in the nation," manager Don Reed announced. Providing an outlet for farm products and some year-round jobs, Skyland incidentally helped a number of kids through college. Because the fruit-freezing season coincides beautifully with school vacation, a number of the shift workers were students piling up money for next semester. Inadvertently this work also provided an intense incentive to stay in college, once enrolled. As one graduate remembers, "Repeating the two motions that operated that peach-slicing machine for eight solid hours on the graveyard shift was so ghastly depressing I resolved do anything on God's earth to stay in school and not end up at that machine or something like it for the rest of my natural life."

A man who made millions out of garbage—apple peels and cores—built a vinegar plant near the sources of the raw material, Skyland Foods and the Delta

Canning Company. Victor Speas diverted the river-disposal flow of waste up through oak fermenting vats primed with yeast.

Speas supplied wholesalers. Finished vinegar was shipped out in wine cars to be bottled under almost any label you might see on the grocery shelf. In peak years, the plant produced over four hundred thousand gallons.

At first the pulp remaining after extracting the juice was dumped as sewage into the river, and then it was sold as cattle feed, creating still another profit tributary. Cows, Speas discovered, love the sweet chewy stuff. Seeing the bonus in that by-product, Skyland began doing its own pressing, producing sweet cider for people as well as "taffy" for cattle.

Nobody discovered a profitable use for the vinegar "mother" formed in the brewing process. They dumped the grayish stuff in the similarly colored 'dobe hills.

In the surrounding mountains, lumbering began while the trees still belonged to the Utes; Darling's Mill on the Uncompahgre Plateau sawed boards to build Fort Crawford on the reservation. Virgin timber grew on all sides, and people needed "one-bys" to roof their houses and put shelves in their businesses. With sawyers eager to exploit both timber and people, the town remained purely tents and log cabins for only about two minutes.

S. W. Skinner was not the first to harvest the forest for use down along the rivers, but, because of Elmer Skinner's remarkable memory, we know a good deal about his father's lumbering operations.

In early "mills," the boards were hand-sawed. Two men worked the long saw, one standing above the log while the other worked under it, in a hole called a saw-pit. By the time the Skinner family arrived in 1894, steam engines fired with scrap wood were providing the muscle that moved the saw.

The Skinners arrived by immigrant railroad car—a contract arrangement by which many pioneers moved westward. You rented the boxcar for a certain distance on the track and were allowed to put into it as much as you could cram in. Everything the Skinner family owned—bedding, cattle, clothing, cookware, farm implements, furniture, horses, pigs, tools, whatever—was stuffed into that narrow-gauge boxcar, including themselves.

Skinner set up a sawmill on the Plateau and put his sons to doing men's work. Before motor truck made hauling quicker and cheaper, sawmills were located up where the timber was, saving the time and expense of hauling what would be waste—tree bark and edging-strip scrap. Although Elmer was only eleven, he and his younger brother did the trucking for the mill, driving wagons piled high with lumber down the mountain to town. Dangerous work. The road was narrow, cliff-hung, rocky, and in places very steep. With only wood-block brake and breeching to keep the wagon from ramming down onto the teams, and given the equine propensity to spook at anything sudden or strange, the two children had to be constantly ready to deal with disaster.

For most mills, lumbering was summer work, abandoned when snow got deep in the mile-high forests. But some sawed all winter, moving lumber by sled down to the snow line, transferring it to wagons at a mule barn, and wheeling it the rest of the way to town. The Transfer Road, up Uncompahgre Plateau, is named for this strategem and still sports the foundations of the mule barn to prove it. Rollins Brothers, dealing in both coal and lumber, operated year-round by working crews in the warmth of the mine in winter and in the cool of the forest in summer.

Among a dozen or so lumberyards supplying the confluence through the years, Burkey's was notable for its mill pond. When the screen dome of the tall, curving sawdust burner showered sparks into the evening sky, the reflection in the still water was especially lovely.

But Jones Lumberyard goes back farthest in time—sixty-five million years or so. One day, while scouting the location of the next timber cut, Eddie and Vivian Jones found a fragment of dinosaur bone. That find, on Dry Mesa west of town, gave their lives a new direction. Shifting more of the family business onto the shoulders of their grown children, they prowled and dug and discovered. Through them, Dr. James Jensen of Brigham Young University ("Dinosaur Jim" to friends and fellow professionals) organized a series of summer digs.

The beasts that died on that spot were colossal. Year after year, the Jones-Jensen team topped its prior achievements, finding "the largest dinosaur bone in the world"—again. Two nearly complete skeletons of hitherto unknown species went into the archeology books under names given them by Jim Jensen.

Dr. Jim offered a real dinosaur skeleton for exhibition at the confluence, if the town would provide the building to house it. Since the structure would have had to be three stories high, there was no rush to accept the offer.

Coming into the newspaper office with three sugar beets in his hands, J. B. Hart demonstrated that beets would grow big and sugar-rich in the drainage of the confluence rivers. That was in the fall of 1883, the new community's second harvest.

Soon a familiar autumn scene was lines of beet wagons, teams swishing flies while inching toward the loading ramp on the railroad track. Before today's specialized farm machines, beet growing depended upon stoop labor—thinning in spring, weeding during summer, and topping in the fall. The need for such labor soon outgrew the local supply, and the industry told the world where the work was.

The first immigrant beet workers were Russo-Germans who had fled their oppressors to seek a better life in America. Katharine Amsbary Hedgcock noted, "I don't recall what year the mass immigration of Russians took place, but it was not an uncommon sight to see the black-clothed peasant women with scarves tied around their heads plodding past our house laden with heavy staples from the grocery store as the menfolk stalked ahead, empty-handed. Most of these hardworking, frugal people later became solid citizens, acquired land, and prospered."

For instance, the Kiefer brothers went from stoop labor to owning most of Redlands Mesa and developing Kiefer Canal out of the Colorado River.

Then there was the Russo-German couple, a very pregnant young woman and her husband, who got on the train at Delta near Christmastime in 1908. The train was a special, taking beet workers back to their homes in Nebraska. Although Mrs. Bauer was already in labor, she didn't tell anybody, just toughed it out. But at Salida, where the rails changed from narrow- to broad-gauge, trainmen had to carry her between trains. Apparently she was grateful; the baby girl, born as the train topped Marshall Pass, was named Stanley for the D&RG superintendent.

The labor shortage created by World War I was filled by immigrants from Mexico—first those kicked out because they didn't agree with Pancho Villa and then those who had agreed with him all too well. Stoop labor, legal or otherwise, has continued to come mainly from Mexico.

With war cutting off foreign sugar, local beet farms and refineries prospered. Holly Sugar bought the old Grand Junction refinery, soon outgrew its capacity, and was faced with modernizing or replacing it. That was when a group of Deltans, ramrodded by John Davis, got the idea of bringing a Holly Sugar factory to the confluence. After all, the two rivers area was producing most of the beets the refinery used. All those raw beets being freighted off to be transformed into sugar somewhere else! Bring that profitable job- and tax-producing process home.

After a lot of nagging persistence, Holly's President A. E. Carlton promised that if 9,500 acres of land were signed up to beet production, he would build a refinery in Delta. When this commitment was relayed to members of the business community at a noon meeting in the International Order of Odd Fellows (IOOF) Hall, a very young and inexperienced lawyer, Mortimer Stone, appointed John Davis to put on a sign-up dinner for *all* the farmers in two river drainages.

The date of this outsize dinner? The very next day.

John Davis, himself young and feisty, got on the phone contacting all the Ladies Aids in town. They had the know-how—town churches stood as monuments to their abilities to put on big dinners—but none could handle anything that big that quick.

He then appealed to Johnny Arthur's bakery over by the Delta House. Sticking his neck out, Johnny promised to provide roast beef, mashed potatoes, gravy, pie, coffee, and rolls for as many of the county's farm-owning population as Davis could provide roof and tables for. It was February; there was no possibility of an outdoor event.

Davis secured a roof by persuading the Kepler-Laycock Garage's owners to shove all the cars out the door and clean the grease off the floor. No other roofed space in town was big enough. He rounded up chairs, tables, china, and silverware wherever he could get them—churches, homes, hardware stores. Somewhere in there, he cajoled Co-op Telephone operators into calling every farmer in the two valleys.

Four hundred and fifty people came and signed up the necessary 9,500 acres.

The big farmers' get-together proved to be so much fun and so beneficial to the community that the Chamber of Commerce made it an annual February event (with John in charge, of course) known as the "Farmers' Spree." Gradually the event expanded and, renamed Deltarado Days, moved to later in the year, becoming a July weekend celebration of life in general, with bands, floats, barbecue, museum displays, ballgames, and rodeo events.

The Holly Sugar plant was built at the very tip of the delta *D*, where river flows into river. In 1920 money, it cost $2.25 million. Besides being a shipping-free outlet for sugar-beet farmers, the plant provided seasonal employment for many during the fall "run" and all-year salaries for a few.

In keeping with the tacit precept, "Squeeze as much profit out of a product as you can before it leaves the confluence," Holly fattened cattle on the refinery's leftover sugar-beet pulp and sold pulp by the dripping truckload to local cattle feeders.

Migrant workers in beet fields and orchards were housed in the company's "colony" near the Uncompahgre. The colony was built of adobe brick in joined units, *pueblo* fashion; rows of housing were interspersed with rows of trees, forming a parklike complex. You could tell what part of Mexico a family came from by how they kept their unit. If the *madre* swept the earth around her door in neat broom-patterns every morning before going out to the fields, she probably came from the shores of Lake Chapala, where it is the custom to sweep the yard out to the middle of the street each morning.

Though they came in summer when the regular schools were closed, colony children attended classes taught by Spanish-speaking teachers. Their parents off in the fields since dawn, the sleepy children were roused by volunteers who gave them breakfast, tucked them into their clothes, and saw them off to school.

Holly Sugar, coal-fired for years, operated for half a century. Its tall stack plumed autumn smoke, spreading an umbrella over the town in the morning that thinned and moved down the valley and then mistily ebbed back, following those tidelike airflows imprisoned by mountain ranges. No one was concerned about air pollution; factory smoke signaled prosperity.

A by-product of burning coal was cinders. When A. Allen Brown came home from law school full of town-betterment ideas and was elected president of the Young Men's Civic Club, he put those eager fellows to work spreading cinders on Cleland Park's clay tennis courts. Still another profitable tributary of the industrial flow developed, as local companies began converting cinders into building blocks for construction of homes and businesses. The cinder supply ceased when Holly cleaned up its emissions act, switching to natural gas after the cheaper fuel became available from wells not many pipeline miles away.

In 1969, Holly Sugar Company brought in a Kansas firm to build a silo structure capable of holding a year's worth of sugar at the source until the price was right. The tall quadruple tower is actually four joined silos, creating a piece of sculpture at the confluence as awesome as an Egyptian pyramid and just as enigmatic in its evocation of time's transitory nature. Only a few years after going to that expense, Holly Sugar departed from Delta, leaving the silent silos standing there.

The closing of the sugar plant might have hit farmers harder but for Coors Beer. Adolph Coors of Golden, Colorado, contracted for so much barley acreage in confluence valleys that a million-bushel elevator was required to store the product.

Moravian barley proved to be a good crop, easy to grow. Maturing early, it allows the farmer's annual debt to be paid off quickly, saving interest. By contrast, ear-corn is harvested only when the kernels reach a certain dryness and may not pay off until midwinter.

In keeping with the confluence *modus operandi* of trying everything at least once, Coors grew hops. The test patch was spectacular, pole-propped vines leaning out to form what looked like a giant green baking pan. But the climate was too hot for the crop; the bloom fell before attaining just the right flavorful tint of brown.

Another element was blamed three decades later, when Coors pulled out altogether, leaving the elevators empty: "too much protein in Western Slope grown barley for the current malting process." Taste in beer had changed?

Contracting with a large company takes some of the risk out of the risky business of farming. You know what you are going to grow and about how much you will be paid for it; all you have to do is grow it right. But that arrangement entails a more basic risk—you never know when the contractor will pull out. At the confluence, the Holly and Coors disasters resulted in a salutary diversification.

Now cauliflower, lettuce, onions, alfalfa seed—scores of products—keep farmers independent of a single buyer.

Each fall, hunters by the hundreds stream through the confluence, taking only the meat and trophy antlers of the game they have bagged in surrounding mountains. If you could induce them to bring in the hides rather than leave them in the woods to rot—set up a tanning facility—cash in on all that free potential leather. Western Tanning Company, financed by shares sold to town businessmen, was set up in North Delta. Initially run by committee, it staggered profitlessly along until purchased by Jim Mowbray, a former state representative. Enlarging and updating the plant, he invented new products. One creation alone, a soft lining for boots and shoes, almost doubled the plant's customers. Business was so successful that a decade later Western Tanning was handling a hundred thousand hides a year.

Traditionally, tanneries stink. Coming from the north, you could smell Delta several miles before arriving. Neighbors put up with the stench because it meant paying jobs, the "smell of prosperity," but authorities were less lenient. When installation of a waste-treatment facility between plant and river didn't satisfy them, Mowbray pumped refuse to a lagoon dug up in the 'dobes. But policies changed; the new demands could not be met, or meeting them wiped out profit.

Local ingenuity, which had found ways to make money from industrial waste (apple cores, beet pulp, cinders), found no way to profit from stink—that is to recycle the protein-rich scrapings of hair and flesh from a hundred thousand deer and cow hides into some kind of paying product—and do it before they had time to get smelly. The tannery closed.

Commerce at the confluence began with the fur trade—beaver fur pelts snagged by trappers working out of Antoine Robidoux's Fort Uncompahgre trading post. Beaver, fox, coyote, muskrat, and other furs continued to be trapped and traded in the environs of the confluence, but large-scale fur trading in the area resumed only in the twentieth century, with the mink farmers.

One, Charles Bertram, entered the fur trade cold, starting with five mink that, as he put it, he

bought first and learned about afterwards.

There was so much to learn, and no authority to turn to—except the mink itself. You can't go against mink nature. For instance, though they've lived on wire mesh for generations, cage litter never a problem, the mother mink still insists on toilet training her babies to use one certain corner. It takes a lot of her energy by the time she's trained six or seven kits, picking them up one at a time and taking them over to the selected spot until they get the idea.

Bob Stoody's fur farm attained annual pelt harvests exceeding seven thousand, despite a bout with Aleutian disease. "Aleutian disease," Bob explained, "is an inheritable, transmissible, fatal disease of the disease-resistant mechanism itself. The only way to eradicate it is to find the affected animals by blood test and exterminate them."

Another mink farmer, Lloyd Gibson, actually began as a trapper, working his way through Western State College trapping native mink on The Blue, near Gunnison. He gave the fur-loving world a brand new tint of mink—by mistake. In moving his Utah operation to the confluence, he mixed up the pedigree tags on two cages; the resulting illicit marriage produced a shimmery new fur that Lloyd copyrighted as "Creole."

Confluence-grown pelts, and wraps made from them, get top awards and prices in worldwide exhibits and markets, but you almost never see anybody at the confluence decked out in mink. Local mink is sold mainly in Europe, Russia, and the Far East.

With so much trade passing through Delta to get to market, whether by rail to the world or by wagon to the mining communities, the business part of town grew out of all proportion to the residential sections.

For a while, there was a separate business for almost everything. When Annie King went shopping, she visited the bakery for bread, the butcher shop to select a saddle of lamb, the creamery for buttermilk, a grocer for flour and salt, the tinsmith for bargain pie pans, the bootery to have her shoe buttons re-stapled, the Kandy Kitchen for a striped sack of horehound, the drygoods store for twelve yards of taffeta for a new dress, the variety store for soutache braid to trim it, the milliner's to order a hat made to go with it, the dressmaker's to look at charts and decide on its style, and so on. There were stores, such as the Corner Cigar Store, that sold almost nothing but tobacco.

Some businesses, however, doubled up in trades that later became separate. H. K. Correll advertised: "Furniture, Rugs, Ranges, Undertaking" and maintained a black team and coach to carry the casket leading the procession to the cemetery.

Until the advent of chain stores, most groceries gave credit. Customers paid once a month or once a year, depending on how much capital the grocer had to operate on. Annual payers were farmers who charged all year and paid when the crop came in. Even a year's worth of groceries did not involve big money, because so much of the family food was produced in orchard, barn, garden, and chicken coop; and because excess products (eggs, butter, fruit, sweet corn, etc.) were traded in on such exotic items as lemon drops, coffee, and cut-plug tobacco.

Merchants provided delivery service. Light wagons had thin, curved-wood roofs and were seatless, to speed leaping out and dashing off with baskets of merchandise. But it took time to tie the horse to the hitching post. Some delivery boys, notably grocer Bailey's, didn't bother: "Frank Childs left Bailey's horse unhitched Saturday night and it ran away, doing little harm. Monday he was 'rattled' as usual and left it unhitched again. Bailey will have a guardian appointed for him at the next term of court."

There is the story of the woman on Grand Avenue who habitually demanded immediate delivery of insignificant orders—two sticks of cinnamon, a pack of needles. This cut profits; the usual procedure was to let orders stack up through the morning until there was a paying amount. The day she ordered a spool of No. 10 white thread, to be delivered at once, the merchant decided to embarrass her into changing her ways. Instead of sending the light delivery wagon, he hired a freight dray (about the size of a narrow-gauge flatcar) and two very large men to deliver it, with very specific instructions. With the spool occupying the exact center of the dray-bed, they drove up to her house; hitched the team, making a great fuss about it, to attract her attention; and, pinching the spool between their thumbs and forefingers, they heaved it off the dray-bed, lugged it up the porch steps, and deposited it on her kitchen table, gasping and mopping their brows. It didn't cure a thing. Her next order was for immediate delivery of a box of carpet tacks.

When a lady—a real lady—wanted a hat, she didn't paw through racks, trying on one after another; she went to a milliner and had it made. At the confluence, the ultimate milliner was Rose Harrington in Hillman's. Gordon Hodgin, who clerked at Hillman's as a lad, remembers: "Rose had bins and bins of trim. Feathers, flowers, fruit, ribbons, beads." Starting with a hat shell, she would study the face she was going to—Well, you can't say "the face she was going to *frame*," because those hats rode high! Anyhow, she created a hat to *complement* the face, different from last spring's hat and different from any other hat in town.

Founded by the Hillman brothers in 1907, the store became known as the "Neiman-Marcus" of the western half of Colorado. Four times a year, buyers went to New York to bring back the latest fashions. The elegance of the Hillman building survives. Wide stairs with two show-off-your-gown landings, an ornate pressed-metal ceiling, and the "slingshot" cash cups that, by a yank of the cord, would scoot the money up to the bookkeeper on the balcony—all are still there.

The Hillman men married remarkable, but very different, women. Walter

Hillman's wife, Letitia Crabill, a graduate of Oberlin with honors in music, came to town after the hierarchy of musicianship already had been informally set up. She immediately was acknowledged to be the best musician the town ever had had—and was beloved anyhow.

John Hillman's wife Lucy expected to run the town and practically did. Lavishly generous and authoritative, she was misplaced in history; she would have functioned perfectly as a queen in the Victorian age. After the advent of the automobile, Lucy always, *always* backed her Cadillac straight out of the driveway at 821 Main, without looking either way. When Officer Copp (yes, the town marshal happened to be named Copp) finally got up the courage to face her about it, she demanded: "Young man, do you know who I am!" He assured her that he did but said that he had been worried for a long time and just had to do something; somebody was going to get hurt or killed if she kept on backing out—

And Lucy said, "You are fired. I will phone the president. You're fired." She didn't phone the president of the United States, although she could have—she was a National Republican Committeewoman, and presidents weren't cut off from the electorate by phone banks in those days. She decided that it wasn't worth bothering the president about, so she called the governor. He fired Copp with fanfare, then on the side got him a job as a patrolman up at Gunnison.

Lucy Hillman couldn't bear to see a child shivering for lack of warm clothing or gaunt from lack of food. Shooing underclad kids into Hillman's, she would pick out underwear, stockings, coats, mittens. She paid from her purse, stuffed the children into the garments, and sent them off. The girls protested about the ugly long underwear, but Lucy wouldn't listen. Nonsense, she said, keep their legs warm, fewer colds! Once out of her sight, they rolled the legs high up under their new dresses.

County officials understood Lucy very well and shrewdly made her the county welfare officer, knowing that she'd stretch the limited welfare fund—usually about fifty dollars a month, for all the needy—with her own money. And she did. When she had outfitted a child or bought a bushel basket of groceries for a jobless father, she would pay the store a dollar or two out of the welfare money and fish the rest from her own purse.

As the welfare official, it was her responsibility to find homes for homeless children—orphans, neglected children, and foundlings—the latter were always left in a bundle on Lucy's back porch. When an Escalante family was deserted by the father and orphaned by the mother's death from influenza, Lucy found homes for the two little girls. When the body of a young mother was discovered bound with barbed wire under water at Cory bridge, the orphaned infant was left on Lucy Hillman's porch.

As the town was going into its tenth year, Dr. Albert. H. Stockham arrived and bought the house and offices of Dr. McLean. That is about the last you hear of Dr. Stockham as a physician. He financed enlargement of the Hunt Hardware Store and somehow, in the process, it became Stockham Hardware Store. He owned enough Delta State Bank stock to be on the board of directors; he owned enough of the First National Bank to be its president. He was one of the three who financed the Model Block subdivision. With brother Wilson and Zaninetti, he owned the huge Bar I ranch at Cedaredge. He owned and piped irrigation water to the top of the tall island mesa known as Antelope Hill; he floated financing for an electric railway. Dr. Stockham contributed hugely to area development, but he spread himself very thin. The Great Depression got him.

A regular visitor at Stockham Hardware was an ammunition salesman known as "Presh" Ploger, a name that Harry Ploger acquired because his wife called him "precious." Presh was probably the best shot this region of gun experts ever saw. It is unlikely that the Kings would have won so many national shooting prizes if Presh had been an amateur and not a professional. His sales trips drew crowds at the trap club, where he shot dimes out of the air without missing and, using a mirror to aim over his shoulder, traced the profile of an Indian in bullet holes on a copper plate behind him.

Acquired by the Schmidt family, the hardware store went from cast-iron Monarch ranges to microwave ovens without "modernizing" the store out of its heritage. The owners retained the intricate pressed-metal ceiling and the free-standing cherrywood staircase.

The pioneer West was full of bachelors just waiting for a wife before starting to amount to something. George Wilson was perfectly content to drive the North Fork stage on Tuesdays and do a little horse racing at Hank Hammond's track on Sundays—until Ella Brown arrived.

Ella, a graduate of the Brooklyn Conservatory of Music, offered piano lessons and demonstrated her talent by playing on request at any function. In a time when there was no wired-in entertainment, pianists were in great demand for church, club, afternoon tea, or home sing-arounds at piano or pump organ. Ella was good, drawing students from the town's first families, including the daughters of Judges King and Amsbary and little Welland Jeffers, whose mama, as we shall see, was in process of ruining Main Street to protect her sole son from himself.

Spurred by the married state, George Wilson opened a saddlery and harness shop, making everything needed to connect horse to job—traces, collars, hames. Buggy harness with decorative rings and plumes as wanted. Freighting harness, rugged and thick-strapped as needed. Pack, racing, and stock saddles. George developed saddlery into an art, creating saddles of such outstanding quality and style that to own a George Wilson was, and still is, a mark of distinction. Hollywood traces down and buys every George Wilson saddle it gets word of.

If you want to step back into last century, go into the Davis Clothing men's store on the corner of Fourth and Main and ask for a shirt collar and a couple of gold collar buttons. You won't get them, but you'll see them in an old swivel case, because John's son, Mel Davis, saved back a few when a film crew was buying them up for a movie being shot over in Aspen a few years ago.

John Davis never threw anything away, he just stored out-of-date stuff in the basement until it came back in style. He wasn't a collector, so if the filmmakers wanted to buy those collars, why, okay. Did they want the 1920s BVDs, too? They didn't. The muslin BVD was the least sexy of any male undergarment designers ever thought up. Those BVDs still may be down there in the basement waiting to come back in style.

Except for updating the stock, nothing in this store has changed since John opened it in 1912. Shelved merchandise rises to the fourteen-foot ceiling; boxes of shoes and cowboy boots are reached by climbing one of those old rolling ladders. Lever buttons on the ornate silver-gilt cash register will slide open specific cash drawers in the oak cabinet below. Oak-framed glass cases display socks and union suits (if it's winter). The tall triple mirror swings to show you whether your rear lets the coat hang straight in back; if it doesn't, there is a treadle sewing machine for alterations. You sit on the oak and leather settee while the clerk, squatting on a matching foot-rest stool, removes your shoe, measures with a sliding rule, pushes the ladder along its track, and climbs to find your size. If it wasn't for that case of Stetson hats in the middle of the floor, you could see the marks of iron-shod hooves that Shorty Gibson's horse made in the wooden floor eighty years ago, when he came in here shopping on horseback that time.

John Davis came to Paonia in 1893. While attending high school, he worked in the old Paonia Hotel, getting up at 4:30 A.M. to open up, build fires in every room, clean spittoons, and mind the desk until time for school, after which he returned, closing up at 1 A.M. "All the rooms had kerosene lamps. On weekends I would carry the lamps down the back stairs, clean the bowls and chimneys, fill them with oil, and carry them all back up to the rooms." If he also cleaned all the chamber pots, he didn't mention it.

John got a job with Emry Brothers Shoe and Clothing Store at thirty-five dollars a month, with the promise of a five-dollar raise every quarter "if he made good." He made so good that, by 1912, he was lettering his own name on a store in Delta, specializing in such exclusive fabrics as English worsteds, German vicunas, linens, and silks. "At first we carried ladies shoes, but they had so many buttons, eighteen or twenty, and the ladies would want to try on pair after pair. Took too much of the clerk's time doing all the buttoning and unbuttoning."

Known as "Mr. Republican" for the part he played in electing governors and congressmen, John Davis himself was a state senator. Besides his part in getting the sugar plant, he financed the canning factory in one of its several incarnations and was still actively president of the Delta Savings and Loan at age ninety-five.

The store John Davis started is owned in the third generation by Mel's son Bradford. Brad does altering on an electric sewing machine, but behind him is the old machine John Davis treadled to make those fraction-of-an-inch changes that gave Davis Clothing customers a perfect fit.

Beyond helping to finance the Hillman's store building, Walter Hillman never was involved with that emporium. He became a banker. One wonders: had he stayed with Hillman's, would he have died a natural and unequivocal death?

From the first, money itself has been a major business at the confluence. Five months after the first wagons edged through the sagebrush, Col. Harvey Bailey and T. B. Crawford shipped in a safe, set it up in their little shack of a false-front building, and offered people a better place to put spare cash than under the mattress.

Colonel Bailey had no intention of staying small. He drew up plans for an arch-windowed, turret-towered, two-story building on the main corner of Main Street, ignoring the fact that the spot already was occupied by the thriving Williams Grocery. Aside from this, Bailey's plans were so ambitious that it took nine years before his dream for the bank could be realized.

In the meantime, competition moved in. Trew Blachly and Don Baldwin opened the Farmer's and Merchant's Bank across the street from the site upon which Colonel Bailey's dream was predicated. And a Delta branch of the Austin bank— eight miles upriver—was opened by Dr. Austin Miller, a tubercular refugee who had been a founder of the town named for him.

Grocer Williams helped the Bailey dream along by moving over one lot, by agreeing to have his new store function as part of the bank building (though he still retained ownership), and by becoming an official of the bank.

Construction of the Delta County Bank was a show that ran for months on Main Street. Sidewalk engineers watched block-and-tackle booms lift brick and cut stone higher and higher, as the walls went up. John Jeffers, noted for his stonework, shaped cornices and lintels right there in the middle of the street. John's son Welland, in white shirt and knee britches, was among the spectators and might have been learning his father's trade, except that Mrs. Jeffers had other plans for little Welland.

The bank's acanthus-leaf capitals were shipped from Denver, but nobody knows where the polished pink granite corner pillar came from. The story is that the original plan called for a square pillar matching the pilasters; that some stone company owed the bank money and went broke; and that the pillar was all the bank could get out of it, so they used it, even though it doesn't go with anything else and is too slender for its base and capital.

When the Silver Panic struck, the Delta County Bank closed for six days and then reopened with a new name, First National Bank, and new owners, who included Dr. Stockham, president, and Walter Hillman, vice president. Fortunately, another official was lawyer Millard Fairlamb, who would help the group through the awful trouble they got themselves into during the Great Depression.

Ten years after the McCarty Gang robbed the Farmers and Merchants Bank, the First National Bank was the target of a home-grown bank robbery attempt, perpetrated by four "young men-about-town."

Porter Plumb's law office, located behind the First National, had a trap door under the back stairs. Working from there, the four tunneled bankward. As the paper reported: "They tunneled to the vault and had knocked away some of the foundation before anything was suspected." Discovering that they were being watched, the robbers quit but made the mistake of leaving their tools in the hole.

The four were convicted in district court but exonerated in the state supreme court, apparently because of the wording of the prosecution's charge: "feloniously, willfully, maliciously and forcibly broke and entered the First National Bank of Delta." The four had lacked a few inches of actually accomplishing what they were charged with.

12

Coming Together for Good Times

Until the advent of the motion picture and the phonograph, fun was a local product, home-grown and richly various.

In winter there was skating on river ponds, singles and couples swirling to a show-off stop just short of the bonfire and hot cider. There was tobogganing off Garnet Mesa down scary-steep Third Street Hill, barred to buggy and wagon traffic. (Ninth Street Hill traffic is still blocked off in favor of sleds on deep-snow Saturdays). Powered sledding—papa or big brother hooked his saddle horse to a string of sleds and scooted the whole third grade swooping and hollering round and round Courthouse Square. Skiing in those days was hard work, not sport. Called Norwegian showshoes, skis were used to find stray livestock caught in high country by early snow.

Swimming, before water was caged in tempered pools, was risky fun, especially for life-challenging males. The snowmelt chill of rivers, perilous currents to outwit. Hunting and fishing along the two rivers, in lakes and forests in encircling mountains, were not purely fun, because they played such a vital part in putting food on the table, but were all the more satisfying for that.

Picnicking at Fat Man's Misery west of town. You and your club or class rode out there in a hay wagon. On the rim, you unhitched and tied the team to the wagon to munch the hay, then you scrambled down a gully and, holding the picnic stuff over your heads, tried to see if you could squeeze through a slot in the cliff called Fat Man's Misery, because a fat man couldn't. Those who passed the entry test built a fire in the sun pocket down there, reheated the fried chicken, and spread out the other goodies—potato salad, purple eggs (pickled with beets), bacon on biscuit sandwiches, wild gooseberry pie—and proceeded to stuff themselves. The idea was to see how much you could eat and still squeeze back up through Fat Man's Misery. If you couldn't, it was a mighty long walk home the other way.

Horse racing was here before the settlers, who didn't bother with the Ute race courses—they were straight, not oval. The earlycomers laid out their own tracks, slightly before they laid out the town. Hank Hammond's track in North Delta was followed by an official course, when the County Fairground was set aside, west of Fadely's Swamp.

Racing came in all classes. Cowboy horse racing with stock saddles and much whooping and hat whomping had the least social éclat but was the most popular.

Thoroughbred racing, the sport that really brought out the betting money, was big from the start. The Roberts brothers ran blooded mares and studs on the Uncompahgre Plateau even before the settlers arrived. Many of these horses were trained to the track by their man, Ben Lowe. Other pioneers brought favorite winners and studs. Racing wasn't always on the up-and-up. Lung Chung, in addition to his Chinese laundry and an upriver farm, had a threateningly fast horse. In the spring of 1905, he and Harrington were due to match horses at the fairground track, with a lot of Western Slope money riding on the outcome. Chung, advised to hide his horse lest it be doped, did so, but another of his horses died. Suspected poisoning was confirmed by stomach analysis in Denver.

Swankiest of all was sulky racing. The sleek horse skimmed along between the chariot's shafts (and virtually between the driver's braced legs, the way those sulkies were built), pacing or trotting with a fast, elegant aplomb not matched by whooping cowboy or whipping jockey. Confluence owners followed the nationwide circuit of "two-wheel" race events, shipping their horses in special, sumptuous railroad cars. A hazard of the circuit was fire in hay-filled stables. Reward S, sire of many winners, was sole survivor of a stable fire in Illinois that killed all the rest of Silsby and Norton's racers.

After the county (then eight years old) voted to make gambling illegal, horse races were announced in the press circumspectly, sometimes as religious events: "Services were held at Negro Gulch last Sunday. Officiating were Willbank's and Kennicott's horses. Big attendance. Hider (George) happy, other fellows busted, all in the contribution box."

Betting apparently was righteous as long as no cash was involved. The paper openly announced: "If McKinley carries Ohio, Dave Bailey is to do the family washing of Prof. Harris the following week, and in case Bryan carries Ohio, the family washing of Dave Bailey will be done by Prof. Harris. Mrs. Harris and Mrs. Bailey are saving up all the old dirty clothes they can so as to give them good exercise."

Though horse racing is no longer the big thing it was in early days, horse raising is. Thousands of horses are grown at the confluence for specialized purposes. For handling cattle on the range, nothing replaces the horse, but there have been changes. The cow pony is trucked to the site of the day's work, whether driving cattle, assessing grazing conditions, or keeping tabs on the newborns. A few ranchers have tried helicopters for such chores, but, except to check on strays, aerial cow punching hasn't proven efficient.

Outfitters, a growing industry in these valleys, raise horses to put hunters up where the big game is in the fall, and all year provide four-footed transportation for the weekend trail rider who thinks living in view of four mountain ranges is wasted without a quiet, friendly means of exploring them.

Bicycles were only for men at first, being much too costly for mere children. A board fence was erected around the cycle racetrack on Courthouse Square to avert the hazards of stray creatures under wheel and to provide a place for spectators to perch during inter-city cycle club races.

Inevitably people had to find out whether a bicycle could outrace a horse. The race was set for May 8, 1894, from the Delta County Bank corner to Montrose and back. Charley Updegraf was to ride a Cleveland Bicycle, and Clarence Mower his old roan horse, Prince, that he'd bought at a sheriff's sale. If the cycler won, he would receive a new Cleveland of his own; if Mower won, he would get a hundred dollars. School in both towns was let out for the event; cheering wheelmen and horsemen lined the route. Betting was heavy, favoring the cycle.

Prince arrived in Montrose in one hour and twenty-six minutes, the bicycle six minutes later. Everybody in Montrose turned out to yell them in. Prince made it back to the Delta County Bank in three hours and twenty-three minutes, having traveled fifty miles. Charley Updegraf gave up four miles out and came home in a buggy.

The result was laid to the long-windedness of the horse, which was "a common bronco cowhorse about 13 years old." But the cycler's problem, no doubt, was that hooves could deal much better than wheels with the rutty, rocky, winding river road that then connected the towns—actually five miles longer than today's U.S. Highway 50.

Baseball was big. In the early years, the town's baseball team was not composed of high-school kids, but of business and professional men. For example, the Delta lineup against Hotchkiss on Fourth-of-July weekend, 1903, was: pitcher, cattle-man Boss Beckley; catcher, Town Marshal Welch; first base, attorney Plumb; sec-ond base, Mayor Johnson; third base, Judge Amsbary; shortstop, W. B. Stockham; left field, Alderman Travis; right field, Alderman McGrew; center field, William Mathers; umpire, Judge A. R. King. That third baseman was awesome. Of him, the newspaper once noted, "Mr. Amsbary, our fat man, says if he finds the man that stole his clothesline, he'll sit down on him."

Town played town. Entire populations went to games by train, team and band riding on flat cars and pausing at every named siding to tootle their expected vic-tory. The special train hung around until the game was over to bring the folks back home. One such train didn't make it back from Grand Junction. Stranded by a track washout in the canyon some miles north of home, fans and team spent a foodless night and day in the cars and finally were yanked home backwards in a great loop that traversed a large part of the Rockies before reaching home from the opposite direction almost a week later.

These "Town Daddy" ball teams, as they were called, were not as amateurish as the occupations of the players might indicate. Tom Seaton (of the druggist Seatons) was scouted by the Federal League to pitch for Newark and was with the Philadelphia Phillies in the National Baseball League in 1913, the year he won eight straight.

Trapshooting, croquet, poker, tennis, pool, horseshoe playoffs, prizefighting, whist, cock-fighting—if it was competitive, they were into it.

Cock-fighting surfaced at about the same time as the craze for fancy chicken breeds. Before the poultry industry restricted itself to the White Leghorn (and the Leghorn to a lifetime sentence in a two-by-two cage), chickens were various and gorgeous; Silver Wyandottes, Buff Orpingtons, and Rhode Island Reds outstrutted each other at county, state, and national fairs. Growing fighting chick-ens was carefully less ostentatious; Carl Smith raised game cocks for a secret pit club in Grand Junction.

Fun and games in the pioneer era of striving and accomplishing centered on dominance, physical or mental. Boss Beckley outpitches Fred Burritt of Forked Tongue Creek; then both are raucous rooters in the Community Rooms, when Ark Hall outhams Judge King in a straight-faced debate on who the pumpkin belongs to when the vine sneaks across a property line to do its unseemly thing.

There was nothing very competitive about R. E. Eggleston. He was the only one doing his thing—a combination recreation-livelihood. At the confluence, he'd stock his boat with three months' worth of supplies and trap and hunt his way down the Gunnison and Colorado rivers into the Grand Canyon and back. Though

In front of his hardware store E. M. ("Easy Money") Getts admires bearskin that was Old Clubfoot, plague of stockmen on two mountain ranges. Clubfoot had lost some toes in a trap, providing a tracking signature that led to his death in 1902. Courtesy of Delta County Historical Society.

he returned with "loads of pelts," it was never revealed whether he rowed, poled, or packed his way back against the current of those rivers. "The Trapper," he signed himself in humorous letter-articles for the *Delta Chief* describing his discoveries—the mummy of an Indian Maiden, ledges of pure marble, and, of course, placerable gold.

Eggleston was a forerunner in the long use of the Gunnison for leisurely rafting, canoeing rapids, and kayaking. Most notable among those who indulged in this pastime were U.S. President and Mrs. Jimmy Carter, guests of Hank Hotze, who escorted them over Chucker Trail into the gorge and on a fishing-float trip down Black Canyon to Pleasure Forks.

The nine holes of the first real golf course were laid out on a sloping bench of rocky adobe desert, across the river and two miles north of the confluence. Construction began in 1925, with team and scraper clearing off the sage and boulders; then a huge cement roller smoothed the fairways—sort of. That antique piece of construction equipment is still out there somewhere. Most of the "greens" (there never was a blade of grass on the course) were back from the edge, but it delighted the course designers—John Davis, Charlie Parker, and their cronies—to put two of the holes on points jutting out over a deep, stony gulch along the east side.

No. 8, the worst hole, was known as the Ant Hill, the Pimple, or the Blankety-Blank. Surrounded by gully on all sides, the Pimple "green" was only about six strides wide, towering above a jumble of chicken-coop-size lava boulders. If your ball didn't land on the green, forget it. Some players refused to forget it. Preacher Duke Smith, unaided by strong language, took sixteen strokes to get up out of there. Ernest Englehart had better luck; with Charlie Parker standing up on the rim pointing at the hole, Ernie took a swing, managed to miss rocks, and lifted that ball up and right into the cup.

The greens were covered with cottonseed mat, which made them very fast, requiring special putting skills. There were other hazards, too. You were as likely to sink your putt in a prairie dog hole as the cup; mosquitoes in ravenous clouds dimmed (they vowed) the sun; and then there were rattlesnakes. Charles Conklin said, "All those stories about rattlesnakes on the golf course are greatly exaggerated. I doubt they ever killed more than a dozen or so."

Carl Smith, whose memory was longer because it started earlier, recalled, "I used to make money finding balls they lost down in those boulders. Twenty-five cents each. I got the same for killing a rattlesnake." With hazards like these, which the home folks more or less got used to but which visiting players never quite recovered from the shock of, it is little wonder that the Delta Golf Club won almost every meet held on the home course, including the Western Slope Championship.

Most of this early golf course was scraped away when Blake Airport was created. Golf is now played on manicured greens down by the Gunnison River, where there are shady cottonwoods and a welcoming clubhouse.

The Delta Trap Club is just a little upriver from the golf club. It has produced a number of championship gunmen, beginning with the Kings, father and son, in the early days and, more recently, Ben Lowe's grandson, Colorado Hall-of-Famer Jack Lowe.

There is a long tradition of all-male get-togethers at the confluence. It began with the Bachelors' Den, a narrow building on Main Street with a false front, just wide enough to accommodate the door and one window. The elegantly furnished Den was home to young unmarried men (of which pioneer towns had a surfeit), providing an alternative to a lonely, cramped hotel room or a raucous, crowded saloon.

The tradition expanded as male clubs proliferated during the early part of this century. Fraternal lodges—Masons, International Order of Odd Fellows (IOOF),

Elks. Town boosters—Lions, Rotary, Kiwanis. Or just to yak—every cafe and drugstore, with its nameless 10 A.M. coffee coterie.

For a while, Masons rode horseback forty-five miles to Grand Junction to attend lodge meetings. Then, in 1884, they organized Delta Lodge No. 62, with eighteen members. The group met anywhere it could until the turreted First National Bank was built; then lodge rituals were conducted in the meeting room upstairs. It was a fine place for inspiring discourse—those great arched windows, almost floor to ceiling, looking out into the stars. But the building, with its tower and pillars, so elegant when seen from the two street sides, was flawed—there was no inside stairway. The second floor was reached by an open wooden stairway that zigzagged up the alley side. Unfinished lumber steps were hard for the ladies of the Eastern Star to negotiate in the dark; it tripped their slippers, snagged their gowns, put dirt and slivers in their white gloves when they steadied themselves on the raw-lumber handrail. The men couldn't understand their complaints. All second-floor public buildings in town had outside stairs—it was wasteful to put roof and wall on something you used just to get somewhere else, like a sidewalk on the street.

The ladies (after some years) prevailed and were the cause of the Masons acquiring their own hall—one with, they maintained, the only inside public stairs in town.

One of the first things the town's first millionaire, J. Frank Sanders, did with his money was build a place for having fun—the AnnaDora Opera House. Actually, he and Ray Simpson formed the company that financed it, and they named it for their daughters, Anna and Dora, respectively. When you think "opera house," don't think La Scala. The term *opera house* was used at that time for any legitimate theater building, because the show-halls in red-light districts were called *theaters*. The two-story hardware store with theater upstairs was acclaimed as "the most extensive piece of stonework ever done here"—800 perch of brick.

At regular intervals, traveling drama companies—such as the Kempo Komedy Kompany—with a repertoire of several plays each would come to town, stay at the Delta House, and put on their plays, one after another, as advertised ahead of time—*East Lynne, Uncle Tom's Cabin*. The latter came to town several times. Once it came unintentionally, during Christmas week in 1890: "Owing to the fact that the leading man of *Ten Nights in a Bar Room* had on board a larger jag than he could carry last Monday night, the company changed the bill to *Uncle Tom's Cabin*."

Among other performances were a demonstration of levitation by a person named Rose Arthur, a performance by midgets, and the "Nashville Students and Jubilee Singers. Oldest colored organization now traveling." James Connelly, founder of the Irish Socialist Republican party in Dublin, appeared at the AnnaDora the year after Queen Victoria died. He had anticipated the queen's death by staging a procession of thirty thousand protesters behind a black coffin in the year of her Diamond Jubilee. There was no admission charge to listen to Connelly wave the verbal shillelagh in the AnnaDora.

It was generally agreed that the most memorable productions at the opera house were put on by local people. This was not because the imported stuff was so bad or the home folks so good; it was because of Thomas Keirns. Keirns, who was in the bigtime on Broadway for twelve years, had just ended a particularly successful year when he received the medical dictum: "One year to live if you stay in New York, but you are young and your lungs may heal in Colorado, where the sun shines every day."

With the fierce energy that tuberculosis seemed to inspire in its young victims, Keirns taught and directed violin, acting, singing, and dance in schools all over the confluence area and staged at least three productions at the AnnaDora. In her book, *Pioneer Lawyer* (1946), Ula King Fairfield leaves us a picture of the man, the theater, and the times (about 1900):

> When Mr. Kearns [*sic*] looked the AnnaDora over he found a stage, two dressing-rooms, foot-lights consisting of a tin trough holding oil lamps fitted with Rochester burners and tin reflectors.
>
> It was not the kind of an Opera House Thomas Kearns had been used to, but nevertheless, he decided to produce *The Mikado* and his search for local talent began. . . . Among them were Mrs. Charles Botsford, Mrs. Mary Charlton, Miss Cornelia Johnson, all professional musicians schooled at Oberlin, Brooklyn, or Paris.
>
> In transforming twelve freckled-faced country girls into beautiful Japanese geisha girls, Thomas Kearns employed genius and imagination. He sent to New York for bolts of material for our kimonos, which were made by our mothers. We were taught to shuffle in straw sandals, and to flirt with the audience from behind paper fans. An afternoon was spent on our make-up, our hair piled high and decorated with bright ornaments.
>
> All of Delta attended. The front rows were filled with whistling, stamping children, and an overflow of boys sat on the windowsills.

Keirns put on other productions at the AnnaDora—among them, *Pinafore*, *Colonial Extravaganza*, and *A Revolutionary Operetta*—before resuming his career with the New York Opera Company. In the summer of 1901, Elitch Gardens

Theater in Denver featured Thomas Keirns, "famous comedian," as Triplet in "Peg Woffongton." He had to work fast and knew it; he died in 1903.

The AnnaDora was destined to a short life, too. Everybody in town attended the spectacular fire. It started in the hardware store below. Ed January remembered, "That fire was so hot it melted farm machinery in the yard." Esther Stephens recalled the stock of ammunition going off. "Bullets were flying everywhere. We were terrified, but we didn't leave."

Two cultural organizations featuring local talent started in the 1970s: the Valley Symphony Orchestra, which after three decades is still giving wintertime concerts; and the Triangle Theater, which is no more. The latter, after producing some major works *(1776, The Man from La Mancha, Camelot)*, has faded away. No one seems to know whether it was Marty's musicale or something else that led to its demise. That musicale and its reception epitomize so precisely what was happening at the confluence and in the world in the 1970s that it warrants attention.

Marty Conklin Durlin grew up in Delta, the daughter of attorney Charles Conklin, who served as speaker of the Colorado House of Representatives and later headed the U.S. House of Representatives' Committee on Interior and Insular Affairs.

Marty studied flute and organ in Delta, graduated from Colorado Women's College, spent a year at the Austro-American Institute in Vienna, came back to attend Wesleyan University in Connecticut, and then went to Denver, where she worked at public radio station KCFR-FM, where she produced a weekly program of her own. Then she felt a need to come back to Delta and find her roots. Her roots there were very deep indeed; George Conklin, a town founder, was her great-grandfather.

For a living, or to experience all phases of the town milieu, she held several jobs—deejaying an hour of fine music at radio station KDTA, caring for patients in a nursing home, tending bar in a tavern, writing news items for the *Delta County Independent* (DCI) at twenty-five cents a column-inch. Working in the DCI office, she would sit on the floor, legs spread out, her notepad resting on a denim skirt that did not quite cover her bare feet. Ladies bringing in details of formal weddings walked around Marty to get to the editorial desk.

While all this was going on, Marty was recording her cultural collision with her forebears' town in a musicale composed at her kitchen piano, which sat between sink and stove in the old, old house she rented.

Now, Delta had experienced hippies before, but they had been "outsiders" living in tent colonies on the North Fork. They bought communal farms and orchards and religiously practiced a faith locally known as "Equal Opportunity for Weeds and Bugs." They did no orchard spraying; the nutritional quality of every apple was demonstrated by the good health of its resident worm. But the coddling moth cannot be fenced in or out, and the entire North Fork fruit industry was threatened with ruin.

At this time in its history, Delta was in a slough of reactionary apathy, as described elsewhere. Business was bad, many stores were empty, but a certain influential element in town was not entirely dismayed by this. After all, if no new businesses moved into these old structures, they would stay the same. Had a motto been worded for the town at this stage, it might well have been: "Don't change anything." Progress, sure, but hold fast to the good old days of our pioneer forefathers. With equal tenacity, Marty conformed to a tenet of her own sixties generation: "Don't ever do anything the way it's been done before."

The cultural-collision musicale, *Going Home*, was about Marty herself, the town, and her jobs. One bleakly touching song spoke for the nursing home residents:

> *There's lots to do, we eat our meals,*
> *we scribble in our color books,*
> *we look outside, we watch TV . . .*

Another song represented the town's voice:

> *We're very rich*
> *We have a lot*
> *We never want for anything*
> *But we want more*
> *It's only right*
> *We work hard, we deserve it.*

Of Marty's jobs at the newspaper and the tavern, the chorus went:

> *Quarter an inch,*
> *Quarter an inch.*
> *Or you could be a barmaid*
> *At a quarter a pinch.*

The musicale was of professional quality, clever and sad-funny; the cast and orchestra had the area's best voices and instrumentalists, including Triangle Theatre stalwarts. But it didn't go over. The town ignored it. Gene Bond, a member of the cast, says now, "Delta wasn't ready for Marty."

About hippies and the North Fork fruit industry. Each learned from the other, and a compromise has yielded both worm-free apples and a better environment.

When Delta was a year and a half old, it got a newspaper, the *Delta Chief.* Publisher Robert D. Blair had the field to himself for two years. Then county officials, unhappy with his politics, put up five hundred dollars to induce another newspaper to come and present the other side. Blair tried to stop that move, noting that the town couldn't support two newspapers and offering to publish city council news free, but he lost. After a brief interim, the *Delta Independent,* cited as "a paper of no political party," took over the *Chief.*

Publisher during the changeover was Frank Howard, a very young bachelor who apparently was trying to change that status, or so his anonymous piece of August 4, 1885, makes it seem:

A fellow fully realizes the hardness of this life when he walks a mile to church expressly to see his best girl and sees her walk off on the arm of some other fellow who is bigger than him, and when he wends his way homeward in solitude, thinking of how he can get even, he finally reaches the river, and his most strenuous efforts fail to waken the slumbering ferryman on the other side. He then has to straddle an inch wire cable and by almost superhuman effort he drags himself across the river, the seat of his best Sunday pantaloons becomes threadbare and his hands are covered with blisters as big as silver dimes. The paths in this life are thorny and rocky indeed.

The path in this life was very short for young Frank Howard. Joining the Alaskan gold rush, he began publishing the *Record* in Juneau. After commenting in print on how "Roving" Timmons, editor of the *Juneau Torchlight,* had mishandled coverage of a fire, Howard was shot and killed.

An editor might get shot, but he was in no danger of being sued, so editors printed just about anything: "Rumor: J. R. Hall, better known as Arkansaw, is about to commit household felicity. Wow!" "The Rev. Standish was monkeying with the gospel at the Baptist church several evenings this week." "A man came into McGranahan's General Store and bought beans by mistake, instead of sorghum seed. We wonder, upon harvesting his crop, will he order a wind mill instead of a sorghum mill?" "We would advise a certain young man the next time he does the Yum Yum act to pull down the blinds or blow out the light."

Early-day small-town newspapers had a large section of one-sentence news items that kept track of where everybody was and what they were doing: "L. W. Wigram drove up to Iola Sunday. . . . It is said that George Duke will blow the 'swinett' in the town band. . . . Joe Pregent had the nerve to wear the first shirt waist that was worn in Delta."

A descendant of these one-sentence news items written by the editor himself was the "stringer column." For many decades, newspapers paid ten cents a printed column-inch for news of club and family doings, Sunday dinners, trips, illnesses, accidents, and achievements. The "stringer" (usually a housewife) gathered the items by phone, wrote them in longhand, sent them in, and, after they were published, clipped and pasted them together and returned them to be measured and paid for. As more women got jobs outside the home, these columns disappeared, for lack not of writers but of readers. Working women, contacting people directly every day, had less need of neighborhood news items to keep in touch. In addition, as more women began to work, the number of clubs declined. From perhaps a hundred and fifty in the society editor's file—Bide-a-Wee to Xanthos—they dwindled to twenty or so.

Of many publishers at the confluence, one was female. Doris Ebersole went to Linotype school in Kansas, saved her money, and, in partnership with G. F. Roberts, bought the *Delta County Independent*. The paper sold many times during Doris' working life, but, regardless of who the ostensible boss was, Doris and the Linotype ran the place. The machine's top speed was not very fast (after all, it had to take molten lead and mold a line of type out of whatever was keyed into it), and Doris could type exactly that fast all day. Nothing could hurry either her or it. Newspapers are chronically late getting to press, editors and printers chronically frantic as deadline nears. But nothing fazed Doris. She belonged to the Linotype setters' union—which had one member per small town practically all over the literate world—and no matter what the crisis, when break time came, the sweating press crew watched Doris calmly rise and walk out the door to her date with a cup of coffee.

The town's seventy-fifth anniversary came while Jim Cinnamon was publisher. He employed former editor Julie Wise to gather and write the history of the entire area for a long special edition of the newspaper on May 8, 1958. Tackling what was virtually virgin territory, she produced a rich resource for succeeding writers and history students.

When Gene Wells became publisher, both Linotype and flatbed press were junked in favor of an offset press and a pre-computer contraption that punched news onto paper tapes. Then Gene sold the paper to its coverage rival, the *Grand Junction Daily Sentinel*. The DCI continued to be published, but it wasn't the same, and the confluence wasn't the same without a voice of its own. This editorial laryngitis was cured when the Sunderlands brought ownership back home.

"Largest Flat-Top Mountain in the World," it has been called ever since settlers first prowled it. A mile higher than the surrounding valleys, flower-meadowed, forest-shaded, sparkling with two hundred lakes, Grand Mesa cups the cool of spring all summer long.

You can be up there in minutes. It took the pioneers two days by team and wagon, camping overnight at Ginter Grove. With that much effort involved in getting to the top, families stayed awhile—two weeks, a month, all summer. Having established wife and children in cool comfort up there, the working father would ride his horse up to join them on weekends.

Camping and fishing were not restricted on Grand Mesa, except for a brief time when the Englishman William Radcliffe bought, leased, and legislated rights to about everything with fins up there. He protected his "property" with armed guards. One of them shot rancher W. A. Womack and was narrowly saved from lynching. Foiled in trying to kill the killer, the ranchers set fire to everything the Englishman owned. Radcliffe returned to England (after getting the U.S. Congress to reimburse him), and Grand Mesa returned to the people.

When the Radcliffe affair was settled and the ashes cleared away, the deep verandah of a new lodge looked out over the lake, built by the Grand Mesa Resort Company. The company was organized in 1893 by a group of avid anglers who incidentally were business and professional men—Ike Conklin, Ray Simpson, and O. T. Standish among them. Not intended as a profit-making development, the property has remained in the hands of the stockholders, who have cabin-building privileges beside three large lakes.

In 1913, an automobile road was completed to the top of the mesa; at last you could get there in one day instead of two—but just barely. As late as 1945, that road was so bad that, in some of the steep, rocky hairpin turns, the car stood still, chattering up and down at full throttle.

You can still take the Old Road, but the quicker route to that cool heaven is State Highway 65, which slashes through bluffs instead of wriggling around them.

13

Where Cultures Meet

Hispanics compose the largest non-Anglo ethnic group at the confluence of the two rivers. As with other groups of settlers, the earliest arrivals came from other parts of the United States, chiefly the San Luis Valley of Colorado and New Mexico, where they had learned skills that enabled them to play vital roles in the development of new ranches and towns.

Especially valuable, as the new town quickly grew, was the Hispanics' expertise in working clay to make 'dobe brick, fired brick, and tile. And in the difficult job of handling irrigation water, they had generations of know-how gained in shunting the Rio Grande onto fields through *acequias*. This is shovel craft of the trickiest kind. How many laterals will a given ditch support? How, using only your shovel and mud, can you adjust the flow in thirty laterals so accurately that the water in every one of them will reach the end of the field exactly twelve hours later?

A few, though they have Hispanic names (given to their families by Spanish priests centuries ago), take pride in having pure Indian blood. Alfred Gallegos, a Taqua Apache born near Taos, New Mexico, is one. Among the skills he brought with him is the making of Indian bread, which he bakes in an adobe brick oven in his back yard. Neighbors and joggers sniff the morning air for the delicious aroma that announces Gallegos baking day.

During the early days of this century, the immigrating Hispanics were mainly Chihuahuans escaping Pancho Villa's revolutionaries. At that time the best job opportunities were on railroad track-laying and maintenance crews. With their natural sense of rhythm Chihuahuans were good at it. There's a lot of rhythm to pounding spikes and pumping handcars—visualize two men swinging alternate blows to drive one spike, and two men face-to-face bobbing up and down at the handlebars, scooting the little three-wheeled vehicle down the track.

As canning and sugar plants required more "stoop labor" in the fields, groups of Hispanics deep in Mexico moved northward, following the season up across the United States. Most returned home at summer's end, some found steady work, a few acquired farms of their own, and others started businesses or entered professions. Toby Crespín became a printer; Julia Macías head librarian; Jerry García an electrician. The Reverend Henry Archuleta became a missionary-preacher to his people, distributing copies of *Santa Biblia* while raising goats to provide milk and meat for the needy.

Hispanic festivals and ceremonies enrich the community.

Toby Crespín, a native of Delta, is proud of his Mexican heritage and determined to live up to it. At the offset press he was unflappable, but when his son Randy was getting married, the entire newspaper staff got involved in Toby's anxieties as he prepared lists, called people, totaled up sums. Somebody said, "Why so uptight, Tobe? The bride's family takes care of all that stuff."

"In your culture," he agreed. "But in ours it's the bridegroom's father who is responsible for planning everything, paying for everything."

A traditional Hispanic wedding is very beautiful; musical with chanted words, dramatic with slow graceful moves. And different from the typical Anglo wedding. In place of the interchange of rings (or in addition to it), the bridegroom slips a long string of pearls over the bride's head—the symbolic "lasso" that binds her to him for life.

There is the post-Mass wedding breakfast in the St. Michael's social hall. Long tables of elegantly dressed guests, a live band on the little stage (mariachi or rock, depending on the family's taste), the Rosary Society moving about the tables with heaped platters.

There is the ritual of "dragging Main," in which the bridal couple's car, fluttering with flowers and ribbons, is chased through town a couple of times by honking cars full of yelling celebrants.

There is the gala wedding dance, preceded by the wedding march in which the guests circle the bridal couple and then kneel to the floor, leaving the pair standing like figures on a wedding cake. Generously hosted with good music and drink, the dance lasts all night, rising to a peak of total abandonment to fun just short (the host hopes) of tipping over into trouble.

The Crespín wedding dance managed just that. Toby reported Monday morning, "All fun. No fights."

A wave of Greeks immigrated to the confluence in the 1880s, following a wine-grape crop failure in Greece and in response to railroad advertising in Europe for cheap labor to lay rails across the U.S. That first influx of Greeks began as gandy-dancers and section hands on the railroad, then inched out into private enterprise as they saw opportunities. Many went into sheep-raising—a big thing in the old country. A number became merchants. Greek partners, Triantos and Thliveris, started two grocery stores in town, one down by the depot and one on Main Street. Triantos managed the depot store and, to avoid discrimination, he named it Peterson's Grocery, changing his own last name to fit. His son Johnnie, enlarging the store and adding a liquor outlet, proudly kept "Triantos" for himself but left the store the way his father named it—and ran it. As late as 1960, if you didn't see anything you liked in the meat display, Johnnie would go back to the cold room, lug out a quarter of beef, and cut where you pointed.

Sister Rebecca Peterson Shea remembered: "They taught us to cook Greek—eastern breads, *baklava, korambethes.* They made *dolmas,* lamb and vegetables wrapped in grape leaves, and a wonderful lamb stew!"

The partnership broke up, Thliveris taking the Main Street store. He left it only long enough to go to Greece and get a wife. In Greece he was sent to Paris (it was the Greek custom for wise, disinterested people to decide who should marry whom). Athina, the girl he'd been directed toward, asked, "This Delta—is it as big as Paris?" "Yes," said Andy.

As the couple's three children got old enough—around age four—they began helping in the store by stocking shelves. When they protested that they couldn't read the labels, he told them, "Match the pictures on the cans in the box to the cans on the shelf, the words will come." That's how they learned to read. All three went on to earn doctorates in different careers in different countries. By staying simple and cutting corners—Andy did his own butchering, from corral to slicing block—he financed their studies all the way.

You could buy almost anything you needed in Andy's store, but you'd never have guessed it by the window display. It didn't change from month to month: a mound of soggy popped corn, faded boxes of tissue. His best customers couldn't have cared less; they were Greek sheepmen who supplied their camp wagons at his store.

Andy himself, by merely following the merchants' customs of his country, became the store's main display. Any time there were no customers, Andy would be outside, white apron and white hair gleaming in the sunlight, leaning against the parking meter and watching the town go by.

For some immigrants, doing stoop labor in the sugar-beet fields was no dead end, but rather a chance to get paid while looking around for ways to better themselves.

Anton and Anna Schmalz came to Delta in 1906 from the other side of the world—the Volga River in Russia. Their forebears had been homesteaders there, too. In 1792, a German queen—Catherine the Great—married Czar Peter III and moved to Russia, where she discovered much empty land and few Russians as skilled at farming as her own countrymen were. So, a hundred years before our own President Lincoln thought of it, she opened Russian lands for a kind of homesteading. Her terms were: eighty acres of land, no taxes for thirty years, interest-free loans, and freedom from compulsory military and civil service. The offer (available to Germans only) lasted for ten years. This might be called discrimination of the clearest kind, but it paid off, benefiting not only the Germans but also the Russians, through the skills imported.

Catherine, though Great, couldn't rule forever. Under Alexander II, the Germans were stripped of property rights, persecuted for their religion, and exiled to Siberia. Only those who escaped early survived.

Anton and Anna got out in 1906 and came to the Uncompahgre Valley via Portugal, Cuba, Mexico, Texas, and Pueblo, Colorado. Penniless, they worked their way. While pounding railroad spikes in Pueblo, Anton heard about the Gunnison Tunnel and the free lands it would water when finished. Free land, no czar. Between beet-thinning jobs along the Uncompahgre, Anton scouted for a piece of good land nobody had yet claimed—but not on Sunday. On Sunday he joyfully walked ten miles to Sunday Mass, which he could not do in Russia.

Settling on land near the county line, the Schmalz family worked hard, prospered, and increased. Descendants of Anton and Anna now number between 250 and 300. Some of the sons and grandsons acquired farms of their own, and some went into businesses, as the yellow pages of phone books attest.

Those who search property titles are surprised by the number of confluence homes owned by women in the early days. This was not because the ladies owned or ruled the roost, but because the city's governing by-law had been changed by the actions of an immigrant from England.

He was Lionel Wigram, who fled his homeland to escape the consequences of a boyish prank. His father was in charge of the royal horses, many of which were jumpers trained for the steeplechase. Lionel was very adept at handling those super steeds. One day in London, during an event the Queen was attending in the royal carriage, Lionel decided to show off by jumping his horse over the carriage. He didn't quite make it. Carriage and Queen tipped over. About all that Lionel's father could do was get his teenager out of the country quick. In the U.S., Lionel Wigram went into real estate, buying almost all the land that would eventually be Cedaredge. Then he sold off the lots—but only to people he happened to like. Thus he controlled who lived in the town. Fearing that a similar thing might happen in Delta, the city council limited the number of lots one person could own. Thus, if a man wanted to invest in more town real estate, he first would deed the home place to his wife.

Two of the feeder streams at the confluence area were mapped in the 1880s as Nigger Gulch. Sometime after 1959, the U.S. Forest Service and other mappers began to enter them as Negro Gulch. Times had changed, in the confluence as in the rest of the nation. By 1979, the mapped threads of the gulches were appearing nameless on some maps, mute evidence of official uncertainty about what racial terms are or are not currently acceptable.

When the settlers arrived, maps were almost blank. All landscape features had to be tagged quickly, so you could direct travelers or pinpoint where you'd been. Briggs Mesa was named for a racing stud; Buttermilk Creek for its white, hard water; Log Hill for its steepness, which required you to chain a felled tree behind your wagon to keep you from tumbling tail-over-neckyoke to the bottom.

So few of the early settlers were of the ethnic group now called African Americans that a racial designation was name enough for the places where they lived or died. The Negro Gulch on the south side of Grand Mesa was named for a black homesteader. There is no record of who he was, but probably he was a Civil War veteran. For the most part, the blacks who came West during the first postwar decades had toughened their dreams of freedom by fighting for it in the war. He may even have been among the blacks who defended Fort Pillow and survived its capture and ensuing atrocities. This man built a stone cabin not far from the old Ute racetrack and lived by trapping, hunting, and growing his food. Corner-peak remnants of his cabin walls survive.

Another Negro Gulch, west of town, was named for an early-day black whom many people since have "contacted" without knowing it. Several former Delta High School students recall a disassembled human skeleton, used for teaching anatomy in science classes. This is the story of who the bones belonged to and how they got into the high school, as reported in the *Delta Chief* in 1884 and as recalled by child-pioneer Oscar Huffington.

A visitor from Colorado Springs, William Violet, had his horse and saddle stolen from his campsite west of Delta. He tracked the animal almost to Escalante Canyon and came upon it, naked of leather, being pursued by a mulatto on foot, bridle in hand. When Violet claimed the horse, the black man defied him: "Shoot, and be damned." Being mounted, Violet outdistanced the other, caught his horse, went to town, and swore out a warrant.

He and Sheriff Gheen found the man lying under a cedar tree on the rim of a rocky gulch. When Gheen told him to put up his hands, the man threw rocks instead, grazing the sheriff's head. Gheen shot once as a warning and, when the rocks kept coming, shot to kill.

"The fellow was buried near the trail." Oscar remembered. "Years later he was dug up, his skeleton cleaned and displayed in the Delta school when I was a pupil there. Part of our physiology lesson was to put the bones back together."

The earliest Japanese in the area did not migrate, they were sent for. Five men were called in from San Francisco to teach the local farmers how to grow onions. The art was well taught and learned, as is still evident, but the five are chiefly remembered for their food. Finding Anglo dishes unpalatable, they ordered their preferences shipped in—kegs of a special kind of fish and rice by the hundred pounds.

During World War II, when the government was evacuating Japanese from coastal areas, a number were sent to the confluence. Most lived and farmed on California Mesa, but some went commercial. Two families went into the business of beauty. The Taniharas and the Saruwataris established a nursery growing bedding plants for sale and bonsai trees for fun.

Delta's history is no freer of discrimination than any other inch of the earth—Russians kicked out Germans, Germans kicked out Jews, the English made life hell for the Irish, and the Irish made life hell right back.

A Chinese immigrant, Charley Fong, ran a laundry on Main Street during the era when, in many U.S. towns, "out of town by sunset" was strictly enforced against persons of another color. Fong's business filled a need, but a few citizens resented him, and one Saturday they sent word that if he didn't get out of town by nightfall, he would be "ridden out on a rail." Then they repaired to a saloon to work up steam to do the riding.

Hearing about it, Judge King took the gun he always kept under his pillow, went to his office, lit the lamp, and sat there in full view of the Saturday night boardwalk crowds. Four men he suspected of being instigators left the saloon and headed for Fong's laundry. King met them in the street and, fingering his not-quite-invisible gun, asked them where they were going.

"Howdy, Judge," they said, and edged back toward the saloon.

There were, of course, other cases of aggressive discrimination. In the early 1920s, the Ku Klux Klan was the strongest political force in the state of Colorado; some people in the community at the confluence of rivers and races participated. Cathy Boyd recalls her father's accounts of KKK crosses being burned on his lawn because he was sympathetic to the problems of black people.

But things were changing at the confluence and elsewhere. The signs in barbershop windows that once forbiddingly read "No se sirve Mexicanos" (Mexicans not served) changed to inviting "Aquí se habla Español" (Spanish is spoken here).

14

Wars—Snags in the Flow

The Civil War has been called the most fatal war in history, because weapons had been modernized but troop maneuvers to evade them had not. After four terrible years of death and deprivation, peace, when it came, was like a dam released. Men flooded westward, finding gold and silver, joy and freedom in the Wild West of riding and cattle and land free for the taking. A number of confluence settlers were Civil War veterans.

In 1920, the Sterns brothers, publishers of the *Free Press*, brought out a book, *With the Colors*. It gave the names, records, and in most cases the pictures of all known Delta County men who had served in United States wars through World War I. Twenty-four Civil War veterans are listed, all Union men. Undoubtedly as many or more Confederates were among the veterans who helped to establish the new town, but there are no listings to prove it.

Among other naval engagements, C. P. Bragg captained a ship during the Battle of New Orleans. He was taken prisoner and spent ten months in the hell that was a Civil War prison camp, then arrived at the confluence with enough money to build a big house (which later he donated for use as a hospital). He designed the house with a little round window in the third floor gable, from which he could observe the course of town events through his nautical spyglass.

Lt. J. J. Barker of the Missouri Cavalry learned enough about horseshoeing in the cavalry to set up as a blacksmith when he arrived.

Sam Salkeld Fairlamb fought in the 124th Pennsylvania Regiment at all the terrible places—Chancellorsville, Lookout Mountain, Spottsylvania, Antietam, the Wilderness—without a scratch, except that he got the bill of his cap shot off.

He came through law school and subsequent legal battles just as unscathed, to become Judge Fairlamb.

And then there was Cap Smith. A very small man with a whale of a personality, Henry A. Smith enlisted in the Illinois Volunteer Infantry at the age of nineteen, worked his way up through the ranks—corporal, sergeant, first lieutenant—and for a short time served as acting captain, a position that allowed him to be called "Cap Smith" for the rest of his life. He served in fifteen major battles, was wounded three times, was imprisoned briefly, and bore a memento of the war in his body for twenty-one years. A bullet, deflected by the frying pan in his knapsack, entered his chest, apparently incapacitating the wiry little man only briefly. Eventually it worked its way out under a shoulder blade. Cap's favorite war story concerned the time when he was on night guard duty, with strict orders from Colonel Buell to let nobody pass under any pretext, unless they had a pass and knew the countersign, and after a certain hour to let nobody pass even if they had both. Well, one night, Colonel Buell himself came up late, having been outside the lines visiting some pretty girls he'd met. Halted, the colonel asserted his identity, asserted his authority, and asserted that he'd have the upstart guard bound, gagged, and court-marshaled if he didn't let him pass. To no avail. The colonel had to pace up and down the beat with the little guard until the latter was relieved by another detail.

In 1898, Cuba's efforts to win independence from Spain were disrupting U.S. trade. Moreover, treatment of the pro-Spanish Cubans—who were being herded into foodless, shelterless camps—aroused U.S. compassion. The U.S. secretary of war authorized the creation of the Rough Riders, in three cavalry divisions, one of which was headed by Col. Theodore Roosevelt. Distinctive men were recruited for these divisions: "Frontiersmen who have the special qualifications of horsemen and marksmen."

Two adventurous men from the confluence joined the Rough Riders, but neither stormed up San Juan Hill with Teddy Roosevelt. Anticlimactically, William Cofield and Joseph Moore were injured in a railroad wreck in Mississippi en route to the shipping port and had not recovered when that brief but very macho war ended. (Cited as marking the emergence of the U.S. as a world power, the Spanish-American War also may have been the first occasion when this country sent troops to another nation for reasons that included humanitarianism.)

In 1916, seventy-five men made up Company E, 2nd Separate Battalion Infantry, U.S. National Guard, Home Station Delta, Colorado. Company E was part of an expedition ordered to Mexican border duty, in the "little war without a name."

The Delta battalion was headed by Capt. John R. Charlesworth and had a full complement of non-commissioned officers, cooks, buglers, etc. President Woodrow Wilson ordered the expedition, under Brig. Gen. John Pershing, to stop Pancho Villa's raids into lower New Mexico. The outcome was inconclusive, partly because Villa was very popular in Chihuahua and partly because World War I was looming and Pershing was needed elsewhere.

Delta had had a military unit of the National Guard since 1911, meeting wherever there was room—in the Conway building, in the Masonic hall. The unit was meeting in the AnnaDora Opera House in 1916, when it was called into federal service to take care of the ruckus on the Mexican border. Although that war was only a short skirmish, the Delta men did not come home for years, not until World War I was over, having been drafted directly into the U.S. service.

Of 630 area men who served in World War I, thirty-seven died, all but two of them of influenza, not bullets. The flu plague struck just as fatally at home. At times it seemed that the newspaper was nothing but one long obituary column. People wore gauze masks when they went to work or to the store. Others tied little sacks of asafetida around their necks, and it seemed to work—probably because the stinking stuff operated like a quarantine, keeping everybody a mile away. As tuberculosis had earlier, influenza seemed to pick on young people in their late teens and early twenties.

A number of those World War I graves were marked by headstones carved by Cap Smith. A stone mason and carver in addition to being a Civil War veteran, Cap had come west soon after the turn of the century, when the youngest of his nine sons had turned fourteen—the age at which boys then were supposed to be able to be out on their own. Cap built a cabin in Escalante Canyon by laying up three masonry walls against a standing slab that formed the fourth wall, and went into the business of carving tombstones. With four of his sons serving in the armed forces in World War I, Cap Smith spent a lot of his time raising money to help fight that war. He was a familiar figure, riding up and down in his one-horse buggy, selling Liberty Bonds and War Savings Stamps.

Delta, like the rest of America, was totally, hotly, devoutly patriotic in World War I. Home-front organizations—the Red Cross, the Liberty Loan Army, the Civil Council of Defense, and victory gardens—manifested a single-minded national zeal unmatched before or since. "Can the Kaiser" was the admonition on cartoons showing a devilish face with a spear-topped helmet scrunched down inside a Mason fruit jar.

After the war, though there then was no military unit of any kind at the confluence, the area got an armory. The Colorado General Assembly had provided for the building of several state armories and sent a state quartermaster's officer to look Delta over as one of the possible sites. By this time, Captain Charlesworth was Lieutenant Colonel Charlesworth. He told the officer that, if Delta could be given one of the proposed new armories, he would guarantee a rifle company of sixty-five men to occupy and use it. The two-story brick and sandstone structure was built in 1923, in a style now called Egyptian Revival.

The young men of the rifle company trained in the one-floor, two-story-tall armory. Boots sounding like thunder in rhythm, orders cracking like audible lightning. From the balconys above, schoolmates and sweethearts cheered. "It was fun watching them down there," Ione Tyler remembers. Then her voice dwindles: "They didn't know—"

They didn't know that the world's most devastating war—World War II—was just around the corner, waiting for them to get ready, and that many would never return.

Alvin Lee Marts lived on California Mesa, southwest of town, where his family had farmed since coming from Oklahoma in the government resettlement program after the Dust Bowl disaster. Alvin graduated from high school in the spring of 1941, enlisted in the U.S. Navy, got his training in San Diego, and was at Pearl Harbor when the Japanese attacked. He escaped to serve at Midway, Wake, and other South Pacific battles, but he was killed in action off the coast of Salvo Island on November 30, 1942. He served with such distinction that the U.S.S. *Marts* was named for him, his sister Betty going to New York to break the ceremonial bottle of champagne. When the Veterans of Foreign Wars organized a post in Delta, it chose the name "The Lee Marts Post" to honor the boy who would be nineteen forever.

Kelly Calhoun served with equal distinction and even more flair—considering the nature of the man, it could hardly be otherwise. A member of the Navy's Motor Torpedo Boat Squadron in the Southwest Pacific, he reportedly rode that small craft like a mustang at a rodeo. Kelly ramrodded his naval career right through a Presidential Unit Citation, the Purple Heart, and the Silver Star, retiring as a lieutenant commander.

The interminable Korean conflict stretched out beyond meaning for most people; and by the time the war in Vietnam came along, the nation was so far from unquestioning patriotism that it was split right down the middle. And so was Delta, as is exemplified by the writings of two prominent people.

State Sen. Wilson Rockwell and his young son Danny were cattle ranchers east of Black Canyon. Wilson's position in the state capital afforded an overview of the world situation that convinced the Rockwells that the war with Vietnam was wrong. They sold their holdings and moved to Canada. Wilson, author of a number of historical books, also wrote *We Hold These Truths*, explaining the family's decision:

> Although I gladly served for four years in the U.S. Air Force during World War II to help defend this once-great country and its principles against an obvious aggressor, I, as well as my family, were opposed to American's involvement in the Vietnam civil conflict, which we felt was strictly a political war and not in any way necessary for the protection of the United States, its system of government, or its concepts of individual liberty. Paradoxically, it was actually eroding the very fundamentals we supposedly were fighting for. (p. 12)

John M. McGrath—Mike McGrath to fellow high-school students—served as a lieutenant commander in the U.S. Navy, flying armed reconnaissance missions over North Vietnam. On his 178th mission, his plane was shot down, and he was held prisoner of war for six years. When he was released and came home in 1976, he wrote a book, *Prisoner of War: Six Years in Hanoi* describing in words and illustrating with his own drawings the horrible tortures he and his fellow prisoners endured. However Mike McGrath may have felt about the Vietnam War before he entered it, this is how he felt as he wrote the preface to his book: "The Vietnam War—how unpopular it was! Unpopular with the politicians because they could neither explain it nor rally unified national support behind it; unpopular with the armed forces because they were fighting with one arm tied behind their backs, unable to bring the war to a quick and decisive end with the fewest number of casualties."

15

When All the Money–
Rivers Ran Dry

August, 1929. Things had never been better. Riley's trees in Cleland Park were
reaching for the sky; the grass was a thick carpet kids couldn't dent. Cleland Pool
drew a happy, splashing crowd every summer day. The Golf Club was planning a
new clubhouse and laying out another course on top of two-mile-high Grand Mesa,
to be the highest in the world.

Schmidt's Hardware doubled its display space by scooping the second-floor
apartment free of walls. Customers used that elegant cherrywood stairway at will.
The Siecrest twins' battery shop became Siecrest Electric, offering a full range of
appliances and repairs. (When something needed fixing, you could never be sure
which Siecrest you were explaining it to, but whichever one it was would grunt
that it couldn't possibly be done or would take a mighty long time, and then when
you got home, you'd find it had been done already.)

Holly Sugar's new plant was working at full capacity. Anticipating increasing
numbers of migrant workers, the Colony was created, a private street of adobe
houses.

A hundred-thousand-dollar factory to make fertilizer out of the sulfur deposit
was in the works.

Crystal River Railroad was planning to lay track over McClure Pass, a shortcut
from the confluence to Denver. A three-runway airport east of town was in the
planning stage.

Delta County had just swept the State Fair.

The most significant sign of unprecedented boom times was when one of the town's two weekly newspapers went daily. The *Delta County Independent* became the *Delta Daily Independent*. There was that much good news and that many advertisers to support its distribution.

People had more money to spend than they'd ever had before, and all indications were that it would keep on rolling in. Anybody with gumption and two idle dollars was investing in Wall Street, where stocks were rising so fast that you had to tally up your on-paper "take" each week, just to see how much richer you had become since last Friday.

One of the play-it-big boys was a young Denver lawyer named Henry Ricketson. Beginning in 1923 with six hundred borrowed dollars, he built up a chain of thirty theaters, sold out to Fox Intermountain for half a million, and then went to work for Fox as division manager.

In 1927, Ricketson noted that Delta's home-owned Variety Theater, wedged between two stores, wasn't big or classy enough for the crowds coming to watch Tom Mix, Greta Garbo, and the world events depicted in the latest newsreel. So Ricketson built a new theater in Delta. Designed in the era of Grauman's Chinese in Hollywood, the Egyptian too was a "theme" theater. This was soon after the discovery of King Tut's tomb; anything Egyptian was the rage. The theme was carried throughout the building. There were Egyptian figures at work and war in bas-relief on the tapered facade. Heavy cornices adorned roof and marquee. Doors and poster windows were framed in Egyptian hieroglyphics. Carpeting was luxurious. Stairs to the powder room were designed to display gowns and the beauties wearing them (in that era, movie-going was a social event; people came to be seen as well as to see). Luxurious loge seats overlooked the main seating, which swept past Egyptian niche lamps and down to a stage large enough to accommodate vaudeville acts. Invisible except from outside, the stage area towered two stories high, to allow room for pulling up velvet curtains, scenery, and backdrops. The grand opening rites included a pipe-organ prologue, vaudeville acts, and a special showing of *Seventh Heaven*.

In February, Dr. A. H. Stockham sold his share of the flour mill. "To be free to enjoy life," he explained. Nobody noticed that sale until later. But he didn't resign as president of the First National Bank. Nobody noted that, either. Why should they? Profits from farms and orchards were higher than they'd ever been. Money flowed free; new projects leaped to mind and into being with magical ease and speed. The world had come out on a beautiful plateau and was going to stay there forever.

Jack Dempsey was training to come back into the ring after the Tunny "long

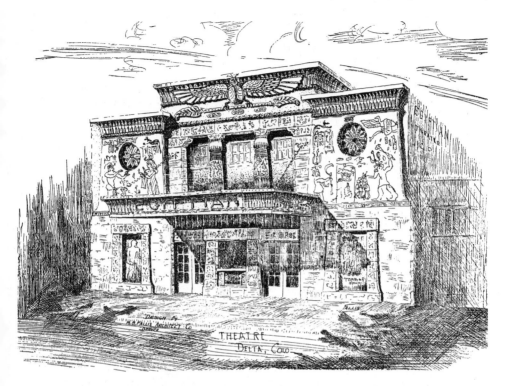

Egyptian Theater, Delta, Colorado, birthplace of the national "Bank Night" craze that saved the country's theaters during the Depression. Drawing by building's architect, M. S. Fallis. From Delta County Independent, *September 28, 1928.*

count." Early in October, 1929, John Maxwell of Delta and Ray Alvis, Dempsey's fight-scheduler, were in Chicago meeting with the Champ concerning future bouts. Whether Jack Dempsey had invested any of his money in Delta is unknown. Like everyone else with any money to play with in those last months of the twenties boom, he had put money in lands and margins, losing over three million dollars in that one year. At least he kept informed—it was from Jack Dempsey, there in Chicago, that John Maxwell learned that Delta's First National Bank was closing its doors, its officers under indictment.

The bank trouble had started almost a year earlier. Cashier Carey B. Adams had been found guilty of using bank money to buy four thousand head of sheep in a deal with his cousin. He was sentenced to five months in jail.

The town took it as an isolated incident, nasty but not indicative of anything bigger. Adams served his months, and that was that. But then the Aetna Casualty and Surety Company canceled its bond with the bank because of "inadequate reporting," leading to withdrawal of city and county funds. At the bank, nothing changed; the flag still flew atop the pointed tower, and the brass door latch and pink granite portico pillar were shining clean.

On Tuesday, September 17, 1929, a bank examiner came to inspect the First National's books—tipped off, it was surmised, by a disgruntled Carey Adams. The bank's officials were present throughout the process: Dr. Albert H. Stockham, president; Walter G. Hillman, vice-president; assistant cashier Seth J. Kyffin; and others of the board. But on Friday it was noted that Walter Hillman was absent. That night his body was discovered at his ranch, a bullet in the head.

On Saturday, early customers found the bank closed and a note on the door that read, in part: "Bank examiners now in charge disclosed the fact day before yesterday that some $22,000 of the funds of the bank had been taken by the vice president, Walter G. Hillman. Besides this there is about $18,000 of paper in the bank due to the operations of Walter G. Hillman."

On the advice of lawyer Millard Fairlamb, this blame-pointing note was quickly removed, but the accusation stuck; in the public mind, Hillman was the culprit, though he had lived an open and exemplary life, had been active in church work, and had served scrupulously as treasurer during the construction of the expensive Methodist church. Dead, he could not defend himself.

The bank went into receivership. The final accounting found it nearly a hundred thousand dollars short. Stockham offered to turn over everything he owned to help make up the loss, but depositors got only thirty cents on the dollar.

Based on accusations by Adams and Kyffin, Dr. Stockham was charged with "conspiracy to violate national banking laws." His accusers also were charged. Kyffin was convicted and served time in Leavenworth. Adams skipped and might have made it to Mexico, except that his wife flubbed by sending his clothes to his new name. He was picked up boarding a steamship and pled guilty to manipulating farm venture funds and embezzling government pension funds.

At Dr. Stockham's trial in the Denver District Federal Court, the "prosecution presented evidence of a robbery plot to cover up the discrepancies and entered in evidence forgeries of the names of several Deltans. In a brilliant defense, Millard Fairlamb presented Stockham as a poor seventy-eight-year-old man who had suffered a fall from a tree in 1923 and was simply unable to run the affairs of a bank." It was noted that Dr. Stockham had raised Carey B. Adams from childhood and had been Hillman's partner for many years. He was acquitted.

The failure of the First National Bank was only the first blow. Soon the town and the world were numb with shock at what was happening.

A week before the bank examiners came to Delta, the president of the bank of Telluride confessed to swindling half a million dollars. Some time previously,

Grand Junction had suffered its first bank failure due to embezzlement, when the Mesa County Bank closed its doors, paying only twenty-five cents on the dollar. Other local banks failed in Delta, Austin, and Crawford.

Three weeks after the Delta bank scandal, the stock market crashed in New York City. Men who had brought it on by similar financial shenanigans began jumping out of skyscraper windows. Three days later, the market crashed again. The Great Depression had begun. On the day the paper carried that news, it also noted that Aimee Semple McPherson was in court for mismanagement of church funds. Being in court didn't faze Aimee. She just went ahead with her plans to visit the Holy Land.

The striking building on the corner of Third and Main never functioned as a bank again. Several businesses have occupied it since. It got an inside stairway after Millard Fairlamb bought the grocery store half and put his law offices upstairs. As for the bank half, Tom Coats sold his bakery and opened a tavern there, calling it "Tom's Inn." He painted that name in big white letters on the cone of the tower; you could see it a mile away. Then he hired Walter Crawley, an expert woodworker, to tour saloons in the old mining towns—Ouray, Telluride, and Silverton—and build in Tom's Inn a bar that would top even those fancy Victorian fixtures. Sometime during subsequent ownerships, the bar was sold to an out-of-towner and removed. The last tavern owners in the building were Daniel and Rosalie Springer, who dubbed it "The Last Chance" and painted *that* name on the tower, where it remained an ironic commentary during the decades when the building stood empty and the town was dwindling.

The Great Depression didn't grind life down as relentlessly at the lush confluence of rivers as it did in the cement deserts of big cities or the wind-scoured deserts of the Dust Bowl. Farm families always had had large vegetable gardens and orchards, and in town the yard between back porch and alley produced a lot of food if carefully planted in rotation. What life-sustaining calories were not grown in town could be traded for from the country folk.

There was, to be sure, almost no cash, but there was barter. If your electric iron quit, you could get it fixed at Siecrest Electric for a bushel of canning tomatoes, or in winter for a dozen quarts of tomatoes you had canned—Myrtle Siecrest to wash and return the Mason jars, of course. But if the iron needed a new cord, Siecrest's parts supplier back in Akron did not take tomatoes. In that case, your children need not go wrinkled to school. You reactivated the old flatirons from doorstop duty and fired up the coal cookstove. Almost every home still had one.

As for coal, it didn't necessarily cost real minted money. After the coal trust price-squeezed small mines into closing, many miners—about the only men still drawing pay checks—lost their jobs. They and other men went into the abandoned tunnels with pick, shovel, and wheelbarrow to dig their winter's supply.

But businesses can't exist on barter or a backyard garden. Stores lowered prices again and again. But bacon at twelve cents a pound, and tennis shoes at thirty-nine cents a pair are no bargain if there aren't that many pennies in your purse. People began stealing food. A truckload of meat, flour, and canned goods was stolen from Delta Market. Robbers took two hundred quarts of canned fruit and vegetables from the Greathouse family cellar on California Mesa.

The D&RG Railroad, running in the red because of the Depression and competition from the automobile, reduced Salt Lake City runs to one every ten days. Then, at the confluence, through runs ceased altogether. With completion of the Dotsero cut-off, the area became a mere siding for cross-continental rails.

Seeing children come to school without the usual lard bucket holding sandwich, apple, and cookie, the PTA begged food donations and, with the Girl Reserves help, made soup available to lunchless children at school. Later the government supplied the food—rice by the ton, a thousand pounds of pork. PTA mothers prepared and dished it out.

The Federal Relief Administration ran out of funds, Colorado was ordered to feed its own poor, and the state passed the order on to the county. But the county tax cupboard was bare. People without money for shoes can't pay taxes. To induce payment, the county offered to forgive interest payments for those who would pay up back taxes. Few could. Moreover, twelve thousand taxable acres of farmland had been abandoned because the land seeped up when drainage ditches could not be maintained.

To run the county and feed the poor, the county issued Unemployment Relief Automobile Tags. The cost of the UR tag was linked to the value of the car. If your auto was worth up to $50, you paid $2; people who owned cars valued from $1,000 to $1,500 paid $20. (At this time, a Model-A Ford sedan cost about $800.) Tags for cars worth over $5,000 cost $60. This definitely was a "tax-the-rich" measure. And the confluence did have its moneyed people right through the Depression, conservative people quietly getting richer under the very conditions that ruined the less well established. UR tags were declared unconstitutional, and all the money had to be refunded.

It wasn't just local residents who needed food. Incoming flatbed railroad cars were fringed with the legs of men desperately ranging the nation trying to find work to feed families back home. Their numbers were so great, their plight so grim, that the railroads ignored them, letting them ride openly for free. At train stops, the men would rove the streets, asking for work and food, door to door, store to store.

Until the Depression, Delta County had cared for its long-term penniless at the county poor farm south of town. Inmates who were able to work tilled the institution's fields and gardens to grow food for all. Those unable to work were cared for at public expense, but there were not many of these; most who might have qualified took pride in proving that they didn't need to. Sadie Dingman, for instance. When Sadie was eight, she lost both hands above the wrists while feeding sorghum stalks into the family molasses mill. Without hands or prostheses, by bending her elbows adroitly, Sadie could write, sew, cook, garden, and milk cows—the latter only when husband and son were out riding the range.

As the Depression ground on, the needs of the poor far exceeded the county's ability to meet them. Some people simply were too old to work. When an old-age pension was set up, sixty-one people put in applications, but only $585 was available; nobody got more than ten dollars. Starr Nelson began holding meetings about the California Townsend Plan, which, years later and with many changes, became Social Security.

When times get desperately bad, two things seem to prosper—a chemical means of escaping unbearable reality, and gambling. Speakeasies were not confined to big cities in the stressful days of the Depression. Though town, state, and nation went dry, certain houses on Columbia Street surreptitiously offered the comfort of oblivion, selling stilled or bathtub gin. Marijuana flourished. Never entirely absent since the first Chihuahuans planted it along the railroad track, marijuana, planted between masking rows of corn, became a main Depression crop on some Peach Valley farms.

As for gambling, if you have only enough money for supper and breakfast, it doesn't seem like such bad money management to spend the breakfast money on a chance to make enough to eat all next month.

Chain letters appealed to that thinking. You got a letter asking that you send a dime to each of the ten people listed and then send a similar request to ten new people, taking off the top name and adding your own. (The letter usually carried a curse for failing to carry through—Jesus or somebody would strike you dead.) The arithmetic was awesome. If only a fourth of the people complied, you'd be rich, and it only cost ten dimes plus a few two-cent stamps. The chain-letter mail got so heavy that post offices all over the United States, just as in Delta, had to hire extra men and trucks to handle it. They passed a law against chain letters.

One of the town's newspapers stayed alive on such desperation-driven gambling. Depression hit newspapers harder than most enterprises. A grocery store might survive because people had to eat, but news is notably indigestible. Subscribers lapsed, and advertisers saw no gain in running ads if people had no money with which to buy.

To stay afloat in the hard times, the *Tribune* tried something that had worked twice before—a popularity contest, with a brand new automobile as the prize. To cast a vote for your favorite among the contestants, you bought a subscription to the newspaper and pressured friends and relatives to do likewise. And, of course, the contestants themselves were out there hustling subscriptions like mad.

In 1916, the prize had been a Ford touring car; in 1926, a Chrysler. This time, desperate in the maw of the Depression, they went all out, putting up a real sedan, a Chevrolet worth $856.

The campaign was a smashing success. So many subscriptions were sold that a permanent bulge was created in the yearly renewal accounts. That annual bulge was apparent even after the *Tribune* was bought by the *Delta County Independent,* as Millie Beale noted when she was DCI office manager thirty-five years later.

The Civilian Conservation Corps (CCC) was set up to educate as well as to provide financial relief. The young men who participated, aged eighteen to twenty-five, were mainly inner-city youths sent into the wilds and woods of America to work hard, study hard, and learn a different way of life. Delta was given a quota of twenty-eight. Each of the boys was issued uniforms and paid about thirty dollars a month, of which twenty-five had to be sent home to help the folks. They lived in tent barracks and had real military officers directing them.

The real military officers, however, had only limited authority. One sergeant was thoroughly nonplussed when he had to stand by while his corps protested a diet of unmitigated rice by rising in unison and leaving the mess tent—a mutiny that in the real army would have put them all in the modern equivalent of leg irons.

There is no evidence in newspapers or memories of any trouble with CCC boys. They did useful and beautiful work. They built the ninety-mile Divide Road, formerly a chuckwagon trail, from end to end of the Uncompahgre Plateau. They cut stone for guard rails and culvert ends as beautifully as that pioneer carver, Jeffers, could have done. For the stone house on Land's End, however, they did not cut the black lava rock but found and fitted angle to angle, as if they were having fun working a jigsaw puzzle.

Of the approximately six thousand Dust Bowl refugees, some 110 families were resettled on eight thousand acres of the Western Slope, many on Uncompahgre Valley acreage that the government selected as having "some of the most productive land in the United States; mild winters, cool summers, freedom from floods, droughts, blizzards, tornadoes, insect pests, and with an abundance of water for irrigation." Just about everything those plains farmers didn't have where they came from. The government built houses for them, still recognizable by their tight, elbows-tucked-in look. Four tiny rooms downstairs, a steep stair to two tiny rooms upstairs under a steep little roof. Though the families received land, farm equipment, a house, outbuildings, and stock, this was not government relief. These settlers' futures were mortgaged, and they paid up. This quiet, almost forgotten deal proved profitable for both the individual and the government.

Almost all of the money the government spent during the Depression to aid people financially also entailed some kind of work on their part that would result in lasting benefit to the community. Works Progress Administration (WPA) men built the bridge across the Gunnison for quicker, easier access to Escalante Canyon. The Rural Electrification Administration brought electricity to farm homes all around the confluence. Buildings erected by the government during those times were designed for beauty, endurance, and immediate aid to the community through worker pay and purchase of materials.

Like other early-day post offices, the one in Delta tended to be located wherever the postmaster lived or did business—in cubbyholes at the back of a drugstore or grocery or in somebody's kitchen. But it had to settle down in one place when the U.S. government decided to help the Depression-paralyzed local economy by erecting a government-financed post office building. The question was where. Only by concentrated force—and buying Mrs. Mathers' Fourth and Meeker corner—did the city fathers keep it from being built twelve long blocks from anything, just because the government already owned some land down at the south end of town.

The structure, made of cream brick and white marble with granite steps, is described as "Starved Classic" on the application for nomination to the National Register of Historic Places. For the National Register, you must always designate type and period of architecture. For instance, the Colorado National Guard Armory (1920) directly behind the post office is labeled "Egyptian Revival," and the old Colorado Bank and Trust building that is now the Delta City Hall is called "Beaux-Arts Vernacular."

The Delta Post Office is cited as "the finest example of a Neo-Classical interpretation in the Starved Classic form in Colorado." Indeed, the wood and tile work are beautiful, and the bas-relief panels at either end of the lobby are without peer among the post offices the government built during that era. And those panels have a story.

During the Depression, the government paid artists and writers not for breathing or being hungry, but for contributing. WPA writers produced books about this nation, describing almost every town in existence. For the Delta Post Office, the WPA paid Mary B. Kittridge to do those two bas-relief murals. They were supposed to be about pioneer days, covered wagons, cowboys, and Indians; and one of them is. The murals were executed a while after the post office was put into use. With people coming in and out, Mary Kittridge put up a bunting screen between her and curious eyes. She had finished one wall and was invisibly at work on the other when Gordon Hodgin lifted the curtain to see how she was doing. He was astonished at what he saw. "Why, those look like—"

"Greek maidens," Mary agreed. "I thought that since Delta gets its name from the Greek letter *D*, it would be appropriate to have Greek maidens on one wall."

The National Register of Historic Places ignored those maidens when it accepted the nomination.

The Great Depression and the wildcat financial operations that brought it on caused many Americans to become permanently distrustful of banks. Sacrificing interest for security, they hid money in their homes—inside slit mattresses, behind loose fireplace bricks, under trap floorboards. When the government, trying to get all that wealth back into profitable circulation, made it illegal to hoard gold, they hid paper money.

One such stash survived the stasher and his memory of where it was. A carpenter and crew discovered it while tearing down a Meeker Street house to make way for a new one. When the men pried off the vertical framing boards around a door, they found that the narrow slot between frame and stud had been stuffed with paper dollars—ones to twenties. No one knew which of several previous owners had done the stashing.

General awareness of such hoarding probably led to what is known as the "hog-pen murder."

Russell Browning, described as "a quiet person who tended strictly to his own business, never confided in anyone, seldom chatted with neighbors," was a bachelor of obvious means, running a good-sized herd of cattle on the Uncompahgre Plateau. But he spent noticeably few dollars and did no banking whatever that anybody knew about, not even after he sold the cattle and moved to a farm and two-story house in North Delta.

The whereabouts of Browning's invisible wealth came under discussion one night in 1933 at a Columbia Street speakeasy shack. After sufficient alcoholic priming, the owner, Lloyd Frady, and customer William Cody Kelly borrowed a car and, with Mrs. Kelly at the wheel, drove to the home of the fifty-three-year-old loner to "hold him up." This was not long after Oklahoma bandit Pretty Boy Floyd had visited Delta, his passage traced and announced by Denver detectives. Perhaps Pretty Boy's visit inspired Frady and Kelly to imitation.

When Browning came to the door, kerosene lamp in hand, to see who had presumed to knock, Kelly lured him out to the pigpens by posing as a Kansas City trucker interested in buying hogs. After putting up a fight that left blood all over the ground and the fence, Browning was knocked out of commission by a bash to the skull and kept that way by barbed wire twisted around his wrists and ankles. His unconscious body was thrown over the fence, where the hogs, it was assumed, would be so ravened by the smell of blood that they would eat him.

Back in the house, Kelly and Frady ransacked the rooms for Browning's hoarded wealth. No one knows whether the old bachelor had any, because, after they ran low on matches, the two killers used twists of lighted paper to see with. The fire got out of hand, and the house burned down.

Browning was not dead when neighbors, roused by the fire, found him, but he died on the way to a doctor. The tire tracks were traced to Frady's shack, and he confessed, detailing the crime in return for promise of a reduced sentence. Kelly and his wife were traced to Kentucky and returned to Delta by the Lockhart family—Sheriff Ray Lockhart and deputy son Ted taking turns guarding the prisoners, Mrs. Lockhart being deputized because it "was compulsory that a matron accompany any woman prisoner being taken from one place to another." Kelly received the death sentence and became the first convict to be executed in Colorado's new gas chamber.

The "soap-kettle murders," the area's other macabre crime, even more gruesome, took place not in Delta County, but over on California Mesa in Montrose County in December, 1917. The crime had such an effect on friends and neighbors and such wide and long-lived publicity that it cannot be omitted from a history of the area. Delta County Undersheriff J. T. Beatty handled the case in the absence of Montrose Sheriff Gill, who was in Kansas at the time testifying in the trial of a World War I draft dodger.

John, aged thirty-four, and his son Otis, then twelve, were living with John's old mother, Nancy Jane, in a crowded boxcar-shaped hovel southwest of town. The boy was accused of taking $1.35 from his grandmother's purse, so John took him out back to punish him. When the boy returned and crawled into bed with his father, he was still whimpering. Later the grandmother was shaken awake by her son; the child had died sometime in the night. "I hurt Otis bad. It was an accident. You've got to help me get rid of the body."

The old woman testified that John held a rifle on her, forcing her to get the cans of lye, mix it with water in the huge iron soap kettle in the back yard, and build the fire to bring it to a boil. Making smooth lye soap of animal fat, flesh, bone, and marrow was part of almost every butchering. They both knew how to do it.

Afterward John went to bed and actually went to sleep, as if what he'd done had drained him. Whether in retribution for his beating her grandson to death, or out of anger at what he had forced her to do, or, as she said at the trial, because she feared that her son would kill her to be free of the only witness to his crime, she decided to get rid of John. She axed him in his sleep and kindled the fire under the kettle again.

But Nancy Jane lacked lye or strength enough to do a thorough job. Fragments of bone discovered by Sheriff Beatty were pronounced human by the Pinkerton detective. She was tried and convicted, but the court, in an early instance of justice taking mental illness into consideration, commuted the death sentence to life in an asylum.

In the middle of the Depression, when businesses of all kinds were failing, when people were standing in line at bakeries to get day-old bread for a quarter per burlap sackful, the nation's movie houses were packed and prospering. Standing outside theater doors from the Atlantic to the Pacific, people waited, tickets in hand, trying to get in.

Bank Night. It began on Delta's Main Street.

Hit by the Depression, the beautiful new Egyptian Theater was on the brink of closing. Manager Harry Moore had tried every trick to get people past the ticket booth. Give-away prizes—dishes, radios, toasters, bicycles, a toy car with a real gasoline motor. Beauty contests, country-store nights, amateur nights, on the theory that people would pay to see their kinfolk perform. Nothing boosted attendance for more than a week.

Moore decided to cut tickets from thirty-five cents to two bits. Fox theater manager Ricketson rushed his man Yeager to Delta to try to prevent the suicidal cut. If the Egyptian—brand new and ranked tops among the company's twenty-eight theaters in five Rocky Mountain states—cut tickets below cost, then Montrose and others still surviving in the chain would follow suit. Something had to be done.

Sitting there in front of the Egyptian, Yeager racked his promotion-geared brain. Some kind of hot-shot promo big enough to make people forget the price hike to pay for it. Money, that's what everybody desperately needed. If you could offer ticket-buyers a chance to win money—big money—

Bank Night. On Tuesdays, the slowest night of the week.

In an article years later in the *Saturday Evening Post,* Forbes Parkhill noted that "Yeager didn't waste time thinking up a name, 'Bank Night' told the story." Unable to be present that first Tuesday Bank Night, Yeager telephoned the Egyptian manager to find out the public's reaction to the price hike.

"Terrible," Moore reported, "everybody's squawking."

"And the box-office take?" Yeager asked hopelessly.

"Oh, we've grossed more tonight than in the entire preceding week. The house is spilling over. A thousand people are waiting outside."

You could buy tickets to Bank Night anywhere in town, and it didn't matter whether you got inside or not, you just had to be within hearing. If you heard your name—drawn from "the hat" by a blindfolded child—you had exactly three minutes to get up on the stage and claim your bag of gold. If you didn't make it, your loss would be added to next Tuesday's pot.

Bank Night swept the nation. At one time, five thousand theaters were paying Yeager and Ricketson royalties for using the patented Bank Night promotion that they had initiated in Delta's Egyptian Theater.

16

Just a Bedroom Town?

When transportation depended on horsepower, towns tended to be spaced the distance apart that the slowest means of transportation—a loaded wagon—could comfortably travel in one day. That is, if you lived halfway between two towns, you could reach either one in a little less than half a day, do your business at store, post office, or smith while refueling your horsepower with nosebags of oats, and still get back home before dark. If the town was much farther than half a day, you had to "stay over," going to the expense of hotel room, meals, livery stable fee, and time lost the next day.

When, with the coming of the first cars, a farmer could get to town in half an hour instead of half a day, he tended to drive right on by the neighborhood town, heading for wider variety and cheaper prices. Bigger towns grew, while the little "between" towns faded away.

Who remembers a town downriver of the confluence, ironically named Pride? Or Appleton to the east? Renamed Saxton by the D&RG, Appleton was a packing-shipping point for fruit wagons, with its own bridge over the Gunnison five miles from Delta. The town of Read once clustered school, store, blacksmith, livery stable, and a hotel with a two-story verandah. Only the hotel, now a dwelling, remains. The cowman's town of Roubideau had all that, plus big stockyards and a renowned saloon. Austin once came near rivaling Delta.

As cars got faster and roads got better, the town-thinning process continued. Towns that had shelved smaller towns were themselves put on the shelf. They became just nice places to live. The few businesses surviving among Main Street's empty buildings were used chiefly to fill unanticipated needs between shopping trips to bigger places.

In the 1960s and 1970s, Delta was in that situation. Smoother, wider highways to the two municipalities it lies between—Montrose and Grand Junction—made it easier for the buying public to bypass the confluence, especially after Highway 50 was made four lanes to Montrose.

Added to that, trade from the North Fork was reduced because of a slow-down in coal mining. The Holly Sugar factory closed. Coors Beer withdrew its backing of barley farming. A coal company took over the Holly Sugar silos and did well for a time, but succumbed to the local 1984–85 depression. Every closing meant lost jobs; the young working population was trickling away like water from a creviced dam.

Agriculture went into a phase called "extraction farming," a form of land mining. Everything possible was utilized to get maximum tonnage out of the ground— bigger, faster equipment (reducing available jobs), poisons to eliminate competitive nibblers (about that time, the cattail marshes lost their blackbird flocks), chemicals to make the earth produce like there was no tomorrow. For some, there wasn't. That a number of these "extraction" farmers went broke by overmortgaging for equipment may have been good for future users of the soil, but it didn't help the current economy.

Perhaps most significantly for the town's sense of self and individuality, its newspaper spoke with an outside voice. Publisher Gene Wells sold the *Delta County Independent* to its rival, the *Grand Junction Dailey Sentinel,* in 1971. Under outside ownership, the paper covered news events adequately and was nicely printed, but it lacked home-owned hustle and zeal.

This static or dwindling state was not altogether owing to Delta's placement on the map relative to other towns. The oversolicitude of a pioneer woman for her son spot-blighted Main Street for half a century.

Elida Jeffers was married to John Jeffers, builder of many structures in town. But she was the sharp business head in the family. Ostensibly a milliner, she was far more than that, selling anything in the line of apparel that had a profit in it.

Mrs. Jeffers was a New Yorker. Whether she had lived or worked in New York's garment district or not, she operated as if she had. The sidewalk in front of her shop was a calculated part of the store. Clothesracks of ready-mades—dresses, kimonos, petticoats—fluttered in the breeze and brushed temptingly against ladies squeezing by; crate-tables of right-foot shoes (the left foot stayed inside to keep passersby honest) scented the air with leather when the day warmed up.

Her store changed its address frequently, because she also traded in real estate—selling, buying, and moving without notice or advertising. She didn't need to advertise, all that sidewalk merchandise did it for her. Altogether she ended up buying or building nearly a dozen business places on Main. Many of these stores were "half-shell"—that is, built on the front half of a narrow lot with minimal materials and workmanship, housing barbershop, cigar store, hock shop, watchmaker. She accumulated them and the rents they brought.

With her assets as well as those of her husband, Elida Jeffers died a rich woman, leaving her son Welland fixed for life. She made sure he stayed that way by putting some kind of restriction on every inch of Main Street she owned. Welland was assured of drawing rent from all those store buildings for as long as he lived, because he couldn't sell or raze a one of them.

She needn't have done it. Welland took care of himself very well. He bought farmland, choosing tenant farmers wisely. He helped to finance several successful enterprises, including Potato Growers. He was cashier of the Colorado State Bank, which probably meant that he owned part of it.

As for those little half-shell store buildings on Main, he wasn't interested; if he couldn't sell them or tear them down to build better, he'd be durned if he'd spend good money patching them up. When the roof leaked or a window lintel rotted, let the tenant do the fixing.

Main Street suffered. Enterprising businessmen looking for a profitable place to start up something new tended to take one look at those crummy stores and pass this town up. For as long as Welland Jeffers lived and the restrictions held.

Two other women, with the best of intentions, did the same stultifying thing, on a smaller scale, to the industrial-commercial strip along Highway 92. Genevieve Hartig and a friend, wanting to help homeless children elsewhere in the world, donated several lots to the Pearl Buck Foundation, which apparently didn't know what to do with them. They sat there, among the businesses, thickets of that weed-tree called Chinese elm.

To mark the town's hundredth anniversary in 1981, businesses and organizations sponsored the gathering and writing of the town's history. Authored by Deborah V. Doherty, *Delta, Colorado: The First 100 Years* was printed by Larry Jaeger at the *Delta County Independent*. In view of the situation at the time, it seems inevitable that the work would conclude on a depressing note: "Changes in food and stock raising have been so swift, so drastic in a community that has always appreciated a slower pace, that the independent farmers and ranchers themselves seem to be foundering. The same is apparent in the lives of the businessmen of the community, as they struggle with unfair competition from large nearby population areas that are easily accessible to the highly mobile Delta county resident."

Progress was also bucking an entrenched nostalgia. Most enterprises were owned by sons and grandsons of pioneers; some were loathe to see new projects disrupt

Little Welland Jeffers (white shirt, knee pants) looking on as stone-mason father in 1892 added Delta County Bank building to Main Street. No one knew that the "half-shell" store buildings his mother financed would blight Main until Welland's death. Courtesy of Delta County Historical Society.

the cherished "way things have always been." Using city council and bankers' clout, they bucked the converging currents of change.

When Bob Berry and wife Lurleene ("Toots") came to the confluence from Oklahoma during the Dust Bowl exodus, they operated a laundromat. The business outgrew its dingy space and old fixtures—twenty wringer washing machines, each with two galvanized washtubs for rinsing. Berry, a building contractor back home and later in Delta County, decided to build a large, new, and very modern laundromat. He had the money, he had acquired the land—town lots he bought at Palmer and First, inside the proper zoning lines. All he needed was a city permit. The city wouldn't grant it. "Never gave us any good reason," Toots says now. "Just the 'father-son' kind of town it was then. Bob wasn't a son of anybody on Main street."

After several attempts to get an official okay, Bob started building anyhow, laying up the brick while townspeople stopped by to watch this piece of insubordination in action. Occasionally somebody in authority came to emphasize how illegitimate he was. He just went on laying brick.

The story got started and still circulates that the harassment forced Bob to perch Toots on a pile of brick armed with a shotgun to guard him while he worked. She says that is not true; "Bob just went on working and when he was about ready to put on the roof, the mayor came around and growled, 'Come on down to the city hall and get your building permit.'"

While business was dwindling, city-county government was growing. The city hall and the county courthouse moved several times, each time into structures that at least doubled capacity. The original stockaded log courthouse–town hall, with the adjoining jail that couldn't hold its first prisoner overnight, eventually was replaced by a square two-story brick building on Courthouse Square. But a tighter jail was built first—the enforced discomfiture of prisoners being more important than the comfort of county clerks. The two-man replacement jail, made of planks nailed flat on each other like brick, still exists; you can see it in the fenced courtyard behind the Museum. It successfully resisted every escape attempt. The same can't be said of its larger successor made of soft Rollins brick. The usual getaway procedure was to keep back your supper teaspoon and tunnel through the soft brick after dark. The newspaper, screaming that a new jail was needed more than a water system, grimly tallied nine breakouts in six weeks. The old square courthouse gave place to a three-story, three-winged structure that housed the jail on one floor until government and crime outgrew the space. The new jail, housing people who haven't done right, is almost as large as the courthouse, whose *raison d'être* is doing right by people. Together the two structures and an annex have roofed over most of the grass on Courthouse Square.

Expansion of government and jail facilities is not a reflection of local population growth. In this matter, the confluence is no different from any other community that is a county seat. The business of government grows, almost regardless of population. In particular, the disproportionate expansion of space for prisoners reflects both the nationwide increase in crime and government regulations on how convicts shall be treated. Prisoners have had little luck escaping from the new jail by making holes in it, but a law library is now available to inmates of the county jail and to those in the state Correction Facility (formerly the Honor Camp) who seek legal loopholes.

A watershed in the way the town of Delta would be regarded for the foreseeable future occurred when city and county decided against having another prison in the area. Along with a number of communities with similar survival problems, Delta submitted "bids" for the facility because of the boost it might bring to the local economy—short-term during construction and longer-term in added jobs.

Having a state prison in the area was not all bad, as Delta knew from experience with the one out on the Roubideau. At least not as long as it was run as an honor camp for young "achievers" who had conducted themselves in jails elsewhere in such a manner as to be deemed worthy to "graduate" to a freer, transitional campus preparing them for final commencement rites and return to life outside. These boys contributed many hours of "free" labor to community projects and seldom tried to escape, perhaps because they knew they would have to cross a lot of empty desert wearing shoe-soles cut with a distinguishing mark that reads like a road map.

Proposed site of the second state prison was on land the city acquired when it bought water rights to several stream drainages on the slope of Grand Mesa north of town—land and water it no longer needed after Project Seven brought town water in from the south. To the state, the site was ideal—isolated enough to discourage escape attempts, yet with towns accessible to personnel. Pressured by several town chambers of commerce, state officials narrowed the choice down to Delta and one other bidder.

That was when the opposition got into gear. Protesters pointed out that, with two state prisons—large and subject to unlimited expansion—and with a new county jail just slightly smaller than the Taj Mahal, Delta would be labeled a prison town. Like Canon City to Colorado residents—"Shape up, son, if you don't want to end up at Canon City." Like Leavenworth to Kansans, like Alcatraz to Californians.

The offer was withdrawn, as local people decided to look for other means of survival. The same decision was made in 1994, when once again a state prison was proposed, this time in Peach Valley.

In the 1960s, there was a movement to spruce up the town, modernize it, cover up all those old-fashioned cornices that edged the roofs like crochet done in stone, hide those arched-eyebrow second-story windows that stared at each other across Main Street, making the town look "dowdy and passé."

Storefronts were slicked up with sheets of painted metal. Permanent plastic sidewalk roofs replaced those antiquated canvas awnings that had to be cranked down each morning and cranked up again come night. The spruce-up didn't help, it just smoothed away the character of the store buildings and street.

Rosy Glenn tried everything in the books to hang on, including converting his vast old barn of a building into a mall. To no avail.

Safeway pulled out, but you couldn't blame that altogether on hard times. After decades with Safeway, Manager Frank Voutaz was "terminated" a few months before he was due for retirement. Perhaps somebody in New York, or wherever,

Hitching rail at Hunt's Hardware was scalloped by bored horses with nothing to do but gnaw wood while the boss tended to business. Courtesy of Delta County Historical Society.

thought the financial slump at this one store was Frank's fault. The town didn't agree. Without boycott or concerted action of any kind, folks just stopped going through Safeway's door. J. C. Penny took Frank on and was glad to get him, but not even the town's loyalty to Frank could save Penney's Delta store. Montgomery Ward, too, closed its retail store and catalog office.

The pioneer store called Garrets Mercantile, that had been owned time out of mind by the Renfrow family, sold out for good. But first, trying to stave things off, Mel Renfrow opened a branch store in one of the empty buildings up the street, creating an outlet for goods he could sell at shopper-drawing bargain rates because he bought them at bankruptcy sales throughout the mountain states. That helped for a while.

Remington's shut its doors like closing book covers on two of the town's favorite stories. The first is the double success story of the two partners who created Remington-Elliott Men's Shoes and Clothing Store. Avon Remington, a Yale graduate, came west to be cured of tuberculosis, and was. Although he already had lost one lung, he lived a long and successful life. Caleb Elliott came west to get rich, and did. He began by peddling lamp fuel up and down streets and countryside by horse and buggy—earning him the permanent name of "Coal-Oil Johnnie." While doing so, he kept his eyes open for profitable real estate turns and found them, mainly in Peach Valley, east of town. Nationally publicized by the developing company, the land out there looked good and paid poor. Two or three years was as long as most easterners hung on before moving out and letting the title lapse to the mortgage holder. Coal-Oil Johnnie bought up these turn-backs as often as he could and sold and resold just as often. He got rich—at that and as a full but inactive partner in Remington-Elliott, and by selling insurance. Rich enough to add one more to the row of fine, ornate houses on the rim of Garnet Mesa looking down over the town.

The other story is sad but reflects so poignantly the goodness of this town that it should be included. Librarian Eveline Nutter told the story about the woman with whom she had played games as a child, enjoyed formal teas as a matron, and, like the rest of the town, looked after always. Mrs. Remington, now in her seventies, had crossed the street to the library. Eveline said gently, "Go back home, dear, and change your dress, you've spilled something." When she had gone, Eveline explained:

Sweet, tiny Mrs. Remington, the only child of wealthy Dr. Braisted, had trouble doing things the way other people did, and leaving things lie. When she went downtown, she carried a large purse and would slip almost anything into it—jewelry, a paring knife, a piece of her beef sandwich, a pair of kid gloves. The whole town knew and loved her nonetheless. Mr. Remington knew and said nothing, just passed the word that people should keep track of what she took, and he would return the items or pay for them. The town not being populated entirely by angels, Mr. Remington occasionally may have been billed for things his wife never saw; if so, he didn't complain.

The same leeway was given Elmer Barnes' dog. There was an ordinance against unleashed dogs downtown, but the law wouldn't dream of impounding Elmer's.

Elmer was perpetually middle-aged in a puckish sort of way. He was different, outrageous, and the town loved him for it. At a time of strict coat-and-tie conformity in male attire, Elmer wore a gnomish straw hat with a foot-long pheasant feather jutting back, and in winter a coonskin cap wagging a long tail. He practiced carpentry just well enough to make an easy living at it, but not so well that the world wouldn't let him do anything else. And he preferred—or attracted—non-serious carpentry such as the "therapeutic" stables he built for movie stars' horses when *True Grit* and *How the West Was Won* were being filmed in this area. Every stall had to be identical to the one the inhabiting horse was accustomed to back in Hollywood, so the animal wouldn't get psychotically homesick.

In his yard, Elmer grew primitive corn—that is, corn in which each kernel has its own husk—just as a reminder of the crudities well-bred corn is rooted in. And he performed a similar function for the human race once or twice a year. On these occasions, after eating lunch at Terrill's Cafe with his friend Judge Kelly Calhoun or editor Jim Cinnamon or somebody, Elmer would come outside, stand in front of the open door, and hog-call folks to come and get it, "Here, Piggy, Piggy, Piggy," at the top of his lungs.

That done, Elmer would reach down to touch his dog, releasing it to jump and bark—you could always tell what store Elmer was in, because his dog sat motionless outside like a placemarker—and prepare to say something Elmerish. This time it might be: "Everybody is two people, the person you think you are and the person this town thinks you are. Two entirely different people. They don't even know each other."

One industry that did not dwindle was facilities providing food for people to eat on the spot. Restaurants and eateries of one kind or another opened, closed, and reopened under changed management over and over; but their numbers increased rather than otherwise, as more and more women worked at jobs outside the home. Instead of a home-cooked, after-church Sunday dinner for relatives and friends, the family and guests would eat out. Hamburger, pizza, and quick-chicken places prospered.

Shops dependent upon home sewing—yardage stores, variety stores, sewing-machine outlets—disappeared or holed up in a corner of a department store, as working women found less time to sew. One casualty of the working-woman era was the flowered flour sack. During the Depression, milling companies enticed women to buy bigger by packaging the flour in a square yard of printed cloth. If you bought two sacks, you had enough "free" muslin to make little Betsy a rose-sprigged dress, complete with ruffles and puffed sleeves. This come-on lasted beyond World War II and faded away only as working women began using so little flour they started buying it in five- rather than fifty-pound sacks.

When businesses on all sides were closing or trying to avoid closure by changing hands, McKnight's Jewelry Store stood firm, as if anchored in time and eternity by the tall pillar clock on the sidewalk out front. A street clock was much needed eighty years ago when wristwatches hadn't been invented, pocket watches were too expensive for many people, and dashboards of vehicles—buggies and wagons—were not equipped with timepieces (dashboards were so called because the mud and stuff kicked up by hooves dashed there rather than in your lap). Jeweler C. D. Allen set up the eight-day clock in 1914. Three years later he moved it, when he took over one of Mrs. Jeffers' half-shell buildings. The clock had to be uprooted one more time, when the widening of U.S. Highway 50 pushed it back.

In the process of re-anchoring, cement got into the works, and it has been a four-day clock ever since. The clock continued to tick away during the ownerships of the McKnight and Hebrew families.

As digital watches became popular, making it cheaper to buy a new battery watch than have the old one repaired, a much-respected vocation, that of watchmaker, seemed threatened with extinction. Work now consists mainly of repairing antique watches and sentimental keepsakes. Because their vocation is becoming so rare, much of the McKnight watch making business comes from elsewhere in the west.

One aspect of the watchmaker's trade disappeared when railroads equipped their engines with radio. In the days when the accuracy of a railroad engineer's watch was all that prevented collisions on heavy-traffic rails, one watchmaker in each division town was certified to keep the railroad running on split-second time. Watchmaker Hal Reid had had that certification in Liberal, Kansas, before coming to Delta. His job was to meet the train, compare his watch with the engineer's, and, if they differed, switch watches and take the wrong one back for overhaul.

The Egyptian Theater survived the doldrums, often because of the manager's creative ideas. One was to host a leap-year wedding on-stage. Looking around for a possible bride and groom, he found Dovie Bullock and John Story of Surface Creek ready and eager. "He wanted a bride, and I wanted to get married," Dovie says now, in her perennially little-girl voice. They were married on-stage in a lavish ceremony that included the works: preacher, flowers, organ music, and free rice.

The advent of the self-service gasoline pump, coupled with the price squeeze when big refinery companies built their own service stations, put many local gasoline vendors out of business. Those homey stations—where friendly owner or attendant stuck his head in the car window to pass the time of day, ask if you needed an oil check, and answer questions about the "best eatery"—became empty swaths of cement with pump bases standing lonely as gravestones.

Only the downtown was dying, however. All around were life and growth. People loved living at the focus of these converging valleys. They kept coming. Subdivisions multiplied around the town, making it a small city, though population data for the area within the city limits did not show that growth. Peach Valley, North Delta, Garnet Mesa, California Mesa expanded and comfortably, elegantly sprawled.

A bedroom town. Was that the town's future? Soul and distinction gone. Like a venerable landmark tree, dying amid thickets of rampant underbrush.

Unlike many towns caught in the between-cities predicament, the community at the confluence kept trying. There were those Main Street Christmas trees. Cut from sheets of plywood and painted green, the Christmas trees topped telephone poles set in the median strip from end to end of Main. Each sawtooth branch was tipped with a light bulb. Standing at attention down the middle of town, they towered over traffic like a string of totem poles. They were impressive, if only for being so big and so numerous. For six weeks out of the year, they certainly made the town distinctive—so far as is known, there was nothing like them on earth.

Perhaps it was the trees' very uniqueness that bothered some people, who noted that they *did* rather look like they had been made by giants in kindergarten. New staff in city hall had other ideas—something more tinselly, more like other towns— and cited the money it cost to plug the butts of all those telephone poles into the median strip every year, wire in the lights, then undo it all after New Year's—not to mention storing the bulky things and keeping the green paint green.

Then there were the median-strip petunia boxes. A Delta Woman's Club's project under Nell Abbott, members did the planting (in redwood boxes made by volunteer carpenters) using donated plants. For six or seven seasons, Main Street in summer was festive with a weaving pink ribbon of flowers waving a welcome, "We like you, traveler. Come again." Perhaps best seen from the air, the ribbon of petunias was enjoyed by pilots of the United Airlines fly-over, one of whom wrote thanking the town for the pretty pink squiggle on his daily route.

With no hose connection, the boxes had to be hand-watered with buckets every day—each merchant being responsible for those in front of his establishment. A hot, heavy job. And it was risky, crossing two lanes of interstate highway traffic, stooping, your rear end barely inches from the semi trucks roaring by. The petunias began to look sick from neglect. The project died.

Sweitzer Lake was going to put the town on the map, and indeed the lake is mapped and described in guidebooks as a fun place for boating, water-skiing, fishing, and picnicking a few miles south of the confluence.

The lake was Morgan Sweitzer's dream. Morgan was raised on a ranch drained by a sluggish, cattail-filled stream winding through bare adobes to the Uncompahgre. Wild ducks and blackbirds loved it. Morgan loved it, too, and dreamed of making it into a lake when he grew up. In 1953, he approached the Colorado Fish and Game Department with a proposition: If they would construct a dam on the draw, he would deed them the land. The dam was built, but Morgan never saw the lake. He was killed in a tractor accident before the dam went in.

Picnic and boating facilities were added after Sweitzer Lake was taken over by the Colorado Parks and Recreation Department. The lake remains a handy place for picnics, and barbecues, boating, fishing, and viewing wild waterfowl nesting in cattail backwaters.

The only industry of its kind in the world came to the confluence area in 1954, when Fred E. Fowler brought Mount Sopris Instrument Company to the confluence. The company makes instruments for locating minerals and other elements from the air, on the ground, or in bore holes deep underground. Sopris scintillators are used from airplanes and four-wheelers, or are carried by hand. The bore-hole probe is a long, slender electronic tool that registers on instruments above-ground what it "sees" thousands of feet below the surface.

Used worldwide from Greenland to Australia, Sopris instruments are so well known to the people who need them that they never have to be advertised, other than in an appearance at an occasional electronics trade show. In addition to supplying profit-making companies, Sopris has provided instruments to the United Nations Development Program for use in Third World countries. Engineer Fred E. Fowler started Sopris Instruments in Boulder in 1951, choosing Boulder because then it was still like a small town. When it ceased to be that, he started looking for another small town and chose Delta.

Speaking in an interview in 1970, he summarized the town's problems and deficiencies about as succinctly as possible:

> Delta needs more industries bringing in outside money. I don't mean heavy industry. The last thing we need is a steel or paper mill to spoil the recreational and enjoyment resources of this area, but we do need light, clean industries to keep our young people with us. As it is, our brightest children simply must move elsewhere after their schooling is complete. There is almost nothing here to employ any technical knowledge.
>
> Delta would be an ideal center for small, clean industries bringing in people who appreciate the advantages that small-town and country living offer.

But a few decades later, Sopris moved to California.

Industrial Park, located a few miles east of the confluence, was set up to accommodate the very kind of enterprise Fred Fowler had in mind. Though businesses in the park tend to come and go—as do entrepreneurial businesses anywhere—it remains home to half a dozen or so industries, making such things as diapers and handmade cabinets to store them in.

Californian Mary Pope came to Delta, the home town of her husband Bill. In 1971, they started a business, Associated Cycles, in North Delta, making the site noticeable by putting a huge ape atop the roof.

Describing the town she saw as "destitute," Mary launched a campaign to let people traveling through on U.S. Highway 50 know why they should stop and look around. After researching the background of scenic and historic attractions in the area, she wrote, illustrated, and self-published eight different "Delta" brochures incorporating the material she had unearthed. Included were the McCarty bank robbery, the dinosaur dig, adventure driving to Escalante Canyon and Uncompahgre Plateau, lists and descriptions of places to eat, sleep, and buy collectibles. The four-page brochures had a professional look and read. In what was perhaps the town's first venture in desktop publishing, she ran them off herself and placed them free of charge in businesses where tourists were likely to see and reach for them. She even built racks (using her motorcycle shop equipment) for displaying the brochures. She designed area-promoting placemats, printed them, and furnished them free to eateries. She lettered and put up points-of-interest signs at Cap Smith's cabin in Escalante Canyon and other side-road attractions. She launched confluence area postcards and colorful flower barrels along Main Street.

A small, tightly-built package of energy, Mary Pope was just a motorcycle blur most of the time. She had a lot of help from something she called the PEOPLE Network. PEOPLE never held meetings, had no officers or minutes. It worked, she said, "to do problem solving in a direct way that gets around the bureaucracy."

"People," Mary observed, "are very interested in getting things done, but the bureaucracy—by its design and the kinds of people attracted to it—is not particularly effective." Someone with that much drive invites roadblocks—especially if the *modus operandi* she called bureaucracy is bypassed. Anyhow, all her efforts weren't enough. Mary Pope gave up and went east. Her brochures are now collectibles.

When druggist Bill Heddles became mayor, he got the clout to accomplish some things he'd wanted done ever since he returned to what he saw as a dying town. His first project was to get rid of those giant, telephone-pole Christmas trees, substituting a more conventional style in Noel town-trim. Then he pushed through Paul Shields' project to install a rolling roof over Cleland Pool, with a plant to heat the water. He did some typically mayoral things such as putting in a sewage-collection system on Garnet Mesa and inveigling the Highway Department to fresh-pave and recurb Main Street; then he put a baseball diamond down by the bridge over the Gunnison.

Bill Heddles was born in 1912 up the North Fork in Paonia. His father died when he was twelve, and his mother went to Chicago to find work. He remembered boarding the train with her, carrying all he owned in one small suitcase. During high school, he worked in a drugstore owned by an old German who lent him the money to go through pharmacy school. After serving in drugstores in several states, he returned to the place of rivers he had known as a child, was employed at Dunbar Drug, and then teamed up with Don Cooper to buy O'Dell's Drugstore, which they renamed Comet Drug. By that time, Bill was president of the Chamber of Commerce. The next year he was elected to the city council.

Although baseball always had ranked high in the town's priorities, at this point there was nowhere for kids or men to bat balls at each other, officially or otherwise. Bill Heddles kept looking at an empty wedge of land between Highway 50, the river, and the Holly Sugar grounds. The wedge wasn't really empty; there were about five hundred car bodies that had been left when a used-car-parts enterprise went out of business, plus piles of old brick and cement chunks dumped there when the city was prettying up somewhere else.

Bill got Lady Bird Johnson to clean up the old cars. That is, he got her national cleanup fund to donate thirty thousand dollars toward it. He did the rest, using his own muscle and his powers of persuasion with Chamber of Commerce and Lion's Club. Scrounging used fencing, telephone poles, piping, and pump, they put up a backstop and lights, laid an underground sprinkling system, and planted trees and grass. The kids who played there called it Bill Heddles Ball Park, and the city made the title official.

Heddles had ideas for the rest of that unused, grubby-looking land: a picnic pavilion, tennis courts, rodeo grounds. He drew up plans to implement them, but they remained on paper.

Bill Heddles Ball Park operated for about four years. Another city regime had other ideas and moved the ball field out to the city reservoir on Garnet Mesa. When Bill Heddles died, his dream was dead, the wedge of land beside the river returning to weeds and trash.

The town grew apathetic. Autumn leaves piled up in doorway corners of empty stores. The fading letters on the tower of the empty Last Chance Saloon seemed prophetic.

The fastest major community project in confluence history was pushed through in six months, from inception to completion, when the outdoor historical drama, *Thunder Mountain Lives Tonight,* opened on the evening of June 6, 1986.

Gus Albert, 82, got the idea and presented it to a chosen handful of Deltans on Dec. 6, 1985. Everybody listened, shivered at the work and money involved, and tacitly begged off. Gus heated them up.

Gus Albert was born in Brooklyn and still sounded like it after half a lifetime living somewhere else. He and Dottie came to Delta and bought Scottie's Cabins—the cabins subject to bed-wetting when the river flooded. He put a hex on the river to keep it in place (of course, some dams had been built upriver in the meantime), tore down Scottie's Cabins, built a luxurious hotel-motel with a dining room that looked out at the river flowing by on the other side of some flowery reeds, added a room for display of local antiquities, landscaped camper space under the cottonwoods, put in a miniature golf course for travelers' evening fun, and then leaned back and waited for tourists.

They didn't come, at least not in the numbers Gus had envisioned. So he got the idea of an outdoor drama—something like the Oberammergau Passion Play, but with cowboys and Indians. After all, the history of the confluence is the stuff of drama—beaver trappers, trading posts, Indians, cowboys, sheep-cattle wars, and shoot-out duels. If travelers heard about it, they'd want to see it. If they stopped to see it, they'd stay at least one night. Benefit the whole town.

Abbott Fay, a history professor retired from Western State College, wrote the script for the historical pageant. Gordon Hodgin led the fundraising effort; counting a Colorado Energy Impact grant and donations, fifty thousand dollars had been raised by opening night. Director Sam Lindblad asked for volunteer actors to fill the cast. Other volunteers contrived scenery, props, and costumes. The Delta Roundup Club provided its arena and grandstands east of town.

On opening night, the play was seen by several hundred spectators, including people from thirty-two states and Liverpool, England.

Thunder Mountain Lives Tonight has played every summer since, June through August, varying in tone and content each year with changes in management and directors. At one point, Utes from the Southern Reservation came up and helped with some of the Indian episodes. Dance instructors Linda Dysart and Linda Speedie volunteered help in choreographing the dances. The character of Dellie Blachly, bank-robbery widow, who had come to be portrayed as a backwoods illiterate, was revised to show her as the cultured woman Dellie really was. Soap-opera renditions of the Ben Lowe–Cash Sampson shoot-out were squared with the facts, dramatic enough in themselves.

People who had known for sure that the effort would fail—didn't everything in this place dwindle away like a piece of driftwood fading out of sight downriver?— began to believe that the drama might become a permanent institution after all, and they looked around for something else that might work.

17

The Confluence

The Last Chance Saloon was the crux, the touchstone.

It looked sturdy enough from the outside. Brick walls—hard brick, not that soft Rollins red. Sandstone foundation slabs that had not budged. Perfectly aligned stonework above the window arches. It was filthy with pigeon droppings, of course, especially under the corner portico. From time to time, Esther Stephens, small keeper of a chunk of the town's conscience, would come with broom and mop to clean things up as high as she could reach.

But the building was falling down from inside out. Leaking roof, rotten floors, sagging stairs, buckling inner walls. A decade or so earlier, Sky Fairlamb had moved his office out, for fear that the upper floor would give way—under the tonnage of the law library accumulated during three generations of Fairlamb lawyers—crash through and kill somebody down below.

Even so—even more so in that condition—the towered building was the town's talisman. The thing that made Delta different. A tangible illustration of its pioneer past. Knowing what a fabulous asset such a structure would be to any retail business it housed, any number of prospective buyers had looked at it eagerly, looked it over with growing doubt, and looked back longingly as they drove away. The building wasn't commercially viable. No conceivable profit would pay off what it would take to make it safe and useful.

What to do about the Last Chance?

Tom Huerkamp says that he is the one who voiced the solution at an informal gathering of the more or less interchangeable members of the Chamber of Commerce and the City Council:

Bulldoze it.

"The Last Chance" saloon, symbolic of all small towns' struggle for survival.

Whether Tom meant it or just made the threat to prod the town into action is a moot point. It worked. "I was the heavy," Tom says. "Everybody got mad at me."

Huerkamp, who through the years has added considerably to the endowment that made him a fearsome fullback on his school team in Minnesota, does rather look as if he could accomplish his threat without recourse to mechanical means. He had proved his competitive drive financially—in the space of two decades he made a from-scratch enterprise, Grand Mesa Office Supplies, into a company operating in four states. And he had proved that he could get his way in civic matters. As an appointee of the county commissioners, he is credited with the quick fundraising that launched the campaign to save Pleasure Forks.

Pleasure Forks, fourteen miles upstream from town, was the lovely canyon-walled place where the Gunnison River and its North Fork come together. It had been the fun and fishing getaway place of the area since the first settlers arrived. Enjoyed as much by a lone fisherman casting a line into the reflection of red cliff as by boaters running the rapids above and below, it was the gathering place of families, clubs, and church groups around picnics spread on wild grass in the shade of cottonwoods. In the early days, there was an open dance pavilion, with ladies whirling their long skirts to the music of fiddles and wash-tub drums under strings of lanterns and the moon. Pleasure Forks belonged to everybody, that had always been taken for granted; some used it well, some did not. It briefly came to world attention when the author's *DCI* article about trashing at Pleasure Forks was picked up by *Reader's Digest* in 1974, translated into a score of languages, and circled back around the globe to reappear locally—in Chinese.

Unknown to most, Pleasure Forks was not located on public land. One fall in the 1980s, users were shocked to see "No Trespassing" signs posted by a real-estate agent at the lovely place they had always considered theirs. Quickly, county commissioners put up ten thousand dollars of the county's share of lottery money to secure a six-month right-to-purchase option on the 844 acres, while they figured out whether the county should finance the purchase and, if so, whether it could. Commissioner Charles Hallenbeck formed the Gunnison River Trust Fund (GRTF) Committee to raise money, and put Tom Huerkamp in charge. With good pre-publicity, the GRTF raised twenty thousand dollars in one event, a combined auction and banquet. This, plus the option money and the donation of two hundred acres by owner William McCluskey, put enough local money on the line to warrant trying for grant money. The Colorado Division of Wildlife and the Bureau of Land Management came through.

As for the Last Chance Saloon rescue squad: With "Bulldoze It" Huerkamp focused threateningly in the limelight, the Downtown Urban Renewal Authority (DURA) was created, with Hartland Clubb as president and Tom Huerkamp as vice-president. DURA set about raising money to save the Last Chance and incidentally to remake the town.

DURA persuaded businesses to turn over the share of sales tax (3⅓ percent) that they were entitled to keep as payment for doing the paperwork involved in collecting it. Then DURA and the city used this resource projection to refinance existing city bonds, extending them and reducing interest. By this means, one million dollars immediately became available—a surprising amount, due in part to an unexpected tax escalation.

If the threat of bulldozing the Last Chance scared people into action, that million dollars yeasted DURA members and the whole town, creating a burst of ideas. Richard Englehart was hired to help them decide on priorities and to head the Parks and Recreation Department for the city. What they settled upon was: new sidewalks, beautiful ones with brickwork patterns and ramps for wheels; decorative lampposts standing over stone planters full of flowers at each corner; trees to be planted all up and down Main Street and a block or two up the side streets;

murals to be painted on the blank sides of several stores; two or three miniparks with shady seats where men could wait for women to get through spending their money; a parking lot equipped to handle RV's and their dumping needs; street signs directing visitors to points of interest; and, oh yes, acquisition and restoration of the Last Chance Saloon—the First National Bank Building.

The project also included gifting the Delta County Historical Society with the old brick firehouse, along with funds to create a museum by doubling the size of the building, remodeling it to suit the storage and display needs of its new use, and landscaping the grounds, as described elsewhere.

A low-interest loan fund was set up, enabling merchants to do storefront renovation, which in most cases meant taking off that sheet metal and restoring the original conservatively ornate brickwork. With greater restraint than was shown in some nearby old mining towns, they did not paint the antique masonry patterns in shades of pink and lavender. The 1930s-style stucco spatter-paint finish that makes Delta Hardware a unique memento of those years was retained when the store doubled in size.

The Chamber of Commerce opened a visitors' center in the old First National Bank Building, after it had been shored up inside, evacuated of pigeons, cleaned, and polished, and after the lettering "Last Chance" had been removed from the tower. Officially termed "a rare example of Romanesque Revival," the building is listed in the National Register of Historic Places. DURA's murals project was overseen by M. C. "Mo" Kreutz. After checking goals and pitfalls with a town in Vancouver noted for its murals, Mo lined up his artists. Local painters were chosen, he said, to further interest in area scenes and history, and to have the artist handy for touchups should somebody misjudge while parking a car and ram into the Gunnison River, done in oils on brick.

As a result of these and other improvements, another "mural" eventually appeared along the highways leading into town—signs reading "All-America City Award."

Commercially, things did not change that much. Aspen Computers doubled its space by cutting an arch between the two of Mrs. Jeffers' half-shells it owns. To the antique oak wall cabinets that came with the place, Kelly O'Brien added his own roll-top desk, the contrast of old materials and high-tech computer software creating a startling ambiance. The Paper Works Ink, an office-supply store founded by two women, Cathy Boyd and Colleen Jensen, outgrew its space and moved into larger, more centrally located quarters—the old Garrett Building. But, at the same time, two nearby enterprises closed their doors.

Main Street, with its sapling trees and flower tubs, looked clean and lovely, but lonely. Rather like a Utrillo painting of an empty Paris street, especially on a

Move the center counter and you'll see hoofmarks cut when Shorty Gibson came in here on horseback. Davis Clothing store hasn't changed since John Davis, right, opened it in 1912, nor when son Mel, left, took over. Third generation Brad Davis added one innovation—you don't have to buy your tuxedo, you can rent it. Photo by Muriel Marshall.

rainy day when the reflection of a distant pedestrian stretched toward you on the wet sidewalk.

Town was indeed lovely—after you got to it. But first, approaching from the north, you saw a ghastly mess. The confluence, that final wedge of low ground before the rivers flowed together, had been used for a century or so by people and nature alike, as a place to put unwanted things. There was Old Fadely's Swamp, where the seep of the converging waters sidetracks and lies there undecided—not quite stagnant, not quite moving. Frogs, muskrats, birds, reeds, and willows live and die while it makes up its mossy mind. Citizens had been complaining about it for more than a hundred years: it bred mosquitoes, it smelled. It smelled worse than ever after the sewage treatment lagoons were dug, and not much better after they were abandoned for a better disposal system.

Weeds and trash took over the deserted Holly Sugar grounds; the 'dobe bricks of the migrant "shacks" were sloughing into soil; lime dunes left by the factory were oozing and blowing into everything. Somebody opened a wrecking yard and went away, leaving all the wrecks.

Clean it up? Make a park of it? Bill Heddles dreamed of that and got as far as a small softball field. But Bill had not been the first to dream of a park at the confluence of rivers.

From pioneer days on, residents had felt that the site was made for such a purpose. First came the health spa centered over the sulfur spring between First Street and the river. Then, in 1908, on an island in the Gunnison across from town, they created La Veta Park with a bandstand, seating, dance floor, and picnic tables. A published invitation carries the feel of the times:

> Public school will be in charge of the entertainment at the opening of
> La Veta Park May 1st, and an interesting program has been arranged
> commencing at 8 o'clock. The Delta Concert Band under the direction of
> Prof. Forrest will supply music. In the afternoon and evening there will be
> dancing. Plenty of room and good floor. Everybody is invited to come.
> Bring your basket dinner. Come early and stay late. There will be public
> speakers from home and abroad. Also an especially prepared literary
> program, during the rendering of which Prof Condit will act as master of
> ceremonies. Strict order will be observed. No intoxicants will be allowed
> on the park grounds and no intoxicated person will be tolerated.

River floods wiped out La Veta Park island a couple of years later, but apparently it gave J. C. Cole an idea. In 1912, he created Cole's Lake Resort out of

Cole's Slough, a mile-long, horseshoe-shaped loop in the Gunnison a short distance downriver, near the Campbell Switch bridge. After draining the slough and dragging out the sunken trees and brush, Cole dammed off both ends of the river and filled the lake with water from the cold springs at the upper end. He removed the unloved carp, bullheads, and suckers; built a two-story cement hatchery; and imported 250,000 eastern trout, red speckles and natives, figuring that, when the springs had filled the lake seven feet deep, the water would be cold enough for trout. Among other attractions at Cole's Lake Resort were wild ducks and pelicans.

The resort's day came and went. About three-quarters of a century later, the town council eased toward a similar idea, but upriver at the confluence. As a first step, City Manager Steve Schrock reclaimed the Holly Sugar site. The sugar factory was old and ugly; its tall brick smokestack was not ugly but posed an eventual hazard and had to come down. An immense steel beet-washer wheel was saved as a memento of what Holly Sugar factory had meant in terms of money and jobs, and it was mounted on edge at the corner of First and Palmer streets, where the new entrance to the planned park would be.

The town already owned the seventy acres that had held the sewer lagoons and had plans for converting them into fresh, clean lakes. But the plans kept expanding—a golf course, indoor and outdoor theaters, trails, wildlife area, restrooms, open space. More land was needed.

City officials applied for two grants to buy land but received neither. Perhaps DURA's Main Street project was not yet successful enough to proclaim that this was a town willing to work to better itself, or perhaps the officials didn't yet know the ropes in grantsmanship. The money was out there, like a dammed river waiting to be diverted onto land. In a way, it was a new kind of pioneering.

At the time when Sylvester Huffington and Hank Hammond staked homesteads at the confluence, government funding consisted of a piece of land. The government granted 160 acres to a man seeking to better himself, if the man put up earnest money—that is, $1.25 per acre in cash or the equivalent in time, five years of his life, devoted to improving his piece of land.

The man, the nation, and the government profited immensely. Huffington's heirs got a piece of ground worth ten to fifteen times what he put into it, the nation grew wealthier for every homestead that developed into a farm, and the government could levy taxes on the improved property forever.

Besides "free" land, the vital resource in arid sections of the West was streams of water. But this wealth could be accessed only by specialists—engineers who knew how to dam and tap the streams and then channel them to those landowners who showed themselves qualified, by doing their earnest-work (in this case, by digging their own lateral ditches).

When government funding took the form of money instead of land, a new kind of pioneering was born, and a new vocation. Specialists, grant-tapping "engineers," understood the lay of the federal, state, and private funding landscape, knew which streams of money were available to serve what purposes, and were adept at tapping into these waiting reservoirs of cash.

Such grant "engineers" were not unknown to the confluence community. For quite some time, the schools had had salaried specialists in this field, skilled in locating the fund reservoirs, and setting up the channels (paperwork) to bring the streams of money home.

With "engineer" Maria Forester heading the fund-tapping crew, the next time city officials applied for a grant (1988), they got it. By the time the new park was ready for its grand opening in 1991, seven streams of outside money had converged at the confluence, and an eighth fell out of the blue.

Three were from federal sources: HUD's Community Development Block Grant, administered through the state Department of Local Affairs; U.S. Soil Conservation augmented by funds from hunter-members of Ducks Unlimited; Energy Impact grants from mineral severance taxes on coal and other mines. The State of Colorado contributed through the Economic Development Administration and through its Division of Wildlife "Fishing Is Fun" license fees funds. U.S. West telephone company contributed from its private philanthropy funds. The seventh contributory was through pure chance you might say—Lotto money administered by Colorado Greenways.

Grants and gifts totaled about $1.5 million—in addition to several thousand dollars of front money put up by the city, some of which came from lottery returns and some from selling acreage along U.S. Highway 50 for industrial use.

What did all that money buy?

It bought that extra 195 acres. The sewer lagoons became a 70-acre fishing-boating lake. Incidentally, the bottom turned out to be commercial-grade gravel, so excavation cost the city nothing, since the gravel was a product that the excavators, Delta Sand and Gravel, could resell. The lake is deep enough for cold-water trout and is kept well stocked. Dead cottonwoods were sunk in the lake-bottom to provide a habitat for bass and sunfish. The lake is equipped with boat-launching facilities (only hand-rowed or quiet electric-powered boats allowed, thank you) and a pier for fishing from wheelchairs. There is a sand-surfaced bathing beach.

William McCrea Bailey was hired to build a scaled-down approximation of Antoine Robidoux's fur-trading post, originally located somewhere a little farther downriver. Bailey builds log cabins for a living, almost anywhere in the West, and restores historic log structures for museums. He is an authority on Antoine

Robidoux, having traced the Frenchman's career from Canada to the Midwest, the Southwest, and the Rocky Mountains. Now, shaded by big cottonwoods and within hearing of the flowing Gunnison River, the Living History Museum Fort Uncompahgre contains trade goods, storage buildings for hides and goods, sleeping quarters for trappers, a blacksmith, stock pens, and adobe *hornos* for baking.

Townspeople made the money go farther by volunteering practically eons of their time. The amount of volunteer labor that went into the creation of Confluence Park may be estimated from the fraction of it involved in building Fort Uncompahgre. Bill Bailey kept track—more than a thousand hours were volunteered on that one project alone.

The money built a commons and an amphitheater that seats fifteen hundred and is complete with storage for stage props and screens. New home of the historical pageant *Thunder Mountain Lives Tonight,* the amphitheater grounds received a Ute tribal blessing ceremony before the first performance. Though the drama involves Indians, it does not include actual sacred dances performed by them, so surface earth is not removed after each performance as might otherwise be necessary.

A wildlife area was created, or rather things were left the way they were, except for threading trails and clearing vistas where you can watch cranes refurbishing last year's nests and mother ducks trailing flotillas of ducklings. After you sway on the swinging bridge across the Uncompahgre, you come to an untouched area that someday may be an archery range. And if you come before they carry out their intentions here, you can glimpse an old-time way of dealing with rivers that refuse to stay within their banks: a riprap of lined-up car bodies. Only a few are left, 1930s Fords and Chevys. Buried to their brows in decades of earth embankment, their pop-eyed headlamps peer out like moles.

Five miles of trail linking all these facilities have been surfaced with gravel. They thread their way through wild lands and open space, alongside the lake, and, at intervals, past drifts of landscaped turf and flowerbeds.

A large rectangle of land at the south end of the lake is horse country. This section of the park is set aside for the Delta Horse Country Committee, which received funds from U.S. West to build an arena and other equine facilities here. The grant came after the financial contribution of this enterprise had been demonstrated—horses and related industries are estimated to add $3.5 million dollars annually to the county economy. Though the Horse Country Committee is relatively new, founded by Pat Stroud in 1988, horse breeding has been both hobby and industry at the confluence for almost three centuries, counting those extraordinary horsemen, the Utes. Besides standard breeds, there always have been specialties—Lauri Hick, with her Iceland ponies; Hubert Hallock, with the miniature mules that he would bring to town on leashes and tie like puppies to a parking meter; and the paint horses that Peggy Gilbert breeds because no two look alike, "so parents can pick out their own kids performing down there in the dust and melee of the arena."

The whole Confluence Park complex began with a simple intention: to clean up the Holly Sugar mess and turn the sewer lagoons into a fishing pond. The same mushrooming of goals occurred when the city decided to replace Cleland Pool. The pool was seventy years old, leaky and hard to keep aseptic and attractive. It had to be replaced with another or—like the Last Chance—bulldozed and planted to grass. The city appointed a task force to study the pool situation. The more it studied the project, the bigger the project became, just as with the Last Chance Rescue Squad that achieved the All-America City Award and the Sewer Lagoons Clean-up Crew that somehow came up with a 265-acre developed park.

The task force went into retreat and split into two groups—one to decide what was needed, the other to figure out how to pay for it. The project kept on growing. The pool became a six-laner, then separate pools for therapy and tots were added. Those who preferred to take their exercise dry (except for sweat, of course) spoke up, arguing for equal facilities—a gymnasium with basketball court and bleachers, a room for dance aerobics, a weight room (for taking it off, that is), and a couple of racquetball courts. By this time, they needed an architect, so they got Rich Sales. With his help, they added a meeting room, an activity room, a snack bar, and a childcare room to free mothers to concentrate on restoring the figures that childbearing had somewhat altered. All this would require quite a staff of instructors and maintainers, so a cluster of offices was placed in the center of the building that Sales was designing as he listened.

The finance half of the task force had not been idle. What they came up with was a ballot creating a one-cent sales tax on everything sold within the city limits. And they got it passed.

The facility was named the Bill Heddles Recreation Center, for the druggist who built a softball diamond here while dreaming that it would evolve into a park, but who only lived to see his diamond bulldozed out of existence.

In the midst of construction, that eighth source of money fell from the sky, literally. The country of Kuwait pledged $100,000 toward the Bill Heddles Recreation Center. Ambassador Al-Sabah delivered the pledge in person and was met at the airport by a color guard of area armed forces recruiters, the Delta High School Band, Desert Storm veterans, and others. Delta was the first stop on the ambassador's national "Thank You, America" tour following Desert Storm.

As homesteaders once went to the land office to "prove up on the claim" by presenting proof of compliance with regulations, city fathers and friends journeyed to the League of Cities Competition at Charlottesville, North Carolina. Their "proof" was a videotape: before-and-after views of Main Street, Confluence Park, the Recreation Center, high-school students working in the new Technical Centers.

Those Technical Centers played a big part in the video presentation. School officials are firm about crediting the students themselves. If it is the school system that brought Delta to international attention, as in that technology conference in Germany, it is the individual students who keep the schools in the public eye— and not for gang wars and gun-toting freshmen, but for competence. Delta's middle and upper schools regularly enter teams in the brain game called the Knowledge Bowl. The home team scores nationally and outplays other state teams with gratifying frequency.

Taken together, the factors in that video "proof" won the 1992 All-America City Award for the town at the confluence.

But a wonderful park and a superior school system do not necessarily mean a prosperous town. The new generation of pioneers is aware of that. Part of the plan for Confluence Park, and prominent in its financing, was the creation of a Commercial Park, with the city selling business and industrial lots bordering Highway 50.

When the town cleaned up the mess of lime pits, cattle corrals, and weedy debris where the Holly Sugar factory was, they left the huge silo and the igloo-shaped building called the Dome. These are included in the Commercial Park Subdivision. Though built to be strictly utilitarian, the quadruple silo and dome nevertheless enhance both parks by their massive size and the simplicity of their architecture. They are used as a mill by Del-Mesa Farms, the area's newest large industry, which produces chickens and eggs in a dozen or so multi-structure units in the valleys.

First to build in the Commercial Park was Gibson's, which was erected so close to the river that there is only room for the park trail and a bit of landscaping between the store and flowing water. Kentucky Fried Chicken brought its wickedly delicious odors from the other side of town to a new building here, and City Market moved from an overcrowded store uptown to a new $3 million supermarket in the Commercial Park. The new Diamond Shamrock service station and convenience store occupies a park corner at First and Main. Perhaps the soundest indication that the Commercial Park has a firm financial future came when McDonald's arched its golden endorsement over the development. But there is an even stronger omen—word that Fred Fowler's Mount Sopris Instruments is coming back.

Like their homesteading forerunners, town leaders have done the groundwork, staked out their objectives, done the plowing and planting, and diverted the funding "streams" to make the financial desert thrive. They did it! Now it is time to stand back and see whether the crop catches hold, time to step back and ponder what the harvest will be; time to—No, wait a minute! They're doing something out there on the south forty. They're channeling a new grant for "Operation Enterprise," to help small industries and businesses get started and keep going through the first five touch-and-go years.

Just what Fred Fowler ordered.

Sources

Personal interviews by the author for series and single articles that appeared in the *Delta County Independent,* the *Grand Junction Daily Sentinel, Reader's Digest, Westworld Magazine,* and the *Denver Post* between 1965 and 1987.

Nell Abbott, Charles Aldridge, Uhlan Austin, Elmer Barnes, Rev. A. Blanchard Boyer, Lurleene ("Toots") Berry, Charles Bertram, Dr. Gerald Burgess, J. P. Bushnell, Audrey Cheatum, Rick Cooley, John Davis, W. D. ("Buster") Dailey, J. D. Dillard, Marty Conklin Durlin, Ira Edwards, Paul Edwards, Bill Fairfield, Fred E. Fowler, Lloyd Gibson, Tom Gibson, Ed Hanson, Louis Hebrew, Katharine Amsbary Hedgcock, Lauri Hick, Gordon Hodgin, Tom Huerkamp, Nelson Huffington, Dr. James Jensen, Ethel Porter Johnson, Eddie Jones, Vivian Jones, Katherine Kawamura, Eileen Kempf, Roy Long, John (Mike) McGrath, Jim Mowbray, Bernice Musser, Eda Musser, Eveline Nutter, Edith Castle Parker, Halbert Reid, Francis B. Riozzari, Martha Savage, Margaret Scheetz, Ann Schmalz, Winifred Castle Schmidt, Lee Schull, Maxine Schull, Myrtle Siecrest, Elmer Skinner, Carl Smith, Minnie Womack Smith, Esther J. Stephens, Nellie Stephens, Oliver J. Stone, Robert Stoody, Dovie Story, Andy Thliveris, Ione Tyler, Dexter B. Walker.

Newspapers

Delta Chief
Delta County Independent
Delta County Laborer
Delta County Tribune
Delta Daily Independent
Delta Independent
Denver Post
Grand Junction (Colo.) Daily Sentinel
Montrose (Colo.) Daily Press

Unpublished Works in Author's Collection

Blachly, Lou. "Homestead." Manuscript. N.d.

Cameron, Mary. Collection of interviews, clips and documents, U.S. National Forest Service, Grand Junction, Colo. N.d.

Dillard, J. D. Transcribed audiotape of interview by Judge Fred (Kelly) Calhoun. 1976.

Durlin, Marty Conklin. *Going Home.* Musicale. 1977.

"Facts Concerning Life of Louisa Koppe." Letter. N.d.

Huffington, Oscar. "Memoirs and Diary, 1900–1943."

Malone, Rev. Donald C. "The Delta Bank Scandal of 1929."

"Delta United Methodist Church." N.d.

Rockwell, Wilson. "Delta County: The Formative Years." Manuscript. 1974.

Sinnock, Scott. "Geomorphology of the Uncompahgre Plateau and Grand Valley, Western Colorado, USA." Ph.D. Diss., Purdue University. 1978.

Unpublished Works
in Delta County Historical Society collection

"Early Days as Told by Pioneers." Transcript of audiotaped interviews. N.d.

Geer, Taylor. "History of the Western Slope." Typescript. N.d.

Hedgcock, Katharine. "Growing up in Delta at the Turn of the Century." Typescript. N.d.

"Historical Narrative of the Delta Public Library," 1909–89. Manuscript. N.d.

Price, Adah. "Early History of Delta County." Memoirs. N.d.

Reiher, Jerry. "All-America City Finalist Presentation." Manuscript. 1992.

Books

Lee, R. V. *American Military History, 1607–1958.* ROTC Manual. Washington, D.C.: U.S. Government Printing Office, 1959.

Athern, Robert. *The Denver and Rio Grande Western Railroad.* Lincoln: University of Nebraska Press, 1962.

Austin, Hazel. *Surface Creek Country.* N.p.: privately published, 1977.

Baars, Donald L. *Red Rock Country.* New York: Doubleday, 1972.

Bailey, William McCrea. *Fort Uncompahgre.* Silverton, Colo.: Silverton Standard and the Miner, 1990.

Barcus, Earlynne, and Irma Harrison. *Echoes of a Dream.* Fruita, Colo.: Fruita Triangle, 1936.

Betenson, Lula Parker. *Butch Cassidy, My Brother.* New York: Penguin Books, 1976.

Bradley, Ruth. *Dellie: A Lotus in the Dust.* Berkeley, Calif.: Ber-Cal Publishing, 1967.

Chapman, Arthur. *The Story of Colorado.* New York: Rand-McNally, 1924.

Colorado: A Guide to the Highest State. WPA American Guide Series. New York: Hastings House, 1941.

Conard, Howard Louis. *Uncle Dick Wootton.* 1957. Reprint, Lincoln: University of Nebraska Press, 1980.

Dempsey, Jack. *Dempsey.* New York: Harper and Row, 1977.

Doherty, Deborah V. *Delta, Colorado: The First 100 Years.* Delta, Colo.: *Delta County Independent,* 1981.

Fairfield, Eula King. *Pioneer Lawyer.* Denver: W. H. Kistler Stationery Company, 1946.

Givon, T. *Ute Traditional Narratives.* Ignacio, Colo.: Ute Press, 1985.

Gregory, Marvin, and P. David Smith. *Mountain Mysteries.* Ouray, Colo.: Wayfinder Press, 1987.

Hafen, Leroy R., and Ann Hafen. *The Colorado Story.* Denver: Old West Publishing Company, 1953.

Huscher, Betty H., and Harold A. Huscher. *The Hogan Builders of Colorado.* Gunnison, Colo.: Colorado Archaeological Society, 1943.

Jocknick, Sidney. *Early Days on the Western Slope of Colorado.* Glorieta, N.M.: Rio Grande Press, 1913.

Johnson's Universal Cyclopaedia. D. Appleton Company, A. J. Johnson Company, 1899.

Kelly, Charles. *The Outlaw Trail.* 1938. Reprint, New York: Bonanza Books, 1959.

Lathrop, Marguerite. *Don't Fence Me In.* Boulder, Colo.: Johnson Publishing Company, 1972.

Lee, Willis T. *Coal Fields of Grand Mesa and the West Elk Mountains, Colorado.* U.S. Geological Survey, Washington D.C., 1912.

McGinley, William. *Following the Indians into Grand Valley.* Grand Junction, Colo.: *Daily Sentinel.* N.d.

McGrath, John M. *Prisoner of War: Six Years in Hanoi.* Annapolis, Md.: U.S. Naval Institute Press, 1975.

McNitt, Frank. *The Indian Traders.* Norman: University of Oklahoma Press, 1962.

Mease, Janet. *The Grand Junction Town Company and the Land Dispute with William Keith.* Grand Junction, Colo.: Mesa State College, 1934.

Mills, Enos A. *In Beaver World.* N.p., 1913.

Monroe, Arthur W. *San Juan Silver.* 1940. With inked notations by Stella Fairlamb in Fairlamb family copy.

Musser, Eda Baker. *Trails and Trials.* N.p.: privately printed, 1986.

National Midland Trail Association. *Midland Trail Guide.* 1916. Reprint, Glorieta, N.M.: Rio Grande Press, 1969.

Petit, Jan. *Utes: The Mountain People.* Boulder, Colo.: Johnson Publishing Company, 1990.

Powell, J. W. *The Exploration of the Colorado River and Its Canyons. 1895.* Reprint, New York: Dover Publications, 1961.

Rockwell, Wilson. *Uncompahgre Country.* Denver: Sage Books, 1965.

_____. *The Utes: A Forgotten People.* Denver: Sage Books, 1956.

Rose, Ernie. *Utahs of the Rocky Mountains.* N.p.: privately printed. N.d.

Smith, Anne M. *Ethnography of the Northern Utes.* Albuquerque, N.M.: University of New Mexico Press, 1974.

Smith, P. David. *Ouray, Chief of the Utes.* Ouray, Colo.: Wayfinder Press, 1986.

Soldier and Brave. National Survey of Historic Sites and Buildings, vol. 12, edited by Robert G. Ferris. Washington, D.C.: U.S. Department of the Interior.

Sterns Brothers. *With the Colors.* Delta, Colo.: 1919.

Vandenbusche, David. *The Gunnison Country.* Gunnison, Colo.: B&B Printers.

Viers, Lawrence, and Winona Viers. *Bits and Pieces of Olathe History.* N.p.: privately printed, 1982.

Wood, George Bacon M.D. and Bache, Franklin M.D. *United States Dispensatory.* Philadelphia, 1833.

Articles

Marshall, John B. "Andy Meldrum and the Treasure of the Red Mountains." Published by Denver Westerners in 1967 Brand Book.

Parkhill, Forbes. "Bank Night Tonight." *Saturday Evening Post.* N.d.

Rosenberg, Charles E. "What It Was Like to Be Sick in 1884." *American Heritage* 35 (October–November, 1984): 22.

States, Dr. G. W., "Human Interest Stories of the West." *Delta County Independent* series (1937–38).

Zimmerman, Harold. "Harvesting Peaches with German Prisoners of War." *Journal of the Western Slope* 2 (1987): 18–21.

Index

NOTE: Pages with illustrations are indicated by *italics*.